APACHE CASSANDRA
HANDS-ON TRAINING
LEVEL ONE

Ruth Stryker

Apache Cassandra Hands-on Training Level One

Recommended prerequisites: Experience with databases, application servers, and programming

Unit 8: Modeling Data

Unit 9: Creating an Application

Unit 10: Updating and Deleting Data

Unit 11: Selecting Hardware

Unit 12: Adding Nodes to a Cluster

Unit 13: Monitoring a Cluster

Unit 14: Repairing Nodes

Unit 15: Removing a Node

Unit 16: Redefining a Cluster for Multiple Data Centers

Appendix A: Resources for Further Learning

Appendix B: Answer Key

Appendix C: Setting up the Student Computers

Appendix D: How the Course Virtual Machines Were Built

1

UNDERSTANDING
WHAT CASSANDRA IS FOR

Understanding What Cassandra Is

Learning What Cassandra is Being Used For

Understanding What Cassandra Is

Cassandra is an open source, big data, NoSQL database that allows for massive scalability, always-on availability, fast writes, and fast reads.

As an Apache open source database project, Cassandra is free for people to use.

As a NoSQL (Not only SQL) database, Cassandra is an alternative to relational databases, providing linear scalability with its distributed database model. Instead of having just one very large server for a database, Cassandra distributes the data for a database across multiple servers, allowing for massive storage and ongoing expansion through the easy addition of more servers.

Along with its distributed database design, Cassandra was designed to continue operating even if some of the database servers go down, such as from hardware failure or power outage. This foundational aspect of Cassandra allows for a robust, always-on database, able to serve real-time applications at all times.

Cassandra is a combination of Amazon Dynamo, created as an always-available system, and Google Big Table, created for storing enormous amounts of data.

Exercise 1: Access the Apache Cassandra Website

In this exercise, you navigate to the home of Apache Cassandra.

1. In a **browser**, navigate to `http://cassandra.apache.org`.

2. Peruse the site, noticing that Cassandra is an Apache open source project:

Learning What Cassandra is Being Used For

Cassandra is being used by over 1,500 different organizations for a variety of purposes, from sensor data (CERN, smart meters, Internet of Things) to recommendation engines (Netflix, Spotify, Outbrain, eBay) to gaming to fraud detection (Barracuda Networks, Instagram) to location-based services (Hailo taxi) to online financial products (Intuit).

Many organizations choose Cassandra for projects that require one or more of the following: massive scalability, high availability, and/or an exceptionally high volume of writes.

CERN chose Cassandra for its ATLAS particle physics experiment at the Large Hadron Collider because of Cassandra's scaling capabilities and their need to write massive amounts of sensor data.

Netflix chose Cassandra not only for its scalability, but also for its high availability. With customers accessing Netflix at all hours, Netflix needed a system that could always be available, with no downtime.

Barracuda Networks chose Cassandra for tracking every malicious site on the Internet forever.

Spotify, a streaming music web service, chose Cassandra for its high availability and massive scalability.

Intuit chose Cassandra for its online financial products because of Cassandra's high availability, speed, ability to easily scale, and ease of administration.

Exercise 2: See What Cassandra is Being Used For

In this exercise, you visit Planet Cassandra to learn how Cassandra is being used by various organizations.

1. In a browser, navigate to `http://planetcassandra.org`.

2. Click the **CASES** link.

3. Notice the many use cases:

4. Click the **ALL COMPANIES** link, to see a list of companies using Cassandra.

5. Click the **FUNCTIONAL USE CASES** link, to see use cases listed by function.

6. Click a **Read More** link (e.g. for **Hailo**), to learn more about a use case that interests you.

7. Click the **INDUSTRY USE CASES** link, to see cases listed by industry.

8. Click a **Read More** link (e.g. for **eBay**), to learn more about a use case that interests you.

9. Continue perusing the use cases, as desired.

Summary

The focus of this chapter was on understanding what Cassandra is for:

- Understanding What Cassandra Is

- Understanding What Cassandra is Being Used For

Unit Review Questions

1) Which of these is NOT a reason to select Cassandra as a database?

a. massive scalability

b. no single point of failure

c. proprietary software

d. high volume of writes

2) Which of these scenarios would be appropriate for Cassandra?

a. A company that needs to store, every minute, the temperature of rooms in millions of homes

b. A company that wants to store the online user behavior of millions of customers to provide recommendations

c. A high volume shipping company that needs to be able to trace the status of a package in real-time

d. All of the above

Lab: Open the Main Course Virtual Machine

In this exercise, you open the main virtual machine for this course, which was set up on your classroom computer by your instructor, before the start class.

Note: If you are doing this course as self-paced training, follow the steps in Appendix C to set up the course files on your computer.

1. In the **achotl1** (apache cassandra hands-on training level one) folder on your desktop, locate and double-click the **achotl1_vm1_64-bit** file, to open the main virtual machine for the course:

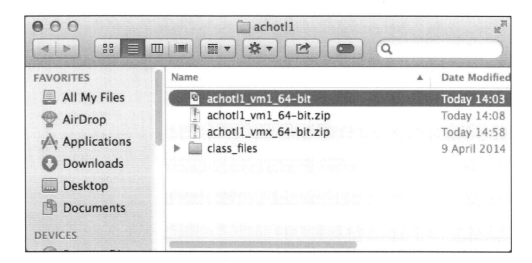

*Windows users: look in the **achotl1_vm1_64-bit.vmwarevm** subfolder to locate and double-click the **achotl1_vm1_64-bit.vmx** file, to open the main virtual machine for the course:*

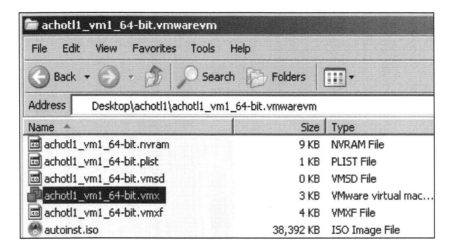

2. If prompted, click the **I copied it** button:

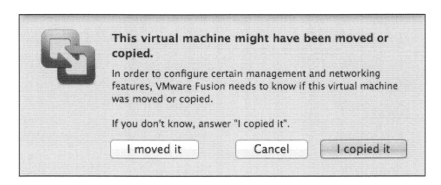

3. Once the virtual machine has launched, enter `ubuntu` in the password field, to access the virtual machine:

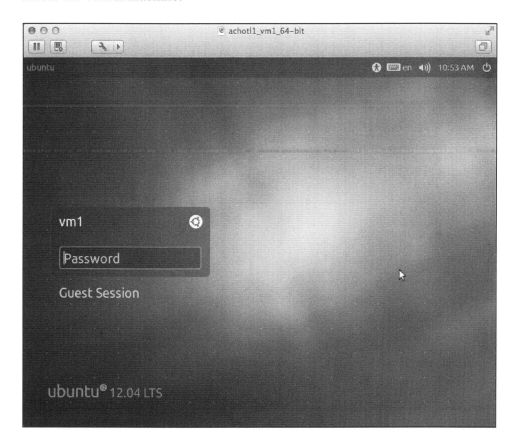

4. Notice that you are now in the course virtual machine, which uses Ubuntu as the operating system. (Ubuntu is a popular Linux distribution, common for running Cassandra.)

GETTING STARTED
WITH THE ARCHITECTURE

Understanding that Cassandra is a Distributed Database

Learning What Snitch is For

Learning What Gossip is For

Learning How Data Gets Distributed and Replicated

Understanding That Cassandra is a Distributed Database

In a distributed database, rather than being constrained to have to fit all of the data onto only one server, the database is spread across multiple servers, allowing for massive horizontal scalability.

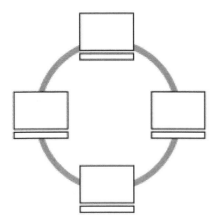

Cluster

In Cassandra, a networked group of nodes (i.e. servers) is called a cluster. Within a Cassandra cluster, there are no master or slave nodes. Each node has the same functionality as the others, which, combined with replication (explained later in this unit) allows for a distributed database with no single point of failure.

A Cassandra cluster can easily be spread across more than one data center, allowing for data availability even if one data center completely goes down.

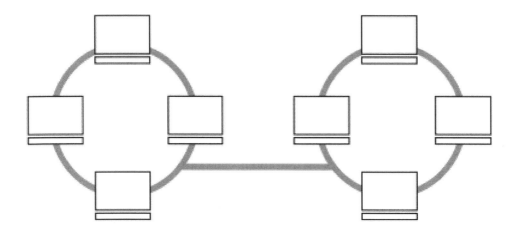

Exercise 1: View Cassandra Documentation

In this exercise, you view the Cassandra architecture documentation provided by DataStax.

1. In a browser, navigate to `http://www.datastax.com/docs`.

2. Click the link for Cassandra Architecture:

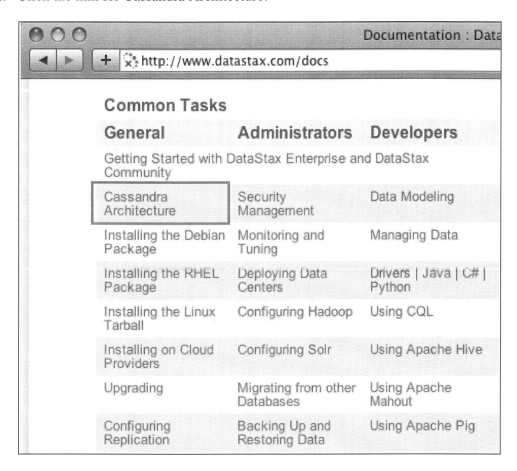

3. Skim through the overview.

Learning What Snitch is For

Snitch is how the nodes in a cluster know about the location of each other.

Ways to Define Snitch

There are a variety of ways to configure snitch, specified in the main Cassandra configuration file on each node. For whichever snitch method is chosen, the same snitch method needs to be used on all of the nodes in the cluster.

- Dynamic snitching
- SimpleSnitch
- RackInferringSnitch
- PropertyFileSnitch
- GossipingPropertyFileSnitch
- EC2Snitch
- EC2MultiRegionSnitch

Each snitch type has its own method of configuration. For example, to use **PropertyFileSnitch**, the IP address, rack, and data center of all the nodes in the cluster are set in the cassandra-topology.properties file of every node.

```
130.77.100.147 =DC1:RAC1
130.77.100.148 =DC1:RAC1
130.77.100.165 =DC1:RAC1
130.77.200.109 =DC1:RAC2
130.77.200.110 =DC1:RAC2
130.77.200.111 =DC1:RAC2

155.23.100.128 =DC2:RAC1
155.23.100.129 =DC2:RAC1
155.23.200.107 =DC2:RAC2
155.23.200.108 =DC2:RAC2
```

For another example, the **GossipingPropertyFileSnitch** (used in Unit 16: Redefining a Cluster for Multiple Data Centers), which uses the cassandra-rackdc.properties file in each node, can be used to just specify the rack and data center information for an individual node. The node's topology is then propagated to the other nodes through gossip. This is an appealing snitch type for a cluster that will be growing.

The default snitch type in Cassandra is **SimpleSnitch**, for single data center deployment only.

More detail about the snitch types is available in the DataStax Cassandra documentation.

Learning What Gossip is For

Gossip is how the nodes in a cluster communicate with each other.

Gossip happens every one second. Every one second, each node communicates with up to three other nodes, exchanging information about itself and all of the other nodes that it has information about from previous gossip exchanges.

While snitch provides a way for nodes to know about the topology of the cluster, gossip provides a way for the nodes to know about the state (e.g. up, down, etc.) of the nodes in the cluster.

Gossip is the **internal** communication method for nodes in a cluster. For external communication (Unit 4: Communicating with Cassandra), such as from an application to a Cassandra database in the cluster, CQL or Thrift are used.

Exercise 2: Check Your Understanding

In this exercise, you check your understanding of snitch and gossip.

1) How do the nodes in a cluster know about the topology of the cluster (e.g. the data center and rack that each node is in)?

a. through the master node

b. through the slave node

c. through cassandra.apache.org

d. through snitch

2) Gossip is how a **client application** talks to a Cassandra database.

a. True

b. False

3) Gossip runs every one:

a. second

b. minute

c. hour

d. day

Learning How Data Gets Distributed and Replicated

Data gets distributed to nodes in a cluster through consistent hashing. Consistent hashing is used to strive for even distribution of data across the nodes.

More specifically, for any row of data that is to be written to a Cassandra database, a hash value is generated by the partitioner (the default partitioner in Cassandra is Murmur3), which then determines which node in the cluster will store that row of data based on the ranges assigned to each node.

To illustrate this concept:

Notice the rows of data to be inserted into the activity table of the home_security database, of alarm activity for various homes:

home_id	datetime	event	code_used
H01033638	2014-05-21 07:55:58	alarm set	2121
H01545551	2014-05-21 08:30:14	alarm set	8889
H00999943	2014-05-21 09:05:54	alarm set	1245

The Murmur3 partitioner (in effect, a hash function) takes the value in the first column to generate a unique number between -2^{63} to 2^{63}. For example, the following might be the token values generated for the home_id values:

```
H01033638 -> -7456322128261119046
H01545551 -> -2487391024765843411
H00999943 -> 6394005945182357732
```

Each node in a cluster is assigned one or more token ranges. For example, in the diagram below, each of the four nodes is assigned a quarter of the -2^{63} to 2^{63} tokens.

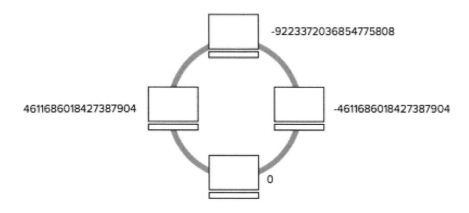

Each node is responsible for the token values between its endpoint and the endpoint of the previous node.

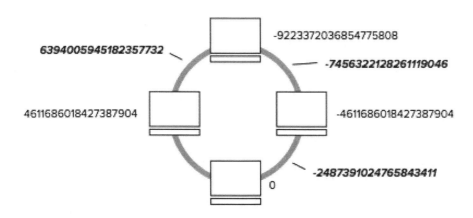

The -7456322128261119046 data is be owned by the -4611686018427387904 node, the -2487391024765843411 data by the 0 node, and the 6394005945182357732 data by the -9223372036854775808 node.

Calculating Token Ranges

For assigning token ranges to the nodes in a ring, to result in even distribution, the following formula can be run on a command line, substituting in the actual number of nodes in the cluster in place of the number 4:

```
vm1@ubuntu:~$ python -c 'print [str(((2**64 / 4) * i) - 2**63)
 for i in range(4)]'
['-9223372036854775808', '-4611686018427387904', '0', '4611686
018427387904']
```

A few people have built and provided calculators on the web, for this same purpose. These can be found by searching in Google (or any Internet search engine) on `Murmur3 calculator`.

Replication

To ensure that a backup exists for data, it is common to specify a replication factor higher than 1 when defining a database in Cassandra. If the replication factor for a database is higher than 1, then, when any rows get written to the database, they will get written to that many nodes.

For example, the diagram below shows a row of data written to three nodes because the replication factor for the database was defined to be 3.

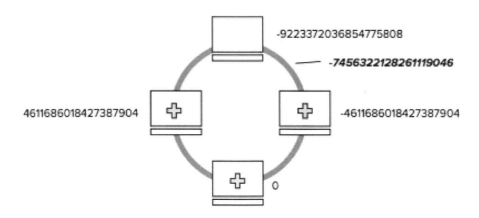

In the case of a replication factor of 3, the data is written to the node that owns it, along with two subsequent nodes.

Replication factor is specified on a per database basis, entered when defining a database (Unit 5: Creating a Database).

Virtual Nodes

Virtual nodes (vnodes) are a newer, alternative way to specify the ranges assigned to nodes in a cluster. With virtual nodes, rather than a node being responsible for just one range of hash values, it is instead responsible for many small range slices.

```
192.168.159.103  rack1  Up  Normal  10.42 MB  36.19%  8995959370875111619
192.168.159.101  rack1  Up  Normal  8.8 MB    30.19%  9067420701225382311
192.168.159.101  rack1  Up  Normal  8.8 MB    30.19%  9087437214801154442
192.168.159.102  rack1  Up  Normal  9.74 MB   33.63%  9114799584639192092
192.168.159.101  rack1  Up  Normal  8.8 MB    30.19%  9124927950302931315
192.168.159.102  rack1  Up  Normal  9.74 MB   33.63%  9128195428643885841
192.168.159.102  rack1  Up  Normal  9.74 MB   33.63%  9131758010915769002
192.168.159.103  rack1  Up  Normal  10.42 MB  36.19%  9190440719116978288
192.168.159.102  rack1  Up  Normal  9.74 MB   33.63%  9211350131645519695
```

Vnodes were created to make it easier to add new nodes to a cluster. Rather than having to double the node count when growing a cluster (which was common in the past, while slicing the token ranges of the existing nodes in half to ensure that the data load would be evenly distributed amongst the nodes in the cluster), adding even just a single node when using vnodes allows for an evenly distributed cluster. When a node is added, it takes on responsibility for its share of the cluster.

The number of token ranges can vary from node to node. This allows for assigning more token ranges to a more powerful computer (e.g. 512) and fewer token ranges to a less powerful computer (e.g. 128). The default is 256.

Vnodes are the default for Cassandra 2.0. The vnodes setting is in the Cassandra configuration file of each node (Unit 3: Installing Cassandra).

Exercise 3: Access Related Documentation

In this exercise, you access the DataStax documentation on data distribution, replication, and vnodes.

1. In a browser, search on `Cassandra 2.0 vnodes`:

> Virtual nodes | DataStax **Cassandra 2.0** Documentation
> www.datastax.com/.../**cassandra/2.0/cassandra/**.../architectureDataDistribu... ▼
> Overview of virtual nodes (**vnodes**). **Vnodes** simplify many tasks in **Cassandra**: You no
> longer have to calculate and assign tokens to each node. Rebalancing a ...

2. Click the link show above, for the **DataStax Cassandra 2.0 Documentation**.

3. Read the virtual nodes overview:

4. Select and skim through related topics: Data distribution and replication, Consistent hashing, Data replication, and Partitioners.

Summary

The focus of this chapter was on getting started with the architecture:

- Understanding that Cassandra is a Distributed Database

- Learning What Snitch is For

- Learning What Gossip is For

- Learning How Data Gets Distributed and Replicated

Unit Review Questions

1) Which of these is NOT a snitch strategy in Cassandra?

a. PropertyFileSnitch

b. GossipingPropertyFileSnitch

c. PartySnitch

d. EC2MultiRegionSnitch

2) What is the default partitioner in Cassandra 2.0 (as well as Cassandra 1.2)?

a. ByteOrderedPartitioner

b. RandomPartitioner

c. MD5Partitioner

d. Murmur3Partitioner

3) The replication factor has to be the same for all databases in a cluster.

a. True

b. False

4) The point of virtual nodes in Cassandra is to:

a. Run Cassandra in the cloud

b. Be able to easily add a new node to a cluster without having to manually adjust the token ranges of existing nodes to have a balanced cluster

c. Use virtual machines instead of physical servers

d. Define one large token range per node

Lab: View the Course Projects

In this exercise, you look at the projects that you will be creating in this course.

1. In the **achotl1** course folder on your desktop, open the **class_files** folder.

2. Notice the folders for various units in the course.

3. In the **unit02** folder, open the **alarm_system_status.pdf** file.

4. See that you will be creating a Cassandra database and application for users to be able to check on the activity and status for their home alarm system:

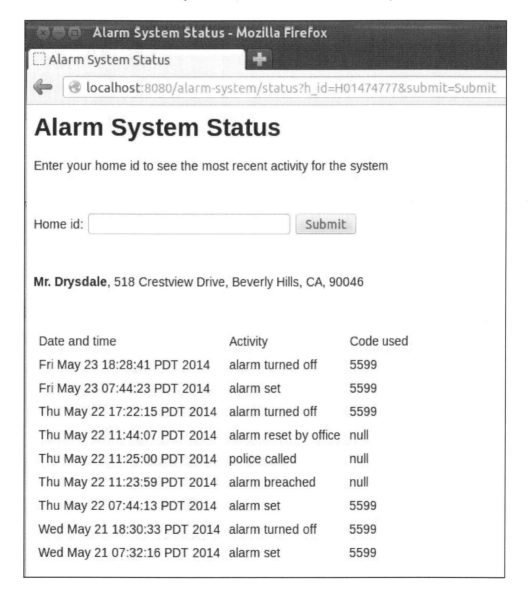

5. In the **unit02** folder, open the **location_tracker.pdf** file.

6. See that you will be creating a Cassandra database and application for a rental car company to be able to check on the location of a car that has not been returned:

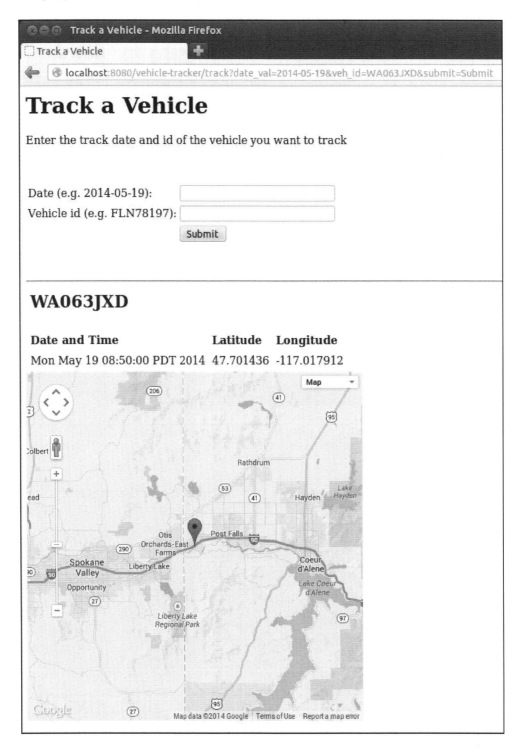

INSTALLING CASSANDRA

Downloading Cassandra

Ensuring Oracle Java 7 is Installed

Installing Cassandra

Viewing the Main Configuration File

Providing Cassandra with Permission to Directories

Starting Cassandra

Checking Status

Accessing the Cassandra system.log File

Downloading Cassandra

The open source version of Cassandra is available for download on the Apache Cassandra home page, located at `http://cassandra.apache.org`.

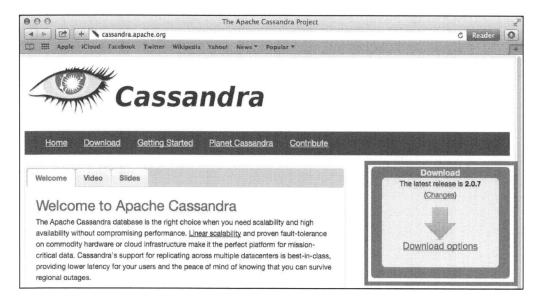

In selecting the Download options link, the download page appears, with a link downloading the tarball file for installing Cassandra on a Debian-based Linux distribution, such as Ubuntu.

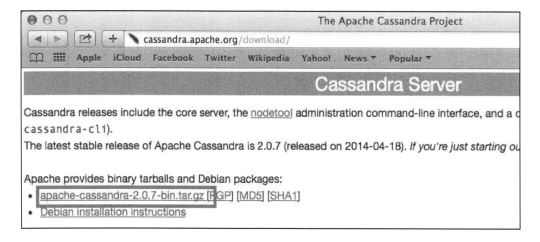

Exercise 1: Locate the Tarball

In this exercise, you locate the open source Apache Cassandra tarball file for installing Cassandra on a Debian-based Linux distribution, such as Ubuntu.

1. In a **browser** in the **virtual machine** (see Firefox icon on the left), navigate to `http://cassandra.apache.org`.

2. Click the **Download options** link on the right, to go to the download page.

3. Click the **apache-cassandra-*x.x.x*-bin.tar.gz** (e.g. apache-cassandra-2.0.7-bin.tar.gz) link.

4. See that you could download the tarball file from any of the mirror sites.

5. Close the browser window, without downloading the file. (The tarball is already downloaded on your virtual machine for you.)

6. Still in the virtual machine, open a terminal window by clicking the **Dash Home** icon (upper-left), typing `Ter`, and then click the **Terminal** application.

7. At the command prompt in the terminal window, enter `cd Downloads` to change to the Downloads directory.

8. Enter `ls` to see the contents of the directory.

9. Notice the tarball file:

```
vm1@ubuntu: ~/Downloads
vm1@ubuntu:~$ cd Downloads
vm1@ubuntu:~/Downloads$ ls
apache-cassandra-2.0.7-bin.tar.gz
```

Ensuring Oracle Java 7 is Installed

Cassandra was written in Java. So, in order to run Cassandra, the Java Runtime Environment (JRE), or Java Development Kit (JDK), is required.

Cassandra 2.0 requires version 7 of the JRE or JDK. Cassandra does not work well with OpenJDK (Open Java Development Kit), so use the Oracle JRE or JDK, not OpenJDK.

The Oracle JRE 7 can be downloaded from the Oracle site at
http://www.oracle.com/technetwork/java/javase/downloads.

To see the steps done to install the Oracle JDK on the course virtual machine, see pages D-6 to D-8 in Appendix D: How the Course Virtual Machines Were Built.

To check that Oracle JRE 7 is the default runtime, the **java -version** command can be used:

```
vm1@ubuntu:~/Downloads$ java -version
java version "1.7.0_55"
Java(TM) SE Runtime Environment (build 1.7.0_55-b13)
Java HotSpot(TM) 64-Bit Server VM (build 24.55-b03, mixed mode)
```

Oracle JRE vs. Oracle JDK

In order to run Cassandra, only the Oracle JRE 7 (Java Runtime Environment) needs to be installed.

In order to develop a Java application, as we will be doing in Unit 9 to create our rental car tracking application, the Oracle JDK needs to be installed, which includes the Oracle JRE in it.

Exercise 2: Check that Oracle Java 7 is Installed

In this exercise, you check that Oracle Java 7 was installed on your virtual machine, so that Cassandra will be able to run.

1. In a browser, navigate to
   `http://www.oracle.com/technetwork/java/javase/downloads`,
   to see that you could download the Oracle JRE or JDK.

2. Close the browser, without downloading the JRE or JDK. (The JDK has already been downloaded and installed on your virtual machine for you. If desired, view Appendix D to see the steps that were done.)

3. In your virtual machine, in the terminal window, enter `java -version` to check that Oracle 7 is set as the default JRE:

```
vm1@ubuntu:~/Downloads$ java -version
java version "1.7.0_55"
Java(TM) SE Runtime Environment (build 1.7.0_55-b13)
Java HotSpot(TM) 64-Bit Server VM (build 24.55-b03, mixed mode)
```

Installing Cassandra

Installing Apache Cassandra can be done via a tarball file or through a package manager.

To install Cassandra using a tarball file downloaded from `http://cassandra.apache.org/download`, you simply unzip the tarball where you would like to install Cassandra.

For example, this screenshot shows unzipping a Cassandra tarball to install Cassandra in a directory named cassandra:

```
~/cassandra$ tar -xvzf apache-cassandra-2.0.7-bin.tar.gz
```

To instead install Cassandra on Ubuntu using a package manager, see the steps at `http://wiki.apache.org/cassandra/DebianPackaging`:

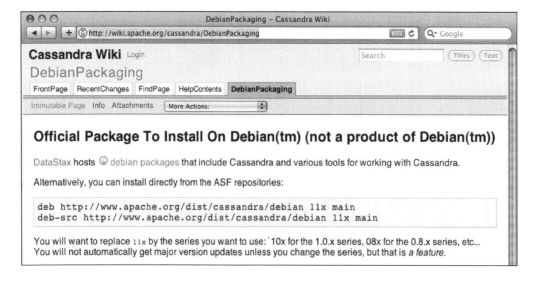

Exercise 3: Install Cassandra

In this exercise, you install Cassandra on your virtual machine using the Apache Cassandra 2.0.7 tarball previously downloaded for you.

1. At the command prompt, enter `cd` to go to the default home directory.

2. Enter `mkdir cassandra` to create a subdirectory, to install Cassandra into.

3. Enter `cd cassandra` to go into the cassandra subdirectory.

4. Enter `mv ~/Downloads/apache-cassandra-2.0.7-bin.tar.gz .` to move the tarball file from the Downloads directory to the cassandra directory.

   Note: Be sure to include the dot in the command.

5. Enter `ls` to see that the file has been moved:

```
vm1@ubuntu:~/cassandra$ ls
apache-cassandra-2.0.7-bin.tar.gz
```

6. Enter `tar -xvzf apache-cassandra-2.0.7-bin.tar.gz` to unpack the file.

7. Enter `ls` to see the new directory:

```
vm1@ubuntu:~/cassandra$ ls
apache-cassandra-2.0.7  apache-cassandra-2.0.7-bin.tar.gz
```

8. Enter `cd apache-cassandra-2.0.7` to navigate to the new directory.

9. Enter `ls` to see the contents of the directory:

```
vm1@ubuntu:~/cassandra/apache-cassandra-2.0.7$ ls
bin            interface   LICENSE.txt   pylib
CHANGES.txt    javadoc     NEWS.txt      README.txt
conf           lib         NOTICE.txt    tools
```

Viewing the Main Configuration File

The main configuration file for a Cassandra node is the **cassandra.yaml** file.

Each Cassandra node has its own cassandra.yaml file, located in the **conf** directory, which is a subdirectory of the **apache-cassandra-2.0.7** directory, which is located wherever Cassandra was installed on the node.

For example, in the screenshot below, the cassandra.yaml file can be seen in the conf directory of the apache-cassandra-2.0.7 directory.

```
vm1@ubuntu:~/cassandra/apache-cassandra-2.0.7$ ls conf
cassandra-env.sh                cqlshrc.sample
cassandra-rackdc.properties     log4j-server.properties
cassandra-topology.properties   log4j-tools.properties
cassandra-topology.yaml         metrics-reporter-config-sample.yaml
cassandra.yaml                  README.txt
commitlog_archiving.properties  triggers
```

To view, or edit, the cassandra.yaml file, any text editor can be used, such as **vim**, a popular Linux text editor.

```
vm1@ubuntu:~/cassandra/apache-cassandra-2.0.7/conf$ vim cassandra.yaml
```

Within the cassandra.yaml file are various settings for configuring a Cassandra node, such as the name of the cluster that the node is to belong to, the type and number of token ranges it is responsible for, the partitioner used, where data is written, and the snitch type.

```
vm1@ubuntu: ~/cassandra/apache-cassandra-2.0.7/conf

# Cassandra storage config YAML

# NOTE:
#   See http://wiki.apache.org/cassandra/StorageConfiguration
#   full explanations of configuration directives
# /NOTE

# The name of the cluster. This is mainly used to prevent mach
# one logical cluster from joining another.
cluster_name: 'Test Cluster'

# This defines the number of tokens randomly assigned to this
```

Exercise 4: View the cassandra.yaml file

In this exercise, you view the cassandra.yaml file, located in the Cassandra configuration files directory.

1. Still in the terminal window, in the apache-cassandra-2.0.7 directory, enter `cd conf` to navigate to the Cassandra configuration files directory.

2. Enter `ls` to see the contents of the conf directory.

3. Notice the cassandra.yaml file listed.

4. Enter `vim cassandra.yaml`, to open the cassandra.yaml file in vim.

    Note: If you needed to edit the file, rather than just open it in read-only mode, you would enter `sudo vim cassandra.yaml` *and then provide the sudo password of* `ubuntu` *if prompted.*

5. **Scroll** through the cassandra.yaml file, noticing various configuration settings, such as **cluster_name** (line 10, specifying Test Cluster as the name of the cluster that this node belongs to), **num_tokens** (line 24, specifying virtual nodes, with 256 token ranges for this node), **partitioner** (line 91, specifying Murmur3Partitioner as the partitioner), **data_files_directories** (line 96, specifying the location of any Cassandra database data stored on this node), and **endpoint_snitch** (line 564, specifying SimpleSnitch as the snitch type).

6. When done perusing the cassandra.yaml file, press the **Esc** key and enter `:q` to exit vim.

Providing Cassandra with Permission to Directories

Cassandra writes various files to the **/var/lib/cassandra** directory (e.g. database data) and **/var/log/cassandra** directory (e.g. log entries).

In order for Cassandra to be able to write to these locations, permission for these directories needs to be granted.

To create the directories, the `mkdir` command can be used:

```
$ sudo mkdir /var/lib/cassandra

$ sudo mkdir /var/log/cassandra
```

To set permissions for the directories, the `chown` command can be used:

```
$ sudo chown -R $USER:$GROUP /var/lib/cassandra

$ sudo chown -R $USER:$GROUP /var/log/cassandra
```

Exercise 5: Provide Cassandra with Permission to Directories

In this exercise, you provide Cassandra with permission to the /var/lib/cassandra and /var/lib/cassandra directories, so that Cassandra will be able to run.

1. Still in the terminal window, at the command prompt, enter `sudo mkdir /var/lib/cassandra` to create a cassandra subdirectory under the /var/lib directory.

2. If prompted, enter the sudo password of `ubuntu`.

3. Enter `sudo mkdir /var/`**`log`**`/cassandra` to create a cassandra subdirectory under the /var/log directory.

4. Enter `sudo chown -R $USER:$GROUP /var/lib/cassandra` to allow Cassandra to write to the /var/lib/cassandra directory.

5. Enter `sudo chown -R $USER:$GROUP /var/`**`log`**`/cassandra` to allow Cassandra to write to the /var/log/cassandra directory.

Starting Cassandra

Cassandra can be started by entering the `bin/cassandra` command in the directory where Cassandra is installed.

```
vm1@ubuntu:~/cassandra/apache-cassandra-2.0.7/conf$ bin/cassandra
```

By default, this command runs Cassandra in the background.

To run Cassandra in the foreground, to make it easier to stop if desired, the `bin/cassandra -f` command can be used instead.

Stopping Cassandra

If Cassandra is running in the foreground, it can be stopped by simply entering **Ctrl-C** in the terminal window that it is running in.

If Cassandra is running in the background, it can be stopped by doing these steps:

1. Entering `ps aux | grep cass` to find out the process id:

```
      vm1@ubuntu: ~
vm1@ubuntu:~$ ps aux | grep cass
vm1        4670   7.5 10.9 1664516 166632 pts/1   Sl
/jdk1.7.0_55/bin/java -ea -javaagent:bin/../lib/jar
adingEnabled -XX:+UseThreadPriorities -XX:ThreadPri
```

2. Entering `kill {pid}`, replacing {pid} with the process id found in step 1:

```
vm1@ubuntu:~$ kill 4670
```

Exercise 6: Start Cassandra

In this exercise, you start and stop Cassandra.

1. Still in the terminal window, at the command prompt, enter `cd ..` to navigate up one directory, to the apache-cassandra-2.0.7 directory.

2. Enter `bin/cassandra` to start Cassandra.

Stop Cassandra from running in the background:

3. In a new terminal window, enter `ps aux | grep cass` to find out the process id:

4. Enter `kill 4670` to stop Cassandra, **substituting** 4670 for your process id.

5. Enter `ps aux | grep cass` to see that the process is gone:

Run Cassandra in the foreground:

6. Back in the previous terminal window, enter **Ctrl-C** to get to the command prompt.

7. Still in the ~/cassandra/apache-cassandra-2.0.7 directory, enter `bin/cassandra -f` to run Cassandra in foreground mode.

Stop Cassandra:

8. In the directory where Cassandra is running in the foreground, enter **Ctrl-C**, to stop Cassandra.

9. In either terminal window, enter `ps aux | grep cass` to see that the process is gone.

10. Enter `bin/cassandra -f` to start Cassandra in the foreground again.

Checking Status

To check the status of nodes in a Cassandra cluster, `nodetool status` can be used.

```
vm1@ubuntu:~/cassandra/apache-cassandra-2.0.7$ bin/nodetool status
Datacenter: datacenter1
=======================
Status=Up/Down
|/ State=Normal/Leaving/Joining/Moving
--  Address    Load       Owns (effective)  Host ID
UN  127.0.0.1  94.73 KB   100.0%            e7ef5ab4-2b5e-47df-80f7
```

Nodetool is a command line tool installed with Cassandra, in the bin subdirectory where Cassandra was installed, that provides a number of useful options for managing a Cassandra cluster.

For example, along with providing the ability to check on the status of the nodes in a cluster, nodetool can also be used to view the token ranges assigned to each node, to decommission a node, or to repair a node. To view a list of all nodetool options, `nodetool help` can be used.

```
vm1@ubuntu:~/cassandra/apache-cassandra-2.0.7$ bin/nodetool help
usage: java org.apache.cassandra.tools.NodeCmd --host <arg> <command>

 -a,--include-all-sstables    includes sstables that are already on the
                              most recent version during upgradesstables
 -c,--compact                 print histograms in a more compact format
 -cf,--column-family <arg>    only take a snapshot of the specified table
                              (column family)
 -dc,--in-dc <arg>            only repair against nodes in the specified
                              datacenters (comma separated)
 -et,--end-token <arg>        token at which repair range ends
 -h,--host <arg>              node hostname or ip address
```

Exercise 7: Check Status

In this exercise, you check the status of the node.

1. In a terminal window other than the one Cassandra is running in, enter `cd ~/cassandra/apache-cassandra-2.0.7` to navigate to the directory where Cassandra is installed.

2. Enter `bin/nodetool status`, to check on the status of the cluster.

3. Notice that the node is Up, running Normal:

```
vm1@ubuntu:~/cassandra/apache-cassandra-2.0.7$ bin/nodetool status
Datacenter: datacenter1
=======================
Status=Up/Down
|/ State=Normal/Leaving/Joining/Moving
--  Address      Load      Owns (effective)  Host ID
       Rack
UN  127.0.0.1  94.46 KB    100.0%            109d2cf8-bcef-4b26-81a8
```

4. For more detail about the node, enter `bin/nodetool info -h 127.0.0.1`:

```
vm1@ubuntu:~/cassandra/apache-cassandra-2.0.7$ bin/nodetool info -h
 127.0.0.1
Token                 : (invoke with -T/--tokens to see all 256 tokens)
ID                    : 109d2cf8-bcef-4b26-81a8-b5f9b94c896b
Gossip active         : true
Thrift active         : true
Native Transport active: true
Load                  : 94.46 KB
Generation No         : 1398780331
Uptime (seconds)      : 1253
Heap Memory (MB)      : 26.01 / 736.00
```

5. To see the 256 token ranges assigned to the node, enter `bin/nodetool ring`:

```
vm1@ubuntu:~/cassandra/apache-cassandra-2.0.7$ bin/nodetool ring

Datacenter: datacenter1
==========
Address    Rack      Status State   Load       Owns       Token
                                                           91249279
127.0.0.1  rack1     Up     Normal  94.46 KB   100.00%    -9167187
127.0.0.1  rack1     Up     Normal  94.46 KB   100.00%    -9121291
127.0.0.1  rack1     Up     Normal  94.46 KB   100.00%    -9111321
```

6. To see additional options available through nodetool, enter `bin/nodetool help`.

Accessing the Cassandra system.log File

The Cassandra **system.log** file is located in the **/var/log/cassandra** directory by default.

Since the log file is a text file, it can be viewed in any text editor. For example, vim could be used to see the contents of the system.log file.

```
vm1@ubuntu: /var/log/cassandra
 INFO [main] 2014-04-29 07:05:32,383 ThriftServer.java (line 99) Usi
ng TFramedTransport with a max frame size of 15728640 bytes.
 INFO [main] 2014-04-29 07:05:32,390 ThriftServer.java (line 118) Bi
nding thrift service to localhost/127.0.0.1:9160
 INFO [main] 2014-04-29 07:05:32,408 TServerCustomFactory.java (line
 47) Using synchronous/threadpool thrift server on localhost : 9160
 INFO [Thread-2] 2014-04-29 07:05:32,415 ThriftServer.java (line 135
) Listening for thrift clients...
                                                290,101        Bot
```

Changing the Settings for the system.log File

The settings for the log file are in the **log4j-server.properties** file, which can be found in the **conf** subdirectory where Cassandra was installed.

```
apache-cassandra-2.0.7/conf$ vim log4j-server.properties
```

To change the location of the system.log file, the **log4j.appender.R.File** property in the log4j-server.properties file can be edited.

```
# Edit the next line to point to your logs directory
log4j.appender.R.File=/var/log/cassandra/system.log
```

Additional settings, like the logging level and the log file size, can also be set in the log4j-server.properties file.

Exercise 8: Access the Cassandra system.log File

In this exercise, you access the Cassandra **system.log** file.

1. Create a new terminal window.

2. Enter `cd /var/log/cassandra` to navigate to where the Cassandra **system.log** file is.

3. Enter `ls` to see the system.log file listed:

```
⊗ ⊖ ⊡   vm1@ubuntu: /var/log/cassandra
vm1@ubuntu:~$ cd /var/log/cassandra
vm1@ubuntu:/var/log/cassandra$ ls
system.log
```

4. Enter `vim system.log` to view the contents of the log file.

5. Scroll to the bottom to see the most recent entries.

6. Press **Esc** and enter `:q` to exit the file.

7. Enter `cd ~/cassandra/apache-cassandra-2.0.7/conf` to navigate to the conf directory.

8. Enter `ls` to see the log4j-server.properties file listed:

```
vm1@ubuntu:~/cassandra/apache-cassandra-2.0.7/conf$ ls
cassandra-env.sh                    cqlshrc.sample
cassandra-rackdc.properties         log4j-server.properties
cassandra-topology.properties       log4j-tools.properties
```

9. Enter `vim log4j-server.properties` to view the file's content.

10. On line 35, notice that the value of the log4j.appender.R.File property is **/var/log/cassandra/system.log**:

```
log4j.appender.R.File=/var/log/cassandra/system.log
```

11. Press **Esc** and enter `:q` to exit the file.

Summary

The focus of this chapter was on installing Cassandra:

- Downloading Cassandra

- Ensuring Oracle Java 7 is Installed

- Installing Cassandra

- Viewing the Main Configuration File

- Providing Cassandra with Permission to Directories

- Starting Cassandra

- Checking Status

- Accessing the Cassandra system.log File

Unit Review Questions

1) How can Cassandra be installed?

a. via a tarball

b. as a package

c. either a or b

d. none of the above

2) What is needed in order for Cassandra 2.0 to run?

a. OpenJDK

b. Oracle JRE (or JDK) 7

c. Oracle JRE (or JDK) 6

d. JRE 5 or above

3) What is the name of the main Cassandra configuration file?

a. main.yaml

b. config.yaml

c. conf.yaml

d. cassandra.yaml

4) What command can be used to check if Cassandra is running?

a. runcheck

b. ps aux | grep cass

c. bin/cassandra

d. Ctrl-C

4

COMMUNICATING
WITH CASSANDRA

Understanding Ways to Communicate with Cassandra

Using cqlsh

Understanding Ways to Communicate With Cassandra

To communicate with Cassandra, such as to define a database, define a table, write data, read data, etc., the common way is to use CQL (Cassandra Query Language), either on the command line using cqlsh or through a client driver (Unit 9: Creating an Application).

CQL

CQL is a SQL-like query language for communicating with Cassandra, created to make it easy for people familiar with SQL to work with Cassandra.

For example, to retrieve all the rows for the columns named home_id, datetime, event, and code_used, in a table named activity, a select statement could be used:

```
SELECT home_id, datetime, event, code_used FROM activity;
```

Like SQL, CQL commands are not case-sensitive.

However, although CQL looks similar to SQL, it does **not** have all of the same options as SQL, due to the distributed nature of a Cassandra database. A complete list of the CQL commands can be viewed in the DataStax CQL for Cassandra 2.0 documentation.

Thrift

Historically, the way to communicate with Cassandra was through Thrift, a low-level API. Thrift is still supported in Cassandra, available on the command line through cassandra-cli or via a client driver. However, although Thrift is still supported by Cassandra, most people new to Cassandra choose to use CQL.

JMX for Administration

To communicate with Cassandra to do administrative activities, such as cluster monitoring (Unit 13: Monitoring a Cluster) and management tasks, tools built on JMX (Java Management Extensions) are commonly used.

Exercise 1: View CQL Commands

In this exercise, you view the list of CQL commands.

1. In Google (or any Internet search engine), search for `Cassandra 2.0 CQL commands`.

2. Click the link for the CQL for Cassandra 2.0 documentation:

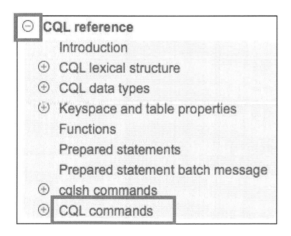

3. On the left, in the table of contents, expand **CQL reference**:

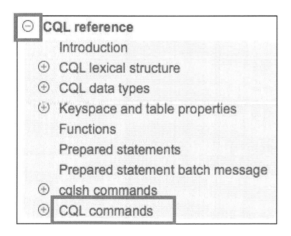

4. Click on **CQL commands**.

5. Notice the list of commands:

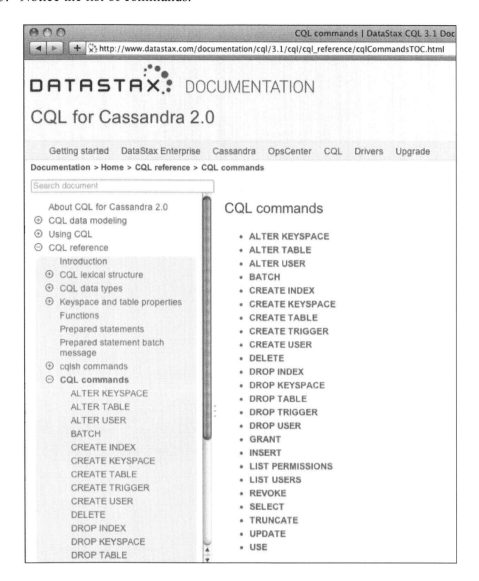

6. Click on any command (e.g. CREATE TABLE) to learn about it.

7. If desired, continue clicking on CQL commands to learn about them.

Using cqlsh

In order to communicate with Cassandra using CQL on the command line, cqlsh can be used.

For executing CQL commands, cqlsh comes with Cassandra, available in the bin subdirectory where Cassandra is installed.

To enter cqlsh, simply reference it in the bin subdirectory.

```
$ bin/cqlsh
```

Once in cqlsh, the cqlsh prompt displays.

```
cqlsh>
```

Once in cqlsh, CQL commands can be run.

To exit cqlsh, simply type exit.

```
cqlsh> exit
```

Cqlsh Commands

Along with being able to run CQL commands in cqlsh, cqlsh commands can also be run.

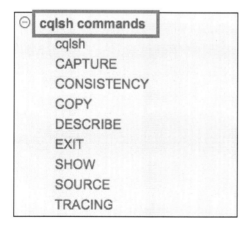

```
cqlsh commands
    cqlsh
    CAPTURE
    CONSISTENCY
    COPY
    DESCRIBE
    EXIT
    SHOW
    SOURCE
    TRACING
```

Exercise 2: Access cqlsh

In this exercise, you enter and exit cqlsh.

1. In a terminal window, in the ~/cassandra/apache-cassandra-2.0.7 directory, type `bin/cqlsh` to enter cqlsh.

2. Notice that you are now in cqlsh:

```
vm1@ubuntu:~/cassandra/apache-cassandra-2.0.7$ bin/cqlsh
Connected to Test Cluster at localhost:9160.
[cqlsh 4.1.1 | Cassandra 2.0.7 | CQL spec 3.1.1 | Thrift
Use HELP for help.
cqlsh>
```

3. Enter `DESCRIBE CLUSTER;`, to try out running a cqlsh command:

```
cqlsh> DESCRIBE CLUSTER;

Cluster: Test Cluster
Partitioner: Murmur3Partitioner
Snitch: SimpleSnitch
```

4. Enter `exit`, to exit cqlsh.

5. Notice that you are no longer in cqlsh (you are back are the regular command prompt):

```
cqlsh> exit
vm1@ubuntu:~/cassandra/apache-cassandra-2.0.7$
```

Summary

The focus of this chapter was on communicating with Cassandra:

- Understanding Ways to Communicate with Cassandra

- Using cqlsh

Unit Review Questions

1) CQL has all of the commands that SQL has.

a. True

b. False

2) CQL stands for:

a. Cassandra Query Library

b. Cassandra Quotient Library

c. Cassandra Query Language

d. Cute Quirky Laugh

Lab: Use cqlsh

In this exercise, you enter cqlsh, run a command, and exit cqlsh.

1. In a terminal window, in the ~/cassandra/apache-cassandra-2.0.7 directory, type `bin/cqlsh` to enter cqlsh.

2. Notice that you are now at the cqlsh prompt.

3. Enter `SHOW HOST;` to see the name of the cluster that cqlsh is connected to, as well as the server name and port number of the connecting host:

```
cqlsh> SHOW HOST;
Connected to Test Cluster at localhost:9160.
cqlsh>
```

4. Enter `HELP;`, to see the list of cqlsh and CQL commands:

```
cqlsh> HELP;

Documented shell commands:
===========================
CAPTURE        COPY   DESCRIBE    EXPAND   SHOW       TRACING
CONSISTENCY    DESC   EXIT        HELP     SOURCE

CQL help topics:
================
ALTER                           CREATE_TABLE_OPTIONS    SELECT
ALTER_ADD                       CREATE_TABLE_TYPES      SELECT_COLUMNFAMILY
ALTER_ALTER                     CREATE_USER             SELECT_EXPR
ALTER_DROP                      DELETE                  SELECT_LIMIT
ALTER_RENAME                    DELETE_COLUMNS          SELECT_TABLE
ALTER_USER                      DELETE_USING            SELECT_WHERE
ALTER_WITH                      DELETE_WHERE            TEXT_OUTPUT
APPLY                           DROP                    TIMESTAMP_INPUT
ASCII_OUTPUT                    DROP_COLUMNFAMILY       TIMESTAMP_OUTPUT
BEGIN                           DROP_INDEX              TRUNCATE
BLOB_INPUT                      DROP_KEYSPACE           TYPES
BOOLEAN_INPUT                   DROP_TABLE              UPDATE
COMPOUND_PRIMARY_KEYS           DROP_USER               UPDATE_COUNTERS
CREATE                          GRANT                   UPDATE_SET
CREATE_COLUMNFAMILY             INSERT                  UPDATE_USING
CREATE_COLUMNFAMILY_OPTIONS     LIST                    UPDATE_WHERE
CREATE_COLUMNFAMILY_TYPES       LIST_PERMISSIONS        USE
CREATE_INDEX                    LIST_USERS              UUID_INPUT
CREATE_KEYSPACE                 PERMISSIONS
CREATE_TABLE                    REVOKE
```

5. Enter `HELP` followed by the name of one of the commands (e.g. `HELP CREATE_KEYSPACE;`), to learn about it:

```
cqlsh> HELP CREATE_KEYSPACE;

        CREATE KEYSPACE <ksname>
            WITH replication = {'class':'<strategy>' [,'<option>':<val>]};

        The CREATE KEYSPACE statement creates a new top-level namespace (aka
        "keyspace"). Valid names are any string constructed of alphanumeric
        characters and underscores. Names which do not work as valid
        identifiers or integers should be quoted as string literals. Properties
        such as replication strategy and count are specified during creation
```

6. Enter `exit` to leave cqlsh.

5

CREATING A DATABASE

Understanding a Cassandra Database

Defining a Keyspace

Understanding a Cassandra Database

In Cassandra, a database is defined by a keyspace. This is similar to how the word schema is used in other database systems to reference a database.

Within a keyspace, tables can be defined, to store data in the database.

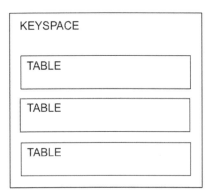

Viewing Existing Keyspaces

To see a list of the keyspaces that already exist in a cluster, the DESCRIBE KEYSPACES; command can be used.

```
cqlsh> DESCRIBE KEYSPACES;

system   system_traces
```

As shown above, when Cassandra first gets installed, two initial keyspaces exist: system and system_traces. The **system** keyspace contains tables for storing data for running the Cassandra node, whereas **system_traces** contains tables for storing data generated when the TRACE command is turned on.

To see the definition for a keyspace, DESCRIBE KEYSPACE *keyspacename;* can be used.

```
cqlsh> DESCRIBE KEYSPACE system_traces;

CREATE KEYSPACE system_traces WITH replication = {
  'class': 'SimpleStrategy',
  'replication_factor': '2'
};
```

Exercise 1: View Existing Keyspaces

In this exercise, you view the keyspaces that already exist in your cluster.

1. In a terminal window, in the ~/cassandra/apache-cassandra-2.0.7 directory, type `bin/cqlsh`, to enter cqlsh.

2. At the cqlsh command prompt, type `DESCRIBE KEYSPACES;`.

3. See the two default keyspaces listed:

```
system   system_traces
```

4. If desired, enter `DESCRIBE KEYSPACE system;` to view the tables that exist in the system keyspace.

5. If desired, enter `DESCRIBE KEYSPACE system_traces;` to view the tables that exist in the system_traces keyspace.

Defining a Keyspace

A keyspace can be defined through the CREATE KEYSPACE command.

To use the CREATE KEYSPACE command, a name for the keyspace needs to be entered, as well as values for replication.

```
CREATE KEYSPACE vehicle_tracker
WITH REPLICATION = { 'class' : 'NetworkTopologyStrategy',
'dc1' : 2, 'dc2' : 2};
```

class

The **class** property defines whether the cluster can be spread across one or more data centers (**NetworkTopologyStrategy**) or just one data center (**SimpleStrategy**).

In general, use NetworkTopologyStrategy so that, even if you are starting with just one data center for your database, you can easily expand to more than one.

In using **NetworkTopologyStrategy**, the replication factor is specified per data center. For example, the code below declares a keyspace that has a replication factor of 3 replicas in the first data center and 2 replicas in the second.

```
CREATE KEYSPACE vehicle_tracker
WITH REPLICATION = { 'class' : 'NetworkTopologyStrategy',
'dc1' : 3, 'dc2' : 2};
```

replication_factor

The **replication_factor** property is used with **SimpleStrategy**. For example, this code declares a keyspace named vehicle_tracker in a single data center with a replication factor of 3:

```
CREATE KEYSPACE vehicle_tracker
WITH REPLICATION = {'class' : 'SimpleStrategy',
'replication_factor' : 3};
```

Or, in the following example, a keyspace using SimpleStrategy with a replication factor of 1 is defined:

```
cqlsh> CREATE KEYSPACE vehicle_tracker WITH REPLICATION =
{'class' : 'SimpleStrategy', 'replication_factor' : 1};
```

Using SimpleStrategy with a replication factor of 1 is common when getting started with Cassandra, like on a development machine running a single node cluster, but not common in production due to the lack of replication.

Case-Sensitivity

CQL is generally not case-sensitive, and the commands themselves are never case-sensitive. However, keyspace names are case-sensitive in that, whenever a keyspace name is referenced, Cassandra lowercases it if it is not in quotes. So, if any capital letters are used when defining a keyspace name, then, to reference the keyspace, it must be referenced with the matching case and be in quotes.

An easy way to avoid dealing with the case-sensitivity of keyspace names is to simply name keyspaces in all lowercase.

Deleting a Keyspace

A keyspace can be deleted with the `DROP KEYSPACE` command. For example, `DROP KEYSPACE vehicle_tracker;` could be used to delete a keyspace named vehicle_tracker.

Exercise 2: Define a Keyspace

In this exercise, you define a keyspace for our rental car tracking database.

Note: For now, our keyspace will be defined with SimpleStrategy, with a replication factor of 1, for development on our 1-node development cluster. In Unit 16: Redefining a Cluster for Multiple Data Centers, we will have more nodes, modify the snitch type, and change the strategy to NetworkTopologyStrategy, so that our cluster can expand to be across more than one data center.

1. At the cqlsh command prompt, for development on our single-node cluster, enter the following to define a keyspace for our rental car tracking database:

   ```
   CREATE KEYSPACE vehicle_tracker WITH REPLICATION = {'class' :
   'SimpleStrategy', 'replication_factor' : 1};
   ```

   Tip: As you type the CREATE KEYSPACE command, you can press the Tab key to see how auto-completion can help you with the typing and syntax.

2. Enter DESCRIBE KEYSPACES; to see that the vehicle_tracker keyspace has been defined:

   ```
   cqlsh> DESCRIBE KEYSPACES;

   system   vehicle_tracker   system_traces
   ```

3. Enter DESCRIBE KEYSPACE vehicle_tracker; to see the definition for the car_tracker keyspace:

   ```
   cqlsh> DESCRIBE KEYSPACE vehicle_tracker;

   CREATE KEYSPACE vehicle_tracker WITH replication = {
     'class': 'SimpleStrategy',
     'replication_factor': '1'
   };
   ```

UNIT 5: CREATING A DATABASE

5-7

Summary

The focus of this chapter was on creating a database:

- Understanding a Cassandra Database

- Defining a Keyspace

Unit Review Questions

1) The name of the strategy that allows a keyspace to span across more than one data center is called:

a. LocalStrategy

b. DataCenterStrategy

c. SimpleStrategy

d. NetworkTopologyStrategy

2) The replication factor has to be the same for all of the data centers referenced in a keyspace:

a. True

b. False

3) The names of keyspaces are never case-sensitive.

a. True

b. False

Lab: Create a Second Database

In this exercise, for a large home alarm security systems company, you create a database for storing the activity of customers' home alarm systems by defining a keyspace named home_security.

Note: For now, our keyspace will be defined with SimpleStrategy, with a replication factor of 1, for development on our 1-node development cluster. In Unit 16: Redefining a Cluster for Multiple Data Centers, we will have more nodes, modify the snitch type, and change the strategy to NetworkTopologyStrategy, so that our cluster will be able to expand to be across more than one data center.

1. At the cqlsh prompt, enter the following command to define a keyspace named home_security that uses SimpleStrategy and a replication factor of 1, for development on our single-node cluster:

    ```
    CREATE KEYSPACE home_security WITH REPLICATION = {'class' :
    'SimpleStrategy', 'replication_factor' : 1};
    ```

2. Enter DESCRIBE KEYSPACES; to see that the home_security keyspace has been defined:

    ```
    cqlsh> DESCRIBE KEYSPACES;

    system   vehicle_tracker   home_security   system_traces
    ```

3. Enter DESCRIBE KEYSPACE home_security; to see the definition for the home_security keyspace:

    ```
    CREATE KEYSPACE home_security WITH replication = {
      'class': 'SimpleStrategy',
      'replication_factor': '1'
    };
    ```

Alternate Lab Steps: Create a Second Database

In this exercise, for a large home alarm security systems company, you create a database for storing the activity of customers' home alarm systems by defining a keyspace named home_security.

Note: For now, our keyspace will be defined with SimpleStrategy, with a replication factor of 1, for development on our 1-node development cluster. In Unit 16: Redefining a Cluster for Multiple Data Centers, we will have more nodes, modify the snitch type, and change the strategy to NetworkTopologyStrategy, so that our cluster will be able to expand to be across more than one data center.

1. Define a keyspace named `home_security` with the replication strategy of `SimpleStrategy` and replication factor of `1`.

2. Use the `DESCRIBE` command to see a list of all the keyspaces defined in the cluster.

3. See that your home_security keyspace is in the list.

4. Use the `DESCRIBE` command to see the definition of the home_security keyspace.

CREATING A TABLE

Creating a Table

A table can be created in Cassandra by using the CREATE TABLE command.

In order to use the CREATE TABLE command, Cassandra needs to know which keyspace the table is being created for. This can be done with the USE command.

Getting into a Keyspace

The USE command is for specifying which keyspace any subsequent CQL commands are for. For example, USE home_security sets the home_security keyspace to be the current keyspace.

```
cqlsh> USE home_security;
cqlsh:home_security>
```

The command prompt then displays the name of the keyspace.

Column Family

Column family, from the days of Thrift, is the old phrase for what is now called a table. If you read older books or blogs, it is likely that you will come across the term column family. In your mind, simply replace the phrase column family with table.

Dropping a Table

A table can be deleted by using the DROP TABLE command. For example, DROP TABLE activity; would delete the table named activity if there was a table named activity in the current keyspace.

Exercise 1: Enter a Keyspace

In this exercise, you enter the home_security keyspace and then start creating a table.

1. At the cqlsh prompt, enter USE home_security;.

2. **Notice** that you are now in the home_security keyspace:

```
cqlsh> USE home_security;
cqlsh:home_security>
```

3. At the prompt, type CRE and press the **Tab** key.

4. Notice that the word CREATE has been auto-completed.

5. Type TA and press **Tab**.

6. Notice that the word TABLE has been auto-completed.

7. Type activity, to name the table, and a space, and press **Tab**.

8. Notice that the opening parenthesis has been typed for you:

```
CREATE TABLE activity (
```

9. Go on to the next topic to continue defining the table.

Defining Columns and Data Types

The `CREATE TABLE` command allows for defining columns in a table, including column names and the type of data that can be stored in each column.

For example, this table might be used to store home alarm systems' activity:

home_id	datetime	event	code_used
H01474777	2014-05-21 07:32:16	alarm set	5599
H01474777	2014-05-21 18:30:33	alarm turned off	5599
H01474777	2014-05-22 07:44:13	alarm set	5599
H01474777	2014-05-22 11:23:59	alarm breached	
H01474777	2014-05-22 11:25:00	police called	
H01474777	2014-05-22 11:44:07	alarm reset by office	

In Cassandra, there does not need to be data in every column of a row.

Defining Columns

To create the columns in the table above, we could define a column to store the id of the alarm system, a column for the event date and time, a column for the type of event, and a column for the access code that was used, if any (e.g. there might be more than one access code for an alarm system, like for different individuals).

```
CREATE TABLE activity (
home_id text,
datetime timestamp,
event text,
code_used text,
...
```

CQL Data Types

In the example above, the text and timestamp data types are used, specifying what type of data can be written to each column. Other common data types include boolean, int, and varchar (same as text). For detail on all the pre-defined data types, see the DataStax CQL for Cassandra 2.0 documentation.

ascii
bigint
blob
boolean
counter
decimal
double
float
inet
int
list
map
set
text
timestamp
uuid
timeuuid
varchar
varint

Exercise 2: Define Columns and Data Types

In this exercise, you define columns and specify data types for the home alarm systems' activity table.

1. Continuing to define the activity table, enter `home_id text,` to define a column named home_id that can contain text values:

    ```
    CREATE TABLE activity (
    home_id text,
    ```

2. Continue entering the following, to define columns for datetime, activity, and code_used:

    ```
    CREATE TABLE activity (
    home_id text,
    datetime timestamp,
    event text,
    code_used text,
    ```

3. Go on to the next topic to continue defining the table.

Defining a Primary Key

Like in relational databases, a primary key in Cassandra is for having a way to uniquely identify a row of data in a CQL table.

To specify a single column as the column that will hold the primary key values for rows in a CQL table, there are two ways to do it. One way is to simply put the phrase PRIMARY KEY after the column definition.

For example, in the home table below, the phrase PRIMARY KEY could be added right after the data type for the home_id column.

```
CREATE TABLE home (
home_id text PRIMARY KEY,
address text,
city text,
state text,
zip text,
owner text,
phone text,
alt_phone text,
email text,
phone_password text,
main_code text,
guest_code text
);
```

Or, another way to define the primary key for a table is to create a separate entry for PRIMARY KEY, followed by the name of the column(s) in parenthesis.

```
CREATE TABLE home (
home_id text,
address text,
city text,
state text,
zip text,
owner text,
phone text,
alt_phone text,
email text,
phone_password text,
main_code text,
guest_code text,
PRIMARY KEY (home_id)
);
```

Compound Primary Key

If the values of more than one column need to be combined in order to create a unique identifier for each row in a table, a compound primary key can be defined.

To create a compound primary key, enter more than one column name in the parentheses that follow the PRIMARY KEY entry.

```
CREATE TABLE activity (
home_id text,
datetime timestamp,
event text,
code_used text,
PRIMARY KEY (home_id, datetime)
);
```

Having more than one column specified for the primary key makes the combined values of the columns the primary key for the row.

Exercise 3: Define a Primary Key

In this exercise, you define a compound primary key for the activity table, so that there is a way to uniquely identify each row in the CQL table.

1. Continuing to create the location table, enter the following code to specify that the values of the home_id and datetime columns will be combined to create the primary key for each row in the CQL table:

```
CREATE TABLE activity (
home_id text,
datetime timestamp,
event text,
code_used text,
PRIMARY KEY (home_id, datetime)
```

2. Go on to the next topic to continue.

Recognizing a Partition Key

The first column listed in a primary key defines the partition key.

```
CREATE TABLE activity (
home_id text,
datetime timestamp,
event text,
code_used text,
PRIMARY KEY (home_id, datetime)
);
```

As you may recall from Unit 2, the partition key is hashed by the partitioner to determine which node in the cluster will store the partition.

Clustering Columns

In a primary key declaration, any columns beyond the partition key are referred to as clustering columns. For example, in the code above, datetime is a clustering column. The clustering column affects how the data is stored in the partition.

How Data is Stored Internally

All of the CQL rows that have the same partition value are stored in the same partition. For example, all of the activity for home_id H01474777 is stored in the same partition.

```
RowKey: H01474777
=> (name=2014-05-21 07\:32\:16-0700:, value=, timestamp=1398€
=> (name=2014-05-21 07\:32\:16-0700:code_used, value=3535393€
=> (name=2014-05-21 07\:32\:16-0700:event, value=616c61726d2€
=> (name=2014-05-21 18\:30\:33-0700:, value=, timestamp=1398€
=> (name=2014-05-21 18\:30\:33-0700:code_used, value=3535393€
=> (name=2014-05-21 18\:30\:33-0700:event, value=616c61726d2€
=> (name=2014-05-22 07\:44\:13-0700:, value=, timestamp=1398€
=> (name=2014-05-22 07\:44\:13-0700:code_used, value=3535393€
=> (name=2014-05-22 07\:44\:13-0700:event, value=616c61726d2€
```

In the old days of Thrift, a partition was referred to as a row. Hence the label of RowKey in the screenshot above.

Exercise 4: Recognize a Partition Key

In this exercise, you recognize the partition key in a table definition.

1. In the definition of the activity table, **notice** that the primary key has more than one column name listed:

```
PRIMARY KEY (home_id, datetime)
```

2. **Realize** that the first column listed, **home_id**, will contain the partition key values for the activity table:

```
PRIMARY KEY (home_id, datetime)
```

3. On page 6-7, in the **home** table definition, **notice** that there is only **one** column defined as the primary key (home_id).

4. **Realize** that, because the primary key only has one column specified, it will be the partition key column for that table.

5. **Know** that each table has its own partition key column.

   Note: It is a coincidence that both the activity table and the home table happen to each have a column named home_id and that they both happen to use their home_id column as their partition key column. There is no relationship between the two tables.

Specifying a Descending Clustering Order

When defining a table in Cassandra, it can be defined to store the data in ascending (default) or descending order. For example, to have the most recent security alarm events at the top of the activity table, descending can be specified.

Specifying an order is done through the presence (as well as absence) of the WITH CLUSTERING ORDER BY clause. (If the clause is not present, the clustering order is ascending.)

```
CREATE TABLE activity (
home_id text,
datetime timestamp,
event text,
code_used text,
PRIMARY KEY (home_id, datetime)
) WITH CLUSTERING ORDER BY (datetime DESC);
```

Specifying descending causes writes to take a little longer, as cells are inserted at the start of a partition, rather than added at the end, but improves read performance when descending order is needed by an application.

```
 home_id  | datetime                 | code_used | event
----------+--------------------------+-----------+-----------------
 H01474777 | 2014-05-23 18:28:41-0700 |      5599 | alarm turned off
 H01474777 | 2014-05-23 07:44:23-0700 |      5599 |        alarm set
 H01474777 | 2014-05-22 17:22:15-0700 |      5599 | alarm turned off
```

Altering an Existing Table

Although some changes can be made to an existing table, such as an adding a column through the ALTER TABLE command (e.g. ALTER TABLE activity ADD status text;), changing the clustering order of a table is not an option. (It would require the rewriting all of the table's data on disk in a different order.) To change the clustering order of a table, the table would need to be deleted and then created with the desired clustering order.

Exercise 5: Specify a Descending Clustering Order

In this exercise, you use the optional WITH CLUSTERING ORDER BY clause to specify a descending clustering order for the activity table, so that the most recent activity is on top.

1. Continuing to create the activity table, enter the bolded code to specify that the data will be in descending order, based on the datetime column values:

```
CREATE TABLE activity (
home_id text,
datetime timestamp,
event text,
code_used text,
PRIMARY KEY (home_id, datetime)
) WITH CLUSTERING ORDER BY (datetime DESC);
```

2. Press the **Enter** key, to generate the table.

3. To check the definition of the table, enter DESCRIBE TABLE activity;.

4. See that the table has been defined:

```
cqlsh:home_security> DESCRIBE TABLE activity;

CREATE TABLE activity (
  home_id text,
  datetime timestamp,
  code_used text,
  event text,
  PRIMARY KEY (home_id, datetime)
) WITH CLUSTERING ORDER BY (datetime DESC)
```

Summary

The focus of this chapter was on creating a table:

- Creating a Table

- Defining Columns and Data Types

- Defining a Primary Key

- Recognizing a Partition Key

- Specifying a Descending Clustering Order

Unit Review Questions

1) What is the command to create a table?

a. DEFINE TABLE

b. FORM TABLE

c. CREATE TABLE

d. MAKE TABLE

2) Which of these are CQL column data types?

a. string, integer, and boolean

b. string, text, and int

c. text, integer, and double

d. text, varchar, and int

3) If defining a primary key as `PRIMARY KEY (meter_id, date, timestamp)`, which column(s) contain(s) the **partition** key?

a. meter_id

b. meter_id, date

c. meter_id, date, timestamp

d. None of the above

Lab: Create a Second Table

In this exercise, you define a table to store the home and owner contact information for each home that the home security alarm company monitors.

1. At the cqlsh prompt, **see** that you are in the **home_security** keyspace:

```
cqlsh:home_security>
```

2. Use the CREATE TABLE command to start creating a table named **home**:

```
CREATE TABLE home (
```

3. Add column definitions to the table definition, to be able to store information about homes in the home table of the home_security database:

```
CREATE TABLE home (
home_id text,
address text,
city text,
state text,
zip text,
contact_name text,
phone text,
alt_phone text,
phone_password text,
email text,
main_code text,
guest_code text,
```

4. Specify the home_id column as both the primary key column and partition key column:

```
CREATE TABLE home (
home_id text,
address text,
city text,
state text,
zip text,
contact_name text,
phone text,
alt_phone text,
phone_password text,
email text,
main_code text,
guest_code text,
PRIMARY KEY (home_id)
```

5. Enter the closing parenthesis and semi-colon, to finish and enter the command:

```
...
PRIMARY KEY (home_id)
);
```

6. Enter `DESCRIBE TABLE home;` to check that the table was created:

```
cqlsh:home_security> DESCRIBE TABLE home;

CREATE TABLE home (
  home_id text,
  address text,
  alt_phone text,
  city text,
  contact_name text,
  email text,
  guest_code text,
  main_code text,
  phone text,
  phone_password text,
  state text,
  zip text,
  PRIMARY KEY (home_id)
```

Alternate Lab Steps: Create a Second Table

In this exercise, you define a table to store the home and owner contact information for each home that the home security alarm company monitors.

1. Ensure that you are in the **home_security** keyspace.

2. Start creating a table named `home`.

3. Define columns named `home_id`, `address`, `city`, `state`, `zip`, `contact_name`, `phone`, `alt_phone`, `phone_password`, `email`, `main_code`, and `guest_code`, all with a data type of text, to be able to store information about individual homes in the table.

4. Specify the **home_id** column as both the **primary key** column and **partition key** column.

5. Finish creating the table.

6. Use the `DESCRIBE TABLE` command to check that the table was created, as shown here:

```
cqlsh:home_security> DESCRIBE TABLE home;

CREATE TABLE home (
  home_id text,
  address text,
  alt_phone text,
  city text,
  contact_name text,
  email text,
  guest_code text,
  main_code text,
  phone text,
  phone_password text,
  state text,
  zip text,
  PRIMARY KEY (home_id)
```

7

INSERTING DATA

Understanding Ways to Write Data

There are a number of ways to write data to a Cassandra table.

One way is to use the `INSERT INTO` command, which is a CQL command that is handy for writing a single row. It can be used in cqlsh on the command line, or via a client driver that supports CQL, such as the DataStax Java driver (Unit 9: Creating an Application).

For importing rows from a .csv file, the cqlsh `COPY` command can be used. This command is used to import, or export, data in the .csv format.

For bulk loading, the sstableloader tool can be used. The sstableloader tool streams SSTable files to a live cluster. (SSTable is the file storage structure for how Cassandra stores data on disk, viewed later in this unit.) In order to use sstableloader, the data needs to be in the SSTable format.

Using the INSERT INTO Command

The `INSERT INTO` command is handy for writing a single row, like from a client application, or manually on the command line.

To use `INSERT INTO`, the name of the table that the data is to be written to, the names of the columns that the data is to go into, and the data that is to be written all need to be specified.

For example, the code below could be used to write a row of data into a table named activity that has columns named home_id, datetime, event, and code_used:

```
INSERT INTO activity (home_id, datetime, event, code_used) VALUES
('H01474777', '2014-05-21 07:32:16', 'alarm set', '5599');
```

Using SELECT to Access Data

The `SELECT` command can be used to access data in a table. For example, to select all the rows with data in any of the columns in the activity table, `SELECT * FROM activity;` could be used.

To select rows with data in specific columns, the `SELECT` command, combined with specific column names, can be used. For example to only bring back data for the home_id, datetime, and event columns, `SELECT home_id, datetime, event, code_used FROM activity;` can be used.

Exercise 1: Use the INSERT INTO Command

In this exercise, you use the `INSERT INTO` command to write a row of data to the activity table.

1. At a cqlsh command prompt, in the home_security keyspace, enter the following code (can copy the code from the **ex01.txt** file in the achotl1/class_files/**unit07** folder on your desktop) to insert an alarm system event into the activity table:

```
INSERT INTO activity (home_id, datetime, event, code_used)
VALUES ('H01474777', '2014-05-21 07:32:16', 'alarm set',
'5599');
```

Note: the home_id has a zero, not an 'O'.

2. Enter `SELECT * FROM activity;` to see the row in the table:

```
cqlsh:home_security> SELECT * FROM activity;

 home_id    | datetime                   | code_used | event
------------+----------------------------+-----------+-----------
 H01474777  | 2014-05-21 07:32:16-0700   |      5599 | alarm set
```

3. Enter `SELECT home_id, datetime, event FROM activity;` to just retrieve data from those three columns:

```
cqlsh:home_security> SELECT home_id, datetime, event FROM activity;

 home_id    | datetime                   | event
------------+----------------------------+-----------
 H01474777  | 2014-05-21 07:32:16-0700   | alarm set
```

Using the COPY Command

The COPY command can be used to import data (COPY FROM) from a .csv file or export data (COPY TO) to a .csv file.

To use the COPY command to import CSV data, the values in each row of data in the .csv file need to be delimited by a character. For example, in the .csv file in the screenshot below, the values are delimited by the pipe (|) character:

```
● ○ ○                     events.csv
home_id|datetime|event|code_used
H02257222|2014-05-21 05:29:47|alarm set|1566
H01474777|2014-05-21 07:32:16|alarm set|5599
H01033638|2014-05-21 07:50:22|alarm set|2121
H01033638|2014-05-21 07:50:43|alarm turned off|2121
H01033638|2014-05-21 07:55:58|alarm set|2121
```

To use the cqlsh COPY FROM command, the location and name of the .csv file need to be specified and the name of the Cassandra table and columns that the data is to go into need to be specified.

```
COPY activity (home_id, datetime, event, code_used) FROM
'/home/vm1/Desktop/class_files/unit07/events.csv' WITH header =
true AND delimiter = '|';
```

In addition, through the WITH clause, whether the first row is a header or not can be specified, and a delimiter can be specified (default is a comma).

Exercise 2: Use the COPY Command

In this exercise, you use the COPY command to import rows from a .csv file to the activity table.

1. On the **desktop** of your **virtual machine**, in the **class_files** folder, in the **unit07** folder, notice that there is a file named **events.csv**.

2. In a new terminal window, at a regular command prompt (i.e. not cqlsh), enter `vim Desktop/class_files/unit07/events.csv` to view the .csv file in a text editor:

```
vm1@ubuntu:~$ vim Desktop/class_files/unit07/events.csv
```

3. Notice that there are 32 rows of data, with a header row at the beginning of the file, and with the pipe character separating the values in each row:

```
home_id|datetime|event|code_used
H02257222|2014-05-21 05:29:47|alarm set|1566
H01474777|2014-05-21 07:32:16|alarm set|5599
H01033638|2014-05-21 07:50:22|alarm set|2121
H01033638|2014-05-21 07:50:43|alarm turned off|2121
H01033638|2014-05-21 07:55:58|alarm set|2121
H01545551|2014-05-21 08:30:14|alarm set|8889
H00999943|2014-05-21 09:05:54|alarm set|1245
H01033638|2014-05-21 13:02:11|alarm turned off|1919
```

4. Press the **Esc** key and enter `:q` to exit the file.

5. In a terminal window at the **cqlsh** prompt, in the **home_security** keyspace, enter the following command to import the data from the events.csv file to the activity table:

```
COPY activity (home_id, datetime, event, code_used) FROM
'/home/vm1/Desktop/class_files/unit07/events.csv' WITH header
= true AND delimiter = '|';
```

6. Notice that the data imported:

```
cqlsh:home_security> COPY activity (home_id, datetime, event,
code_used) FROM '/home/vm1/Desktop/class_files/unit07/events
.csv' WITH header = true AND delimiter = '|';
32 rows imported in 0.114 seconds.
```

7. Enter `SELECT * FROM activity;` to see the rows in the activity table:

```
cqlsh:home_security> SELECT * FROM activity;

 home_id    | datetime                  | code_used | event
------------+---------------------------+-----------+--------------------------
 H01474777  | 2014-05-23 18:28:41-0700  |      5599 |         alarm turned off
 H01474777  | 2014-05-23 07:44:23-0700  |      5599 |                alarm set
 H01474777  | 2014-05-22 17:22:15-0700  |      5599 |         alarm turned off
 H01474777  | 2014-05-22 11:44:07-0700  |      null | alarm reset by office
 H01474777  | 2014-05-22 11:25:00-0700  |      null |            police called
 H01474777  | 2014-05-22 11:23:59-0700  |      null |           alarm breached
 H01474777  | 2014-05-22 07:44:13-0700  |      5599 |                alarm set
 H01474777  | 2014-05-21 18:30:33-0700  |      5599 |         alarm turned off
 H01474777  | 2014-05-21 07:32:16-0700  |      5599 |                alarm set
 H01033638  | 2014-05-22 07:45:28-0700  |      2121 |                alarm set
 H01033638  | 2014-05-21 19:01:46-0700  |      2121 |         alarm turned off
 H01033638  | 2014-05-21 16:58:39-0700  |      1919 |                alarm set
```

8. Notice that the rows are sorted within each partition based on the datetime values, in descending order.

Seeing How Data is Stored in Cassandra

To view how data is stored in Cassandra, `cassandra-cli` can be used. Cassandra-cli is the older command line interface for communicating with Cassandra, used by Thrift, the low-level API for working with Cassandra. (CQL is a high-level language, created to make it easier for people to work with Cassandra.)

Within cassandra-cli, keyspaces and tables can be accessed with the `USE` and `LIST` commands.

```
vm1@ubuntu:~/cassandra/apache-cassandra-2.0.7$ bin/cassandra-cli
Connected to: "Test Cluster" on 127.0.0.1/9160
Welcome to Cassandra CLI version 2.0.7

The CLI is deprecated and will be removed in Cassandra 3.0.  Cons
CQL is fully backwards compatible with Thrift data; see http://ww

Type 'help;' or '?' for help.
Type 'quit;' or 'exit;' to quit.

[default@unknown] USE home_security;
Authenticated to keyspace: home_security
[default@home_security] LIST activity;
Using default limit of 100
Using default cell limit of 100
-----------------
RowKey: H01474777
=> (name=2014-05-23 18\:28\:41-0700:, value=, timestamp=13989581£
=> (name=2014-05-23 18\:28\:41-0700:code_used, value=35353939, ti
=> (name=2014-05-23 18\:28\:41-0700:event, value=616c61726d207475
=> (name=2014-05-23 07\:44\:23-0700:, value=, timestamp=13989581£
=> (name=2014-05-23 07\:44\:23-0700:code_used, value=35353939, ti
=> (name=2014-05-23 07\:44\:23-0700:event, value=616c61726d207365
```

The cassandra-cli interface shows how data is stored internally in Cassandra.

Each partition has the label of RowKey, not to be confused with rows in CQL. Each cell in a partition has a timestamp for the data it stores.

Comparing CQL Rows and Internal Storage Rows

In CQL, a row's primary key value is what makes it unique. Internally, a partition key value (in Thrift, referred to as a row key value) is what makes an internal storage row unique.

CQL rows

home_id	datetime	event	code_used
H01474777	2014-05-22 07:44:13	alarm set	5599
H01474777	2014-05-21 18:30:33	alarm turned off	5599
H01474777	2014-05-21 07:32:16	alarm set	5599

Internal storage row

H01474777	2014-05-22 07:44:13 alarm set 5599	2014-05-21 18:30:33 alarm turned off 5599	2014-05-21 07:32:16 alarm set 5599

Understanding how data is stored internally in Cassandra is helpful when data modeling.

Exercise 3: See How Data is Stored in Cassandra

In this exercise, you see how the data in the activity table is stored in Cassandra.

1. In another terminal window, in the directory where Cassandra is installed (~/cassandra/apache-cassandra-2.0.7), enter `bin/cassandra-cli` to go into cassandra-cli:

```
~/cassandra/apache-cassandra-2.0.7$ bin/cassandra-cli
```

2. Notice you are now in cassandra-cli:

```
vm1@ubuntu:~/cassandra/apache-cassandra-2.0.7$ bin/cassandra-cli
Connected to: "Test Cluster" on 127.0.0.1/9160
Welcome to Cassandra CLI version 2.0.7

The CLI is deprecated and will be removed in Cassandra 3.0.  Cons
CQL is fully backwards compatible with Thrift data; see http://ww

Type 'help;' or '?' for help.
Type 'quit;' or 'exit;' to quit.

[default@unknown]
```

3. Enter `USE home_security;` to specify the home_security keyspace:

```
[default@unknown] USE home_security;
```

4. See that you are now in the home_security keyspace:

```
Authenticated to keyspace: home_security
[default@home_security]
```

5. Enter `LIST activity;` to view the data in the activity table:

```
[default@home_security] LIST activity;
```

6. Notice that the data is stored by partition (labeled as RowKey):

```
RowKey: H01474777
=> (name=2014-05-23 18\:28\:41-0700:, value=, timestamp=1398!
=> (name=2014-05-23 18\:28\:41-0700:code_used, value=3535393!
=> (name=2014-05-23 18\:28\:41-0700:event, value=616c61726d2(
=> (name=2014-05-23 07\:44\:23-0700:, value=, timestamp=1398!
=> (name=2014-05-23 07\:44\:23-0700:code_used, value=3535393!
=> (name=2014-05-23 07\:44\:23-0700:event, value=616c61726d2(
=> (name=2014-05-22 17\:22\:15-0700:, value=, timestamp=1398!
=> (name=2014-05-22 17\:22\:15-0700:code_used, value=3535393!
=> (name=2014-05-22 17\:22\:15-0700:event, value=616c61726d2(
=> (name=2014-05-22 11\:44\:07-0700:, value=, timestamp=1398!
=> (name=2014-05-22 11\:44\:07-0700:event, value=616c61726d2(
=> (name=2014-05-22 11\:25\:00-0700:, value=, timestamp=1398!
=> (name=2014-05-22 11\:25\:00-0700:event, value=706f6c69636!
=> (name=2014-05-22 11\:23\:59-0700:, value=, timestamp=1398!
=> (name=2014-05-22 11\:23\:59-0700:event, value=616c61726d2(
=> (name=2014-05-22 07\:44\:13-0700:, value=, timestamp=1398!
=> (name=2014-05-22 07\:44\:13-0700:code_used, value=3535393!
=> (name=2014-05-22 07\:44\:13-0700:event, value=616c61726d2(
=> (name=2014-05-21 18\:30\:33-0700:, value=, timestamp=1398!
=> (name=2014-05-21 18\:30\:33-0700:code_used, value=3535393!
=> (name=2014-05-21 18\:30\:33-0700:event, value=616c61726d2(
=> (name=2014-05-21 07\:32\:16-0700:, value=, timestamp=1398!
=> (name=2014-05-21 07\:32\:16-0700:code_used, value=3535393!
=> (name=2014-05-21 07\:32\:16-0700:event, value=616c61726d2(
-------------------
RowKey: H01033638
=> (name=2014-05-22 07\:45\:28-0700:, value=, timestamp=1398!
=> (name=2014-05-22 07\:45\:28-0700:code_used, value=3231323!
=> (name=2014-05-22 07\:45\:28-0700:event, value=616c61726d2(
```

7. When done viewing the data, enter `quit;` to exit cassandra-cli.

Seeing How Data is Stored on Disk

When data is written to a table in Cassandra, it goes to both a commit log on disk (for playback, in case of node failure) and to memory (called memcache).

Once the memcache for a table is full, it is flushed to disk, as an SSTable.

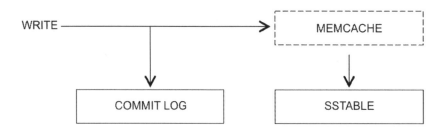

Viewing an SSTable

The SSTables for a table are stored on disk, in the location specified in the cassandra.yaml file. (By default, in the /var/lib/cassandra/data directory.)

```
vm1@ubuntu:/var/lib/cassandra$ ls data/home_security/activity
home_security-activity-jb-1-CompressionInfo.db
home_security-activity-jb-1-Data.db
home_security-activity-jb-1-Filter.db
home_security-activity-jb-1-Index.db
home_security-activity-jb-1-Statistics.db
home_security-activity-jb-1-Summary.db
home_security-activity-jb-1-TOC.txt
```

Any SSTables, and their supporting files, are stored under /var/lib/cassandra/data by default.

To see the contents of an SSTable, sstable2json can be used.

For example, the code below could be used to see the contents of an SSTable named home_security-activity-jb-1-Data.db.

```
bin/sstable2json
/var/lib/cassandra/data/home_security/activity/home_security-
activity-jb-1-Data.db
```

Exercise 4: See How Data is Stored on Disk

In this exercise, you navigate to where the data for the activity table is stored, and then view the data in an SSTable file by using sstable2json.

1. In a terminal window, at a regular prompt, enter `cd /var/lib/cassandra`.

2. Enter `ls` to see the data directory listed:

```
vm1@ubuntu:/var/lib/cassandra$ ls
commitlog  data  saved_caches
```

3. Enter `ls data`, to view the contents of the data directory.

4. Notice the directories for the keyspaces:

```
vm1@ubuntu:/var/lib/cassandra$ ls data
home_security  system  system_traces
```

5. Enter `ls data/home_security` to see the contents of the home_security directory.

6. Notice the directories for the tables:

```
vm1@ubuntu:/var/lib/cassandra$ ls data/home_security
activity  home
```

7. Enter `ls data/home_security/activity` to see the contents of the activity directory:

```
vm1@ubuntu:/var/lib/cassandra$ ls data/home_security/activity
vm1@ubuntu:/var/lib/cassandra$ 
```

8. Notice that the directory is empty, which means there are not yet any SSTables for the activity table.

9. In another terminal window, in the directory where Cassandra is installed, enter `bin/nodetool flush home_security` to flush the memcaches for the home_security keyspace to disk:

```
cassandra-2.0.7$ bin/nodetool flush home_security
```

10. Back in the previous terminal window, re-run `ls data/home_security/activity` to see the SSTable files that now exist:

```
vm1@ubuntu:/var/lib/cassandra$ ls data/home_security/activity
home_security-activity-jb-1-CompressionInfo.db
home_security-activity-jb-1-Data.db
home_security-activity-jb-1-Filter.db
home_security-activity-jb-1-Index.db
home_security-activity-jb-1-Statistics.db
home_security-activity-jb-1-Summary.db
home_security-activity-jb-1-TOC.txt
```

11. Back in the second terminal window (where Cassandra is installed), enter the following code to use sstable2json to view the contents of the SSTable:

```
bin/sstable2json
/var/lib/cassandra/data/home_security/activity/home_security-
activity-jb-1-Data.db
```

12. See the contents of the SSTable:

```
vm1@ubuntu:~/cassandra/apache-cassandra-2.0.7$ bin/sstabl
e2json /var/lib/cassandra/data/home_security/activity/hom
e_security-activity-jb-1-Data.db
[
{"key": "483031343734373737","columns": [["2014-05-23 18\
\:28\\:41-0700:","",1398958151067000], ["2014-05-23 18\\:
28\\:41-0700:code_used","5599",1398958151067000], ["2014-
05-23 18\\:28\\:41-0700:event","alarm turned off",1398958
151067000], ["2014-05-23 07\\:44\\:23-0700:","",139895815
1050000], ["2014-05-23 07\\:44\\:23-0700:code_used","5599
",1398958151050000], ["2014-05-23 07\\:44\\:23-0700:event
","alarm set",1398958151050000], ["2014-05-22 17\\:22\\:1
```

Summary

The focus of this chapter was on inserting data:

- Understanding Ways to Write Data

- Using the INSERT INTO Command

- Using the COPY Command

- Seeing How Data is Stored in Cassandra

- Seeing How Data is Stored on Disk

Unit Review Questions

1) Which command is for inserting a single record into a Cassandra table?

a. WRITE

b. COPY

c. INSERT INTO

d. WRITE ONCE

2) Which command is for inserting data from a .csv file into a Cassandra table?

a. WRITE

b. COPY

c. INSERT INTO

d. WRITE MANY

3) What command line tool can be used to view, at a low level, how data is stored internally in Cassandra?

a. cassandra-cli

b. view-inside

c. cqlsh

d. inside-cassandra

4) By default, where are Cassandra SSTables stored on disk?

a. /home/data

b. /var/lib/cassandra/data

c. /data/cassandra

d. /cass/data

Lab: Insert Data

In this exercise, you insert data into the **home** table in the home_security database. First you use the INSERT INTO command to write one row of data to the table. Then you use the COPY command to import rows of data from a .csv file.

1. At the cqlsh prompt, in the home_security keyspace, enter the following to insert a row into the **home** table:

   ```
   INSERT INTO home (home_id, address, city, state, zip,
   contact_name, phone, phone_password, email, main_code,
   guest_code) VALUES ('H01474777', '518 Crestview Drive',
   'Beverly Hills', 'CA', '90046', 'Jed Clampett', '310-775-
   4011', 'oil', 'jclampett@bhb.com', '5599', '7778');
   ```

2. Enter SELECT * FROM home; to see the row in the table:

   ```
   cqlsh:home_security> SELECT * FROM home;

    home_id   | address              | alt_phone | city          | con
   tact_name | email                | guest_code | main_code | phone
        | phone_password | state | zip
   ----------+--------------------+-----------+-------------+----
   ----------+--------------------+-----------+-------------+---------
   ----+--------------------+-------+-------
    H01474777 | 518 Crestview Drive |      null | Beverly Hills | Jed
    Clampett | jclampett@bhb.com  |      7778 |      5599 | 310-775-4
   011 |            oil |    CA | 90046
   ```

3. Enter SELECT home_id, address, contact_name, phone_password, phone FROM home; to just retrieve data from those columns:

   ```
   cqlsh:home_security> SELECT home_id, address, contact_name, phone_
   password, phone FROM home;

    home_id   | address              | contact_name | phone_password |
    phone
   ----------+--------------------+--------------+----------------+
   --------------
    H01474777 | 518 Crestview Drive | Jed Clampett |            oil |
    310-775-4011
   ```

4. At a regular command prompt (i.e. not in cqlsh), enter `vim` `~/Desktop/class_files/unit07/homes.csv` to view the .csv file in vim:

5. Scan through the data, noticing the header row and that the values in each row are separated by the pipe character:

```
vm1@ubuntu: ~
home_id|address|city|state|zip|contact_name|phone|alt_phone|
H01474777|518 Crestview Drive|Beverly Hills|CA|90046|Jed Cla
H00999943|245 East 73rd Street|New York|NY|10021|Carrie Brad
H01545551|565 North Clinton Drive|Milwaukee|WI|53525|Arthur
H01033638|129 West 81st Street|New York|NY|10024|Jerry Seinf
H02257222|1164 Morning Glory Circle|Westport|CT|06880|Darrin
```

6. Press **Esc** and enter `:q` to exit the file.

7. In **cqlsh**, in the **home_security** keyspace, enter the following command to import the data from the **events.csv** file into the **activity** table:

```
COPY home (home_id, address, city, state, zip, contact_name,
phone, alt_phone, phone_password, email, main_code,
guest_code) FROM
'/home/vm1/Desktop/class_files/unit07/homes.csv' WITH header =
true AND delimiter = '|';
```

8. Notice that the data imported:

```
5 rows imported in 0.047 seconds.
```

9. Enter `SELECT * FROM home;` to view the data in the table:

```
cqlsh:home_security> SELECT * FROM home;

 home_id   | address                   | alt_phone    | city
-----------+---------------------------+--------------+-----------
 H01474777 |       518 Crestview Drive |         null | Beverly Hill
 H01033638 |       129 West 81st Street | 212-483-1072 |      New Yor
 H02257222 | 1164 Morning Glory Circle |         null |      Westpor
 H01545551 |    565 North Clinton Drive |        null |     Milwauke
 H00999943 |        245 East 73rd Street | 212-495-5755 |     New Yor
```

View the location of the data on disk:

10. In a terminal window, at a regular prompt, enter `cd /var/lib/cassandra/data/home_security/home` to navigate to the directory for the home table data.

11. Enter `ls` to see that the directory is currently empty:

```
vm1@ubuntu:/var/lib/cassandra/data/home_security/home$ ls
```

12. In a separate terminal window, in the directory where Cassandra is installed, enter `bin/nodetool flush home_security home` to flush the memcache for the home table to disk:

```
$ bin/nodetool flush home_security home
```

13. Back in the previous terminal window, re-run `ls` to see that SSTable files now exist:

```
vm1@ubuntu:/var/lib/cassandra/data/home_security/home$ ls
home_security-home-jb-1-CompressionInfo.db
home_security-home-jb-1-Data.db
home_security-home-jb-1-Filter.db
home_security-home-jb-1-Index.db
home_security-home-jb-1-Statistics.db
home_security-home-jb-1-Summary.db
home_security-home-jb-1-TOC.txt
```

Alternate Lab Steps: Insert Data

In this exercise, you insert data into the home table in the home_security database. First you use the `INSERT INTO` command to write one row of data to the table. Then you use the `COPY` command to import rows of data from a .csv file.

1. Use the `INSERT INTO` command to insert the following record into the **home** table in the home_security keyspace:

   home_id: `H01474777`
   address: `518 Crestview Drive`
   city: `Beverly Hills`
   state: `CA`
   zip: `90046`
   contact_name: `Jed Clampett`
   phone: `310-775-4011`
   phone_password: `oil`
   email: `jclampett@bhb.com`
   main_code: `5599`
   guest_code: `7778`

2. Use the `SELECT` command to view the contents of the home table:

3. In a text editor, view the contents of the **homes.csv** file that is in the **class_files/unit07** folder on the desktop of the virtual machine:

4. USE the COPY command to import the records in the **homes.csv** file to the **home** table.

5. Use SELECT to check that the 5 records were imported:

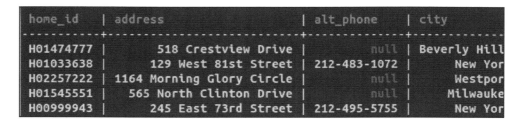

View the location of the data on disk:

6. In a terminal window with a regular command prompt (i.e. not in cqlsh), navigate to the directory where the data for the tables of the home_security keyspace are located.

7. Notice that there are currently no SSTable files for the home table.

8. Flush the memcache for the home table to disk.

9. See that SSTable files for the home table now exist:

```
vm1@ubuntu:/var/lib/cassandra/data/home_security/home$ ls
home_security-home-jb-1-CompressionInfo.db
home_security-home-jb-1-Data.db
home_security-home-jb-1-Filter.db
home_security-home-jb-1-Index.db
home_security-home-jb-1-Statistics.db
home_security-home-jb-1-Summary.db
home_security-home-jb-1-TOC.txt
```

MODELING DATA

Understanding Data Modeling in Cassandra

Understanding Secondary Indexes

Creating a Secondary Index

Defining a Composite Partition Key

Understanding Data Modeling in Cassandra

When data modeling in Cassandra, it is important to understand the implications of working with a distributed database versus a relational one.

No Joins

The fact that joins do not exist in Cassandra is perhaps the most significant data modeling difference between a distributed database versus a relational database. Because the data for a table in a distributed database is spread across the nodes in a cluster (based on the token values generated from the partition values), it would be incredibly slow for a cluster to somehow do joins across multiple tables.

As a result, data modeling in a Cassandra database needs to be done in a way so that all the data for a query is available in one table.

This is not to say that you can only have one table per database. Quite the contrary, it is common to have many tables, often with denormalized data, so that a query request can be handled by a single table.

Instead of data modeling with a data-centric view, data modeling in Cassandra is done by first figuring out what queries will be needed. Then tables are designed to accommodate the queries, so that a query can be answered by a single table.

Understanding Partition Keys and Clustering Columns

As Cassandra is a distributed database with the data organized by partition key, `WHERE` clause queries generally need to include a partition key.

For example, with our previously defined activity table, this query would work:

```
SELECT * FROM activity WHERE home_id = 'H01474777';
```

And this query would work:

```
SELECT * FROM activity WHERE home_id = 'H01474777' AND
datetime > '2014-05-22 00:00:00';
```

But this query would NOT work:

```
SELECT * FROM activity WHERE code_used = '5599';
```

As code_used is not the partition key column, and is not a clustering column, it is not indexed by default, and would therefore be extremely inefficient to reference values of. As a result, Cassandra does not allow the query.

UNIT 8: MODELING DATA

8-3

Exercise 1: Use a WHERE Clause

In this exercise, you attempt to run a few queries with a WHERE clause, to understand when a secondary index would be required.

1. In **cqlsh**, in the **home_security** keyspace, enter the following CQL query to return rows from the activity table only for a specific home:

    ```
    SELECT * FROM activity WHERE home_id = 'H01474777';
    ```

2. Notice that the rows for that home_id were returned:

    ```
    cqlsh:home_security> SELECT * FROM activity WHERE home_id = 'H01474777';

     home_id   | datetime                 | code_used | event
    -----------+--------------------------+-----------+--------------------
     H01474777 | 2014-05-23 18:28:41-0700 |      5599 |   alarm turned off
     H01474777 | 2014-05-23 07:44:23-0700 |      5599 |          alarm set
     H01474777 | 2014-05-22 17:22:15-0700 |      5599 |   alarm turned off
     H01474777 | 2014-05-22 11:44:07-0700 |      null | alarm reset by office
     H01474777 | 2014-05-22 11:25:00-0700 |      null |      police called
     H01474777 | 2014-05-22 11:23:59-0700 |      null |     alarm breached
     H01474777 | 2014-05-22 07:44:13-0700 |      5599 |          alarm set
     H01474777 | 2014-05-21 18:30:33-0700 |      5599 |   alarm turned off
     H01474777 | 2014-05-21 07:32:16-0700 |      5599 |          alarm set
    ```

3. Try entering the following CQL query to only return rows for a specific home for a date range:

    ```
    SELECT * FROM activity WHERE home_id = 'H01474777' AND
    datetime > '2014-05-22 00:00:00';
    ```

4. Notice that only the rows for that home_id and date range were returned:

    ```
    cqlsh:home_security> SELECT * FROM activity WHERE home_id = 'H01474777' AN
    D datetime > '2014-05-22 00:00:00';

     home_id   | datetime                 | code_used | event
    -----------+--------------------------+-----------+--------------------
     H01474777 | 2014-05-23 18:28:41-0700 |      5599 |   alarm turned off
     H01474777 | 2014-05-23 07:44:23-0700 |      5599 |          alarm set
     H01474777 | 2014-05-22 17:22:15-0700 |      5599 |   alarm turned off
     H01474777 | 2014-05-22 11:44:07-0700 |      null | alarm reset by office
     H01474777 | 2014-05-22 11:25:00-0700 |      null |      police called
     H01474777 | 2014-05-22 11:23:59-0700 |      null |     alarm breached
     H01474777 | 2014-05-22 07:44:13-0700 |      5599 |          alarm set
    ```

5. Try entering the following CQL query to only return rows for a particular home for a certain code_used:

```
SELECT * FROM activity WHERE home_id = 'H01474777' AND
code_used = '5599';
```

6. See that, because the code_used column is not a column in the table's primary key, it is not indexed by default and therefore cannot be referenced in a WHERE clause:

```
cqlsh:home_security> SELECT * FROM activity WHERE home_id =
'H01474777' AND code_used = '5599';
Bad Request: No indexed columns present in by-columns clause
with Equal operator
```

Understanding Secondary Indexes

In Cassandra, secondary indexes allow WHERE clauses to reference values in columns other than just the primary key and clustering columns.

By creating an index for columns beyond the partition and clustering columns, values in these other columns can be referenced in WHERE clauses.

However, it is important to know that, contrary to indexes in relational databases, creating indexes for columns beyond the primary and clustering columns, called secondary indexes, does not increase the speed of queries in Cassandra. Secondary indexes simply make it so that WHERE clauses can reference values in columns beyond the primary and clustering columns.

Secondary Indexes Are Not For Speed

Creating a secondary index for a column in a Cassandra table does not increase the speed at which queries return results.

To store a secondary index, Cassandra creates a hidden table, separate from the table that contains the column being indexed.

When a query is run that uses a secondary index, it has to query every node in the cluster, accessing each node's secondary index hidden table.

Creating a Secondary Index

A secondary index can be created for a column by using the CREATE INDEX command. Within the CREATE INDEX command, a name for the index needs to be specified, the name of the column that is to be indexed needs to be specified, and the name of the table that the column is in needs to be specified.

For example, to create an index for the code_used column, the following expression could be run.

```
CREATE INDEX code_used_index ON activity (code_used);
```

Using a Secondary Index

To use a secondary index, simply run a query that references the column that has an index. The name of the secondary index does not need to be specified.

For example, the following query can be run because the home_id column is indexed (because it is the partition key column) and because a secondary index was defined for the code_used column.

```
SELECT * FROM activity WHERE home_id = 'H01474777' AND code_used = '5599';
```

Making Index Tables by Hand

An alternative to having Cassandra create a secondary index for a column through the use of a hidden table, is to define your own table, specifically for a given query.

For example, the following table could be created for a query for the homes in a particular state:

```
CREATE TABLE homes_by_state (
state text,
zip text,
home_id text,
address text,
PRIMARY KEY (state, zip, home_id)
);
```

This handmade table provides a performance improvement over an automatically generated secondary index in that the query can get the needed data from just the relevant nodes rather than having to access every node in the cluster.

One drawback to creating your own index tables, however, is that you are responsible for creating, and updating as necessary, the data in the handmade table as opposed to just having Cassandra automatically create and update a hidden secondary index table.

Exercise 2: Creating a Secondary Index

In this exercise, you create a secondary index for the code_used column in the activity table of the home_security keyspace.

1. In **cqlsh**, in the **home_security** keyspace, enter the following to create a secondary index for the code_used column in the activity table:

   ```
   CREATE INDEX code_used_index ON activity (code_used);
   ```

2. Re-run the query from the last exercise, to see if it will now run:

   ```
   SELECT * FROM activity WHERE home_id = 'H01474777' AND
   code_used = '5599';
   ```

3. Notice that it now works, returning the rows for just the H01474777 home, for just the 5599 code_used:

```
cqlsh:home_security> SELECT * FROM activity WHERE home_id = 'H01474777'
 AND code_used = '5599';

 home_id    | datetime                   | code_used | event
------------+----------------------------+-----------+------------------
 H01474777  | 2014-05-23 18:28:41-0700   |      5599 | alarm turned off
 H01474777  | 2014-05-23 07:44:23-0700   |      5599 |        alarm set
 H01474777  | 2014-05-22 17:22:15-0700   |      5599 | alarm turned off
 H01474777  | 2014-05-22 07:44:13-0700   |      5599 |        alarm set
 H01474777  | 2014-05-21 18:30:33-0700   |      5599 | alarm turned off
 H01474777  | 2014-05-21 07:32:16-0700   |      5599 |        alarm set
```

Defining a Composite Partition Key

A composite partition key is where a partition key is made up of more than one column. If a partition might grow endlessly, such as with a time series use case (imagine collecting the location of a vehicle every second for ever and ever), instead of using the value of just one column as the partition key, the values from more than one column, such as an id and date, can be used to define the partition key.

To create a composite partition key, parentheses are placed around the columns that are to be combined to create the partition key.

For example, in the following code, notice the parentheses around vehicle_id and date.

```
CREATE TABLE location (
vehicle_id text,
date text,
time timestamp,
latitude double,
longitude double,
PRIMARY KEY ((vehicle_id, date), time)
);
```

In using parentheses to define a composite partition key, the values of the columns are combined to create the partition key.

```
RowKey: ME100AAS:2014-05-19
```

Without a composite partition key for time series data, a partition could grow endlessly. For example, if the partition key was only vehicle_id, and the location of the vehicle was collected every second for ever and ever, the partition would grow infinitely.

Time series data can be a good candidate for creating a composite partition key. Although the limit for the number of cells that can be stored in a partition is 2 billion (a fairly large number), it may be better to define a partition key that does not have infinite growth, to avoid the possibility of approaching the limit at some point in time.

In addition, all data for a single partition must be able to fit on disk on a node in the cluster.

Exercise 3: Define a Composite Partition Key

In this exercise, you define a table with a composite partition key.

1. At the cqlsh prompt, enter USE vehicle_tracker; to change to the vehicle_tracker keyspace:

```
cqlsh:home_security> USE vehicle_tracker;
cqlsh:vehicle_tracker>
```

2. Enter the following to create a table named location, noting the parentheses around vehicle_id and date in the primary key declaration.

```
CREATE TABLE location (
vehicle_id text,
date text,
time timestamp,
latitude double,
longitude double,
PRIMARY KEY ((vehicle_id, date), time)
) WITH CLUSTERING ORDER BY (time DESC);
```

3. Realize that the values in the vehicle_id and date columns will combine to define the partition key used to store the data internally.

4. Enter the following command to load data from the coordinates.csv file into the location table:

```
COPY location (vehicle_id, date, time, latitude, longitude)
FROM '/home/vm1/Desktop/class_files/unit08/coordinates.csv'
WITH header = true AND delimiter = '|';
```

5. Notice that the data loaded:

```
30 rows imported in 0.090 seconds.
```

6. Enter `SELECT * FROM location LIMIT 3;` to see the first 4 rows:

```
cqlsh:vehicle_tracker> SELECT * FROM location LIMIT 3;

 vehicle_id | date       | time                      | latitude | longitude
------------+------------+---------------------------+----------+-----------
    ME100AAS | 2014-05-19 | 2014-05-19 08:50:00-0700 |   44.749 |   -67.251
    ME100AAS | 2014-05-19 | 2014-05-19 08:40:00-0700 |   44.746 |   -67.264
    ME100AAS | 2014-05-19 | 2014-05-19 08:30:00-0700 |   44.743 |   -67.343
```

7. In a separate terminal window, in the directory where Cassandra is installed, enter `bin/cassandra-cli` to open the old command line interface for Cassandra:

```
vm1@ubuntu:~/cassandra/apache-cassandra-2.0.7$ bin/cassandra-cli
```

8. Enter `USE vehicle_tracker;` to go into the vehicle_tracker keyspace.

9. Enter `LIST location;` to view the contents of the location table.

10. Notice that each partition key is a combination of the vehicle_id and date:

```
RowKey: ME100AAS:2014-05-19
=> (name=2014-05-19 08\:50\:00-0700:, value=, tim
=> (name=2014-05-19 08\:50\:00-0700:latitude, val
=> (name=2014-05-19 08\:50\:00-0700:longitude, va
```

11. Realize that by having designed the data model so that the location data for each vehicle for each day is in a separate partition, you have avoided creating a partition that grows endlessly.

Summary

The focus of this chapter was on data modeling in Cassandra:

- Understanding Data Modeling in Cassandra

- Understanding Secondary Indexes

- Creating a Secondary Index

- Defining a Composite Partition Key

Unit Review Questions

1) It is common to have denormalized data in Cassandra.

a. True

b. False

2) Secondary indexes make queries run faster in Cassandra.

a. True

b. False

3) It is important to remember the name of a secondary index for referencing it in a WHERE clause.

a. True

b. False

4) What is used to specify a composite partition key?

a. square brackets

b. quotes

c. underscores

d. parentheses

9

CREATING AN APPLICATION

Understanding Cassandra Drivers

Cassandra drivers allow for communicating with Cassandra through various programming languages. For example, an application could be written in Java, C#, or Python, that reads from, and/or writes to, a Cassandra database.

There are Cassandra drivers for many programming languages. These can be found at `http://planetcassandra.org/client-drivers-tools/`.

At the top of the list are drivers certified by DataStax. Further down the list are many more drivers (45+), created by members of the Cassandra community.

Exercise 1: View the Cassandra Drivers

In this exercise, you view the client drivers available for Cassandra, allowing any of fourteen different programming languages to communicate with Cassandra.

1. In a **browser**, navigate to
   `http://planetcassandra.org/client-drivers-tools.`

2. Notice the list of programming languages that have a driver for Cassandra.

3. Notice the list of DataStax certified drivers, at the top of the page.

4. Scroll down the page to see the long list of drivers created by the community.

5. Click on the link for a driver that interests you.

Exploring the DataStax Java Driver

The DataStax Java driver was created to take advantage of the CQL binary protocol introduced in Cassandra 1.2, allowing for CQL queries on a cluster-aware, load balancing, fail over, and asynchronous architecture.

Detail on the driver is available through the DataStax Java Driver 2.0 for Apache Cassandra documentation:

Exercise 2: Explore the DataStax Java Driver

In this exercise, you explore the DataStax Java driver.

1. At the top of the `http://planetcassandra.org/client-drivers-tools` page, click the **DataStax Java Client Driver** link.

2. Scroll down to skim through the page.

3. In a new browser window, navigate to `http://www.datastax.com/download`.

4. Scroll down to the DataStax Drivers section to locate the **DataStax Java Driver** listing:

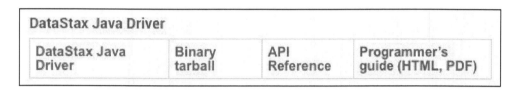

5. Understand that clicking the DataStax Java Driver link goes to the page seen in Step 1.

6. Understand that clicking the Binary tarball link will download the Java driver files as a tarball.

7. Click the **API Reference** link, to view the API reference:

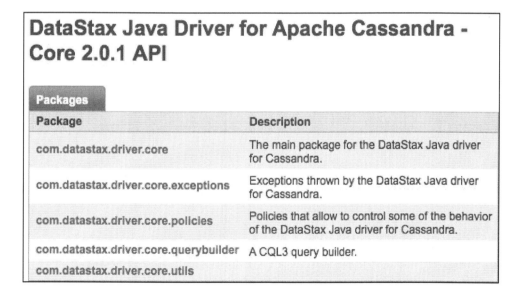

8. Click the **com.datastax.driver.core** link, to see the core classes.

9. Return to the web page with the DataStax Java Driver listing.

10. Access the DataStax Java driver documentation by clicking the **PDF** link (or the HTML link):

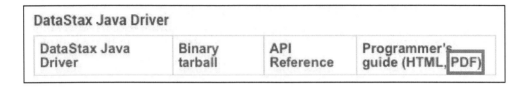

11. In PDF file, scroll down through the file, noting **The driver and its dependencies** section (page 5), **Connecting to a Cassandra cluster** section (page 7), and **Using a session to execute statements** section (page 9).

Setting Up a Development Environment

In order to create an application in your chosen programming language, you will likely want to set up a development environment. For example, to create a Java application, JDK, Eclipse, and Tomcat could be used.

JDK

Oracle JDK allows a Java application to be compiled.

Eclipse

Eclipse, an IDE, provides an environment for writing a Java application.

Tomcat

Apache Tomcat, a web server and servlet container, provides a way to deliver a Java application on the web.

Exercise 3: Access a Development Environment

In this exercise, you first view the steps in Appendix D that were done to create a development environment on your virtual machine. Then you launch the development environment and define a new project for the rental car tracking application.

1. To see what was installed on your class virtual machine to provide you with a development environment for creating Java applications that can communicate with Cassandra, look at the back of this courseware book, in Appendix D: How the Course Virtual Machines Were Built, pages D-6 to D-11.

2. Notice that **Oracle JDK** (pages D-6 to D-8) was installed, allowing you to compile Java applications that you create.

3. Notice that **Apache Maven** (page D-9) was installed, providing an easy way for you to download and use the DataStax Java driver classes in your Java application.

4. Notice that **Eclipse** was installed (page D-10), providing you with a development environment for writing Java application code.

5. Notice that **Apache Tomcat** (page D-11) was installed, providing you with a web server and servlet container for delivering Java applications.

6. In a terminal window, at a regular command prompt, enter `javac -version`, to see that JDK is installed:

```
vm1@ubuntu:~$ javac -version
javac 1.7.0_55
```

7. Enter `cd` to navigate to the default home directory, if not already there.

8. Enter `ls` to see that Eclipse is installed here:

```
vm1@ubuntu:~$ ls
bin
cassandra
conf
Desktop
Documents
Downloads
eclipse
```

9. Enter `ls eclipse` to see the contents of the eclipse directory.

10. Notice the executable file named eclipse:

```
vm1@ubuntu:~$ ls eclipse
about_files    dropins        features       plugins
about.html     eclipse        icon.xpm       readme
artifacts.xml  eclipse.ini    notice.html
configuration  epl-v10.html   p2
```

11. Enter `eclipse/eclipse` to launch Eclipse.

```
vm1@ubuntu:~$ eclipse/eclipse
```

12. In the Workspace Launcher window, click the OK button to use the default workspace:

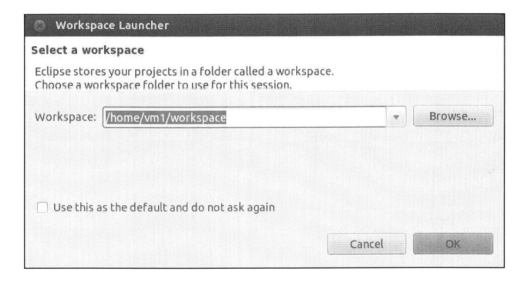

13. In the **File** menu, select **New – Dynamic Web Project** to create a new project:

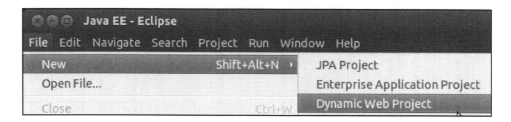

14. For Project name, enter `vehicle-tracker`.

15. In the Target runtime section, see that **Apache Tomcat v7.0** is installed and selected:

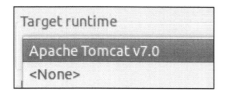

16. Click the **Next** button.

17. Click **Next** again.

18. Select the checkbox for **Generate web.xml deployment descriptor**.

19. Click the **Finish** button.

20. See that the vehicle-tracker project has been created:

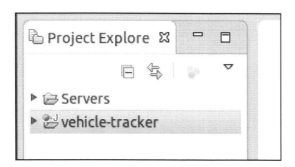

Creating an Application Page

Different programming languages and different development environments have different ways of creating an application page.

For example, a simple Java application page could be created in Eclipse by first defining a Java package, then defining a servlet inside it, writing Java code within the servlet, compiling the servlet, deploying the servlet to a web container, and then interacting with the servlet via a browser. Or, for creating a more robust application, the Java application code could be written using an MVC pattern. (Discussed later in this unit.)

Exercise 4: Create an Application Page

In this exercise, you create an application page in Eclipse for the vehicle-tracker application.

22. In Eclipse, click the **triangle** to the left of the **vehicle-tracker** project, to expand it:

23. Click the **triangle** to the left of **Java Resources**, to expand it:

24. **Right-click** on the **src** folder, to select **New – Servlet**.

25. For Java package, enter `com.vehicletracker.servlet`.

26. For Class name, enter `VehicleTrackerServlet`:

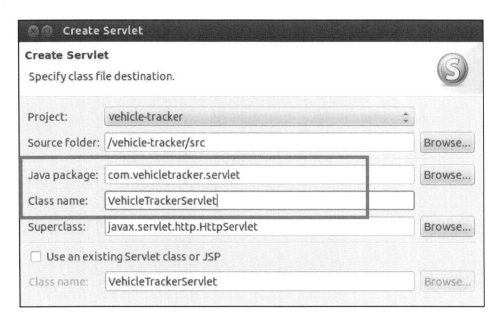

27. Click the **Next** button.

28. In the URL mappings section, select /**VehicleTrackerServlet**.

29. Click the **Edit...** button.

30. Change the pattern to /track:

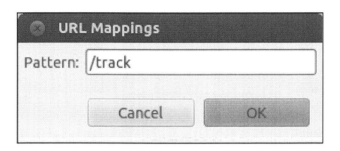

31. Click **OK**.

32. Click **Next**.

33. **Deselect** the checkbox for **doPost**.

34. Click **Finish**.

35. Click the **triangle** to the left of the **src** folder, to see that a package named com.vehicletracker.servlet was created.

36. Click the **triangle** to the left of **com.vehicletracker.servlet** to see that a servlet file named VehicleTrackerServlet.java was created.

37. Notice that the VehicleTrackerServlet.java file is **open**.

38. In the VehicleTrackerServlet.java file, scroll down to locate the **doGet** method:

```
    protected void doGet(HttpServletRequest request, H
        // TODO Auto-generated method stub
    }

}
```

39. At the end of the TODO line, press the **Enter** key twice, to create space to type code within the method:

```
    protected void doGet(HttpServletRequest request, H
        // TODO Auto-generated method stub

        |
    }

}
```

40. Type the following, to output a heading for the application page:

```
PrintWriter out = response.getWriter();
out.println("Vehicle Tracker");
```

41. **Notice** that Eclipse has underlined the unknown PrintWriter class.

42. **Hover** over PrintWriter, to click **Import 'PrintWriter' (java.io)**:

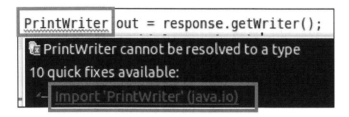

43. At the top of the file, click the plus icon to the left of import java.io.IOException; to see that there is now a statement to import the PrintWriter class:

```
import java.io.PrintWriter;
```

44. Select **File – Save**, to save the VehicleTrackerServlet.java file.

45. **Right-click** on the file, to select **Run As – Run on Server**.

46. Leave Tomcat v7.0 Server at localhost selected, and click **Finish**.

47. Realize that the red text messages at the bottom of the screen, in the Console panel, are likely to be informative messages (not necessarily error messages).

48. Notice that the application page displays in a browser, with the URL of **http://localhost:8080/vehicle-tracker/track**:

Getting the DataStax Java Driver Files

The files required for the DataStax Java driver can be obtained via the DataStax Java driver **binary tarball** link on the `http://www.datastax.com/download#dl-datastax-drivers` page or via Maven.

Needed JAR files include:

- cassandra-driver-core-2.0.1.jar
- netty-3.9.0-Final.jar
- guava-16.0.1.jar
- metrics-core-3.0.2.jar
- slf4j-api-1.7.5.jar

Using Maven

Maven provides an easy way to download and install the DataStax Java driver files.

This can be done in Eclipse by designating the project to be a Maven project and then adding the DataStax Java driver's groupId, artifact, and version information to Maven's pom.xml file.

```
<dependency>
        <groupId>com.datastax.cassandra</groupId>
        <artifactId>cassandra-driver-core</artifactId>
        <version>2.0.2</version>
</dependency>
```

Maven uses its pom.xml file to reference the DataStax Java driver files stored in a repository on Maven Central.

Native Transport

In order to use the DataStax Java driver, the start_native_transport property needs to be set to true in the cassandra.yaml file. This is enabled by default from Cassandra 1.2.5 onwards.

```
start_native_transport : true
```

Exercise 5: Get the DataStax Java Driver Files

In this exercise, you check that the native transport is turned on for your node and then EITHER use Maven to get and install the DataStax Java driver files in your project OR manually install the DataStax Java driver files in your project.

1. In a terminal window, in the directory where Cassandra is installed in your virtual machine, enter `vim conf/cassandra.yaml` to open the cassandra.yaml file in vim:

    ```
    apache-cassandra-2.0.7$ vim conf/cassandra.yaml
    ```

2. Scroll down to **line 310**, to see that native transport is set to true (i.e. `start_native_transport : true`).

3. Press the **Esc** key and enter `:q` to exit vim.

Option 1 (which uses Maven and requires Internet access):

4. In **Eclipse**, right-click on the **vehicle-tracker** project folder to select **Configure – Convert to Maven Project**:

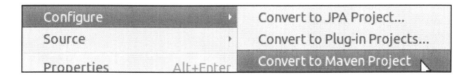

5. In the Create new POM window, leave the defaults and click **Finish**.

6. **Notice** that a pom.xml file has been created and opened.

7. In the pom.xml file, select the **Dependencies** tab:

8. Click the **Add...** button for the **left** column.

9. For Group Id, enter `com.datastax.cassandra`.

10. For Artifact Id, enter `cassandra-driver-core`.

11. For Version, enter `2.0.2`.

12. Click **OK**.

13. **Save** and close the pom.xml file.

Option 2 (which does not use Maven and does not require Internet access):

14. On the **desktop of your virtual machine**, double-click the **class_files** folder, to open it.

15. Double-click the **unit09** folder, to open it.

16. Double-click the **cassandra-java-driver-2.0.2.tar** file, to open it:

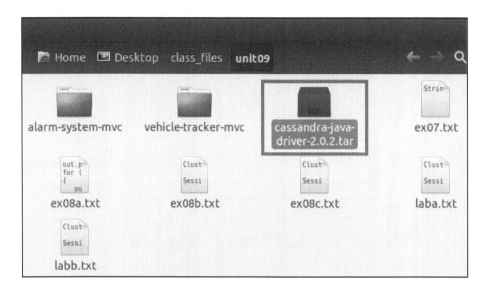

17. Click **Extract**, to unpack the tarball:

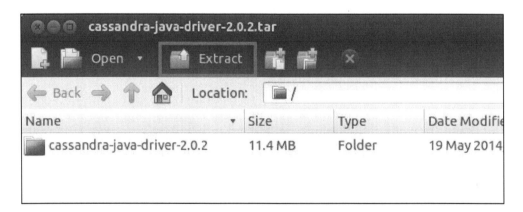

18. In the dialog box that appears, leave the defaults and click the Extract button:

19. Once the extraction is done, click the **Close** button:

20. **Close** the cassandra-java-driver-2.0.2.tar window.

21. **See** that a cassandra-java-driver-2.0.2 folder now exists in the unit09 folder:

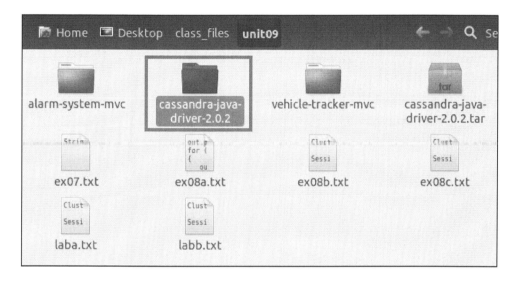

22. **Open** the cassandra-java-driver-2.0.2 folder.

23. **Notice** the **cassandra-driver-core-2.0.2.jar** file:

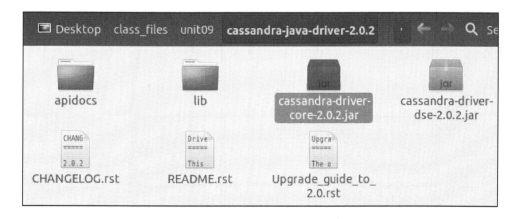

24. Open the **lib** folder.

25. **Notice** the supporting .jar files:

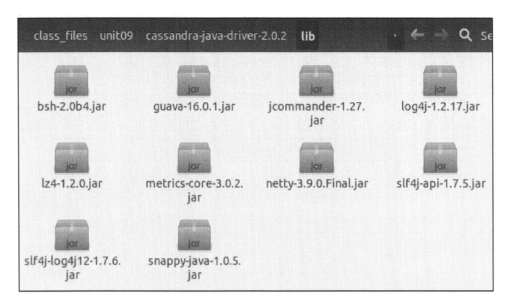

26. In **Eclipse**, in the **vehicle-tracker** project, expand the **WebContent** folder.

27. In the WebContent folder, expand the **WEB-INF** folder.

28. In the WEB-INF folder, notice the **lib** folder.

29. **Drag** the **.jar files** from the class_files/unit09/cassandra-java-driver-2.0.2/**lib** folder to the **lib** folder in Eclipse, to copy them to the vehicle-tracker project.

30. **Drag** the **cassandra-driver-core-2.0.2.jar file** from the class_files/unit09/**cassandra-java-driver-2.0.2** folder to the **lib** folder in Eclipse, to copy it to the project.

31. See that the .jar files are now available in the WebContent/WEB-INF/lib folder of your vehicle-tracker project in Eclipse:

Connecting to a Cassandra Cluster

The Java driver's Cluster class allows an application to communicate with a Cassandra cluster.

To use the Cluster class, a cluster object that references the IP address of at least one node in the cluster needs to be created.

For example, the following code will look on the network that the server running the application is on, to communicate with any one of the IP addresses that are listed, to make an initial connection to a Cassandra cluster.

```
Cluster cluster = Cluster.builder().addContactPoints("127.0.0.1",
"127.0.0.2").build();
```

Once the application has connected to Cassandra through any of the IP addresses, it then knows about all of the nodes in the cluster, including the state of nodes joining or leaving the cluster.

Listing more than one contact point is recommended, so that if one contact point is down, another contact point can be used.

Exercise 6: Connect to a Cassandra Cluster

In this exercise, you use the Cluster class to connect to your Cassandra cluster from your vehicle-tracker application.

1. In Eclipse, in the **VehicleTrackerServlet.java** file, create a blank line after the TODO line:

```
protected void doGet(HttpServletRequest request, HttpSer
    // TODO Auto-generated method stub



    PrintWriter out = response.getWriter();
    out.println("Vehicle Tracker");
```

2. Enter the following code to use the DataStax Java driver Cluster class to create a connection to your Cassandra cluster:

```
Cluster cluster =
Cluster.builder().addContactPoint("localhost").build();
```

   Note: Initially, with our 1-node cluster, we will reference the cluster through localhost. Later, after adding additional nodes to our cluster (Unit 12: Adding Nodes to a Cluster), we will come back to enter two IP addresses.

3. **Notice** that there is a red underline under the word Cluster:

```
Cluster cluster = Cluster.builder().addContactPoint(
```

4. **Hover** over the word Cluster, to select **Import 'Cluster' (com.datastax.driver.core)**:

```
Cluster cluster = Cluster.builder().addConta
```
   - Cluster cannot be resolved to a type
   - 14 quick fixes available:
     - Import 'Cluster' (com.datastax.driver.core)

5. Scroll to the top of the file to see that there is now an import statement for the Cluster class:

```
import com.datastax.driver.core.Cluster;
```

6. **Save** the file.

7. Right-click on the VehicleTrackerServlet.java file to select **Run As – Run on Server**.

8. If a Run On Server dialog box appears, select the checkbox for **Always use this server when running this project** and click **Finish**.

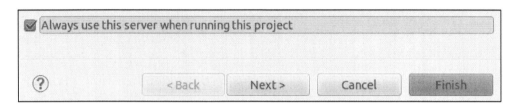

9. If a Server dialog box appears, select the **Continue without restarting** radio button and click OK:

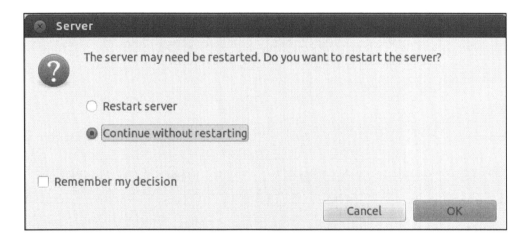

10. See that the application compiles and displays the web page as before, with no errors:

Executing a Query

To execute a query, a few things need to be created. The first is a cluster object (created in the last exercise), the second is a session object, and the third is a query to execute via the session object.

Creating a Session Object

Having a session object allows for CQL queries to be run.

To create a session object, the Session class is used and a cluster connection is passed in. For example, the following code defines a session object.

```
Session session = cluster.connect();
```

In general, only one session object is needed per application.

To limit a session object to a particular keyspace (e.g. for security reasons, to not expose any other keyspaces to the application), the name of the keyspace can be specified when creating the session object.

```
Session session = cluster.connect("vehicle_tracker");
```

Executing a Query

Once a session object exists, a CQL query can be run via the execute query. For example, the following query retrieves latitude and longitude values for vehicle CA6AFL218 on May 19, 2014.

```
session.execute("SELECT time, latitude, longitude FROM
vehicle_tracker.location WHERE vehicle_id = 'CA6AFL218' AND date
= '2014-05-19'");
```

Receiving a Result

In order to use the result of a query, it needs to first be caught by a resultset object. To create a resultset object, the ResultSet class is used.

For example, the following code creates an object named result which stores the result of a CQL query executed by a session object.

```
ResultSet result = session.execute("SELECT time, latitude,
longitude FROM vehicle_tracker.location WHERE vehicle_id =
'CA6AFL218' AND date = '2014-05-19'");
```

Exercise 7: Execute a Query

In this exercise, you create a session object and execute a query to retrieve location data from Cassandra for a vehicle on a certain date.

1. In the **VehicleTrackerServlet.java** file, after the Cluster code, enter the following to create a session object:

```
Session session = cluster.connect();
```

2. Notice that you are passing the cluster connection into the session object.

3. **Hover** over the red underlined Session class to select **Import 'Session'** (**com.datastax.driver.core**):

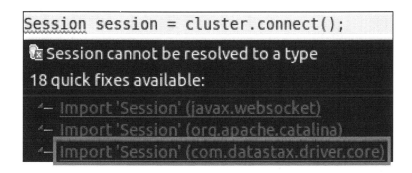

4. On the next line, enter the following to build a query and then run it via the execute method of the session object (can copy from the **ex07.txt** file in the achotl1/class_files/**unit09** folder on your desktop):

```
String vehicleId = "CA6AFL218";
String trackDate = "2014-05-19";

String queryString = "SELECT time, latitude, longitude FROM
vehicle_tracker.location WHERE vehicle_id = '" + vehicleId +
"' AND date = '" + trackDate + "'";

ResultSet result = session.execute(queryString);
```

5. **Hover** over the red underlined ResultSet class to select **Import 'ResultSet'** (**com.datastax.driver.core**).

6. **Save** the file.

7. Right-click on the file to select **Run As – Run on Server**.

8. If prompted, select the **Continue without restarting** radio button and click **OK**.

9. See that the application compiles and displays the web page as before, with no errors:

Displaying Query Results

With the result of a query stored in a resultset object, a row object can be used with a for loop, to iterate through the resultset.

For example, in the following code, the contents of the for loop execute for each row in the resultset object named result.

```
for (Row row : result)
{
   out.println("<tr>");
   out.println("<td>" + row.getDate("time") + "</td>");
   out.println("<td>" + row.getDouble("latitude") + "</td>");
   out.println("<td>" + row.getDouble("longitude") + "</td>");
   out.println("</tr>");
}
```

Row Class

The Row class, useful for accessing rows within a CQL resultset, also includes a number of methods useful for addressing specific column values in a row.

For example, in the code above, the getDate method is being used to access the contents of the time column. Likewise, the getDouble method is being used to retrieve the contents of the latitude and longitude columns.

Exercise 8: Display Query Results

In this exercise, you display query results.

1. **Below** the ResultSet line of code, enter the following (can copy from the **ex08a.txt** file in the achotl1/class_files/**unit09** folder) to loop through the query result, to create a table with a table row for each row in the result:

```
out.println("<table>");
for (Row row : result)
{
    out.println("<tr>");
    out.println("<td>" + row.getDate("time") + "</td>");
    out.println("<td>" + row.getDouble("latitude") + "</td>");
    out.println("<td>" + row.getDouble("longitude") + "</td>");
    out.println("</tr>");
}
out.println("</table>");
```

2. **Hover** over the red underlined Row class to select **Import 'Row'** **(com.datastax.driver.core)**.

3. **Save** the file.

4. Right-click on the file to select **Run As – Run on Server**.

5. If prompted, select the **Continue without restarting** radio button and click **OK**.

6. See the location data display:

```
Mozilla Firefox

http://localhos...e-tracker/track

localhost:8080/vehicle-tracker/track

Vehicle Tracker
<table>
<tr>
<td>Mon May 19 08:50:00 PDT 2014</td>
<td>36.119593</td>
<td>-115.172584</td>
</tr>
<tr>
<td>Mon May 19 08:40:00 PDT 2014</td>
<td>36.044227</td>
<td>-115.181124</td>
</tr>
<tr>
<td>Mon May 19 08:30:00 PDT 2014</td>
<td>35.911527</td>
<td>-115.206312</td>
</tr>
```

7. To see the table display, add opening <html><head></head><body> tags before the Vehicle Tracker heading, and closing </body></html> tags after the closing </table> tag:

```
out.println("<html><head></head><body>");
out.println("Vehicle Tracker");
...

out.println("</table>");
out.println("</body></html>");
```

8. Save the file and rerun it, to see the table display:

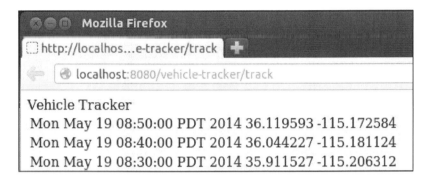

9. Modify the query to return just the first row by adding LIMIT 1 at the end of the query expression:

```
... AND date = '" + trackDate + "' LIMIT 1";
```

10. Save the file, and rerun it, to see that there is just one row being retrieved from the location table:

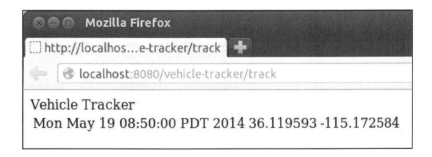

Add additional HTML code to provide a user input form, so that the user can enter a vehicle id and date:

11. **Replace** the contents of the doGet method with the following code, to include a form in the page, for the user to enter the date and vehicle_id of the car they would like to track (can copy from achotl1/class_files/unit09/**ex08c.txt** file):

```
Cluster cluster =
Cluster.builder().addContactPoint("localhost").build();

Session session = cluster.connect();

String vehicleId = request.getParameter("veh_id");
String trackDate = request.getParameter("date_val");
String queryString = "SELECT time, latitude, longitude FROM
vehicle_tracker.location WHERE vehicle_id = '" + vehicleId +
"' AND date = '" + trackDate + "' LIMIT 1";

ResultSet result = session.execute(queryString);

PrintWriter out = response.getWriter();

out.println("<!DOCTYPE HTML PUBLIC \"-//W3C//DTD HTML 4.0
Transitional//EN\"><html>");
out.println("<head><title>Track a Vehicle</title></head>");
out.println("<body>");
out.println("<h1>Track a Vehicle</h1>");
out.println("Enter the track date and id of the vehicle you
want to track");
out.println("<p> </p>");
out.println("<form id=\"form1\" name=\"form1\" method=\"get\"
action=\"\">");
out.println("<table>");
out.println("<tr><td>Date (e.g. 2014-05-19):</td>");
out.println("<td><input type=\"text\" name=\"date_val\"
id=\"date_val\"/></td></tr>");
out.println("<tr><td>Vehicle id (e.g. FLN78197):</td>");
out.println("<td><input type=\"text\" name=\"veh_id\"
id=\"veh_id\" /></td></tr>");
out.println("<tr><td></td><td><input type=\"submit\"
name=\"submit\" id=\"submit\" value=\"Submit\"/></td></tr>");
out.println("</table>");
out.println("</form>");
out.println("<p> </p>");

if(request.getParameter("veh_id") == null)
{
    // blank
}
else if(result.isExhausted())
{
    out.println("<hr/>");
    out.println("<p> </p>");
    out.println("Sorry, no results for vehicle id " +
    request.getParameter("veh_id") + " for " +
    request.getParameter("date_val"));
}
```

```
else
{
    out.println("<hr/>");
    out.println("<table cellpadding=\"4\">");
    out.println("<tr><td colspan=\"3\"><h2>" +
    request.getParameter("veh_id") + "</h2></td></tr>");
    out.println("<tr><td><b>Date and
    Time</b></td><td><b>Latitude</b></td><td><b>Longitude</b>
    </td></tr>");
    for (Row row : result)
    {
        out.println("<tr>");
        out.println("<td>" + row.getDate("time") + "</td>");
        out.println("<td>" + row.getDouble("latitude") +
        "</td>");
        out.println("<td>" + row.getDouble("longitude") + "</td
        out.println("</tr>");
    }
    out.println("</table>");
}

out.println("</body></html>");
```

12. Save the file and rerun it, to see the form display:

13. Enter the date of `2014-05-19` and the vehicle id of `WA063JXD` into the form fields.

    Note: The vehicle id contains a zero, not an "O".

14. Click the **Submit** button.

15. See that the latitude and longitude coordinates for the vehicle were returned from the database:

16. Try entering a date or vehicle id that does not exist (e.g. `2222-01-31` and `QQ123456`).

17. Notice the message that appears:

> Sorry, no results for vehicle id QQ123456 for 2222-01-31

(Optional) Use Google Maps to display the location of the vehicle on a map:

18. **Replace** the contents of the doGet method with the following code (copy from **ex08d.txt**) to display a map with a marker that shows the location of the vehicle:

```
Cluster cluster =
Cluster.builder().addContactPoint("localhost").build();

Session session = cluster.connect();

String vehicleId = request.getParameter("veh_id");
String trackDate = request.getParameter("date_val");
String queryString = "SELECT time, latitude, longitude FROM
vehicle_tracker.location WHERE vehicle_id = '" + vehicleId +
"' AND date = '" + trackDate + "' LIMIT 1";

ResultSet result = session.execute(queryString);
ResultSet result_for_map = session.execute(queryString);

Double lat_for_map = 0.0;
Double long_for_map = 0.0;

for (Row row : result_for_map)
{
    at_for_map = row.getDouble("latitude");
    long_for_map = row.getDouble("longitude");
}

PrintWriter out = response.getWriter();

out.println("<!DOCTYPE HTML PUBLIC \"-//W3C//DTD HTML 4.0
Transitional//EN\"><html>");
out.println("<head>");
out.println("<title>Track a Vehicle</title>");
out.println("<meta name=\"viewport\" content=\"initial-
scale=1.0, user-scalable=no\"/>");
out.println("<script type=\"text/javascript\"
src=\"http://maps.google.com/maps/api/js?sensor=false\"></scri
pt>");
out.println("<script type=\"text/javascript\"> function
initialize() { ");
out.println("var latlng = new google.maps.LatLng(" +
lat_for_map + ", " + long_for_map + "); ");
out.println("var settings = { zoom: 10, center: latlng,
mapTypeControl: true, mapTypeControlOptions: {style:
google.maps.MapTypeControlStyle.DROPDOWN_MENU},
navigationControl: true, navigationControlOptions: {style:
google.maps.NavigationControlStyle.SMALL}, mapTypeId:
google.maps.MapTypeId.ROADMAP}; ");
out.println("var map = new
google.maps.Map(document.getElementById(\"map_canvas\"),
settings); ");
out.println("var companyPos = new google.maps.LatLng(" +
lat_for_map + ", " + long_for_map + "); ");
out.println("var companyMarker = new google.maps.Marker({
position: companyPos, map: map, title:\"Vehicle\" }); ");
out.println("} </script>");
out.println("</head>");
```

```
out.println("<body onload=\"initialize()\">");
out.println("<h1>Track a Vehicle</h1>");
out.println("Enter the track date and id of the vehicle you
want to track");
out.println("<p> </p>");
out.println("<form id=\"form1\" name=\"form1\" method=\"get\"
action=\"\">");
out.println("<table>");
out.println("<tr><td>Date (e.g. 2014-05-19):</td>");
out.println("<td><input type=\"text\" name=\"date_val\"
id=\"date_val\"/></td></tr>");
out.println("<tr><td>Vehicle id (e.g. FLN78197):</td>");
out.println("<td><input type=\"text\" name=\"veh_id\"
id=\"veh_id\" /></td></tr>");
out.println("<tr><td></td><td><input type=\"submit\"
name=\"submit\" id=\"submit\" value=\"Submit\"/></td></tr>");
out.println("</table>");
out.println("</form>");
out.println("<p> </p>");

if(request.getParameter("veh_id") == null)
{
    // blank
}
else if(result.isExhausted())
{
    out.println("<hr/>");
    out.println("<p> </p>");
    out.println("Sorry, no results for vehicle id " +
    request.getParameter("veh_id") + " for " +
    request.getParameter("date_val"));
}
else
{
    out.println("<hr/>");
    out.println("<table cellpadding=\"4\">");
    out.println("<tr><td colspan=\"3\"><h2>" +
    request.getParameter("veh_id") + "</h2></td></tr>");
    out.println("<tr><td><b>Date and
    Time</b></td><td><b>Latitude</b></td><td><b>Longitude
    </b></td></tr>");
    for (Row row : result)
    {
        out.println("<tr>");
        out.println("<td>" + row.getDate("time") + "</td>");
        out.println("<td>" + row.getDouble("latitude") +
        "</td>");
        out.println("<td>" + row.getDouble("longitude") +
        "</td>");
        out.println("</tr>");
    }
    out.println("</table>");
    out.println("<div id=\"map_canvas\" style=\"width:500px;
    height:500px\"></div>");
}

out.println("</body></html>");
```

19. Save the file and rerun it.

20. In the form, enter `2014-05-19` and `ME100AAS` (00 are zeros), to see the map display with the location of the vehicle:

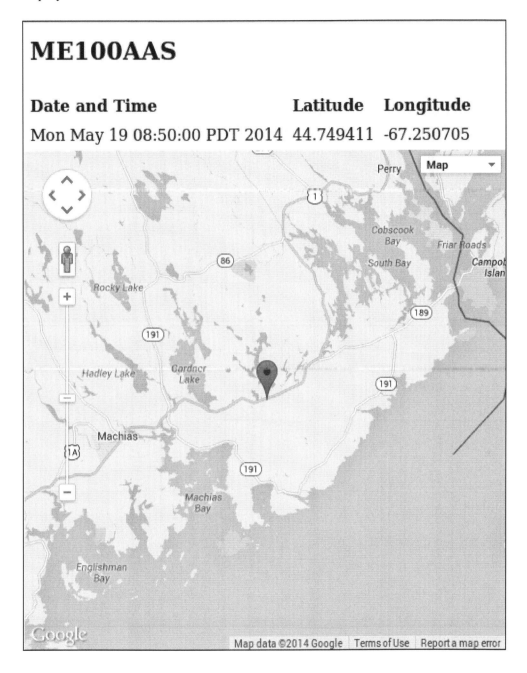

Using an MVC Pattern

MVC, which stands for Model-View-Controller, is a modern design pattern in which the code for an application is separated into its model, view, and controller parts.

Model

Model refers to the data, or backend, aspect of an application. In the case of a Cassandra application, the cluster and session objects for communicating with a Cassandra database would be part of the model code.

View

The view code is for the front-end, or user interface, of an application. The view code determines how the application is displayed to the end-user. In the case of a Cassandra web application, this would likely be HTML/JavaScript code.

Controller

The controller code is for handling the user's interaction with the application. In effect, working between the view and model code. In the case of a Cassandra web application, the controller code would include handling the query requests.

Exercise 9: View an MVC Pattern

In this exercise, you view the Vehicle Tracker application constructed in an MVC pattern, where there are separate files for the model, view, and controller parts of the application.

1. In Eclipse, **close** any open files.

2. Select **File – New – Dynamic Web Project**.

3. For Project name, enter `vehicle-tracker-mvc`.

4. For Project location, **deselect** the checkbox for **Use default location**.

5. Click the **Browse...** button.

6. On the left, select **Desktop**.

7. Double-click the **class_files** folder.

8. Double-click the **unit09** folder.

9. Select the **vehicle-tracker-mvc** folder.

10. Click **OK**.

11. Click **Finish**.

12. **See** that the vehicle-tracker-mvc project now exists.

13. Click the triangle to **expand** the project folder:

14. Click the triangle to the left of **Java Resources**, to expand it.

15. Click the triangle to the left of **src**, to expand it.

16. **Notice** the com.alarmsystem.dao and com.alarmsystem.servlet packages.

17. Click the triangles to **expand** both packages.

18. Notice the files inside:

```
▼ 🗁 Java Resources
   ▼ 🗁 src
      ▼ ⊞ com.vehicletracker.dao
         ▶ 🗋 CassandraAccess.java
         ▶ 🗋 GetsSets.java
         ▶ 🗋 VehicleTrackerDao.java
      ▼ ⊞ com.vehicletracker.servlet
         ▶ 🗋 VehicleTrackerServlet.java
```

19. Double-click **CassandraAccess.java**, to open the model file.

20. Within the code, **notice** the cluster and session objects, for communicating with the Cassandra cluster:

```
Cluster cluster = Cluster.builder().addContactPoint("localhost").build();
Session session = cluster.connect();
```

21. Double-click **VehicleTrackerServlet.java**, to open the view file.

22. **Notice** that there is HTML code, specifying the user interface of the application:

```
PrintWriter out = response.getWriter();

out.println("<!DOCTYPE HTML PUBLIC \"-//W3C//DTD HTML 4.0 Transitional//EN\">
out.println("<head>");
out.println("<title>Track a Vehicle</title>");
out.println("<meta name=\"viewport\" content=\"initial-scale=1.0, user-scalab
out.println("<script type=\"text/javascript\" src=\"http://maps.google.com/ma
out.println("<script type=\"text/javascript\"> function initialize() { ");
out.println("var latlng = new google.maps.LatLng(" + lat_for_map + ", " + lon
out.println("var settings = { zoom: 10, center: latlng, mapTypeControl: true,
out.println("var map = new google.maps.Map(document.getElementById(\"map_canv
out.println("var companyPos = new google.maps.LatLng(" + lat_for_map + ", " +
out.println("var companyMarker = new google.maps.Marker({ position: companyPo
out.println("} </script>");
out.println("</head>");
out.println("<body onload=\"initialize()\">");
out.println("<h1>Track a Vehicle</h1>");
out.println("Enter the track date and id of the vehicle you want to track");
out.println("<p> </p>");
out.println("<form id=\"form1\" name=\"form1\" method=\"get\" action=\"\">");
```

23. Double-click **VehicleTrackerDao.java**, to open the controller file.

24. Notice the query string, for retrieving data from Cassandra:

```
public class VehicleTrackerDao {

    private Session session = null;
    private ResultSet result = null;
    private LinkedList <GetsSets> resultList;

    public VehicleTrackerDao(String vehicleId, String trackDate) {
        getData(vehicleId, trackDate);
    }

    protected void getData(String vehicleId, String trackDate) {
        session = CassandraAccess.getInstance();
        String queryString = "SELECT time, latitude, longitude FROM vehicle_tr
        result = session.execute(queryString);
        resultList = new LinkedList<GetsSets>();

        for (Row row : result) {
            GetsSets location = new GetsSets();
            location.setTime(row.getDate("time").toString());
            location.setLatitude(row.getDouble("latitude"));
            location.setLongitude(row.getDouble("longitude"));
```

25. Double-click **GetsSets.java**, to open a file with additional controller code, which provides Java encapsulation for addressing the columns in the location table:

```
public class GetsSets {
    private String time;
    private Double latitude;
    private Double longitude;

    public String getTime() {
        return time;
    }
    public void setTime(String time) {
        this.time = time;
    }
    public Double getLatitude() {
        return latitude;
    }
    public void setLatitude(Double latitude) {
        this.latitude = latitude;
    }
    public Double getLongitude() {
        return longitude;
```

26. Right-click the **VehicleTrackerServlet.java** file to select **Run As – Run on Server**.

27. See that the application page displays in a browser, with the URL of **http://localhost:8080/vehicle-tracker-mvc/tracker-mvc**.

28. Enter 2014-05-19 and FLN78197, to see that the MVC application works:

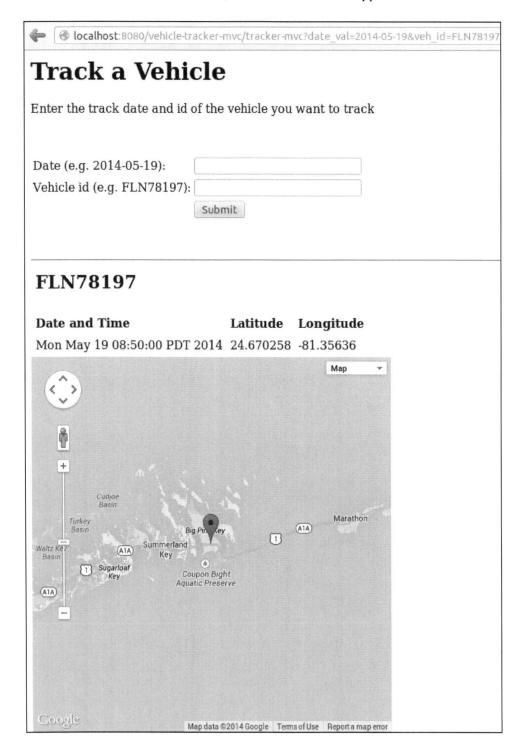

Summary

The focus of this chapter was on creating an application that uses a Cassandra database:

- Understanding Cassandra Drivers
- Exploring the DataStax Java Driver
- Setting Up a Development Environment
- Creating an Application Page
- Getting the DataStax Java Driver Files
- Connecting to a Cassandra Cluster
- Executing a Query
- Displaying Query Results
- Using an MVC Pattern

Unit Review Questions

1) The only client driver that exists for communicating with Cassandra is the DataStax Java driver.

a. True

b. False

2) The DataStax Java driver must be used with Eclipse and Maven.

a. True

b. False

3) When using the Cluster class, it is a good idea to specify the IP address of more than one node so that, if one node is down, an alternate node can be used for the initial connection to the cluster.

a. True

b. False

4) To execute a CQL expression via the DataStax Java driver, a session object is needed.

a. True

b. False

5) The name of the class that receives and holds the result of a CQL query is:

a. Rows

b. Result

c. Results

d. ResultSet

Lab: Create a Second Application

In this lab exercise, you create an application for a person to be able to remotely check on the status of their home alarm system.

1. In **Eclipse**, close any open files.

2. In the **File** menu, select **New – Dynamic Web Project** to create a new project:

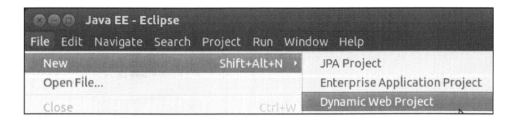

3. For Project name, enter `alarm-system`.

4. In the Target runtime section, see that **Apache Tomcat v7.0** is installed and selected:

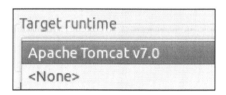

5. Click the **Next** button.

6. Click **Next** again.

7. Select the checkbox for **Generate web.xml deployment descriptor**.

8. Click the **Finish** button.

9. See that the alarm-system project has been created:

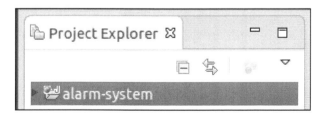

10. Click the **triangle** to the left of the **alarm-system** project, to expand it:

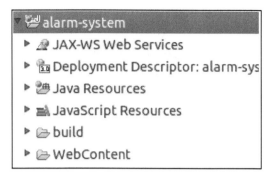

11. Click the **triangle** to the left of **Java Resources**, to expand it:

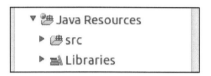

12. **Right-click** on the **src** folder, to select **New – Servlet**.

13. For Java package, enter `com.alarmsystem.servlet`.

14. For Class name, enter `AlarmSystemServlet`.

15. Click the **Next** button.

16. In the URL mappings section, select /**AlarmSystemServlet**.

17. Click the **Edit...** button:

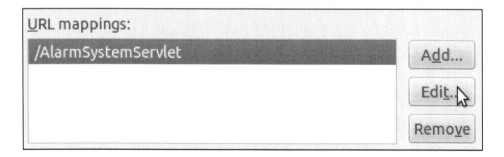

18. Change the pattern to /status:

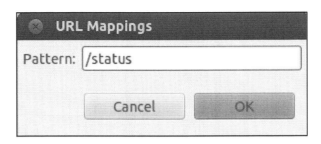

19. Click **OK**.

20. Click **Next**.

21. **Deselect** the checkbox for **doPost**.

22. Click **Finish**.

23. Click the **triangle** to the left of the **src** folder, to see that a package named com.alarmsystem.servlet was created.

24. Click the **triangle** to the left of **com.alarmsystem.servlet** to see that a servlet file named AlarmSystemStatusServlet.java was created:

25. Notice that the AlarmSystemServlet.java file is **open**.

26. In the AlarmSystemServlet.java file, scroll down to locate the **doGet** method:

```
    protected void doGet(HttpServletRequest request, H
        // TODO Auto-generated method stub
    }

}
```

27. At the end of the TODO line, press the **Enter** key twice, to create space to type code within the method:

```
    protected void doGet(HttpServletRequest request, H
        // TODO Auto-generated method stub

        |
    }

}
```

28. Type the following, to output a heading for the application page:

```
PrintWriter out = response.getWriter();
out.println("Alarm System Status");
```

29. **Hover** over PrintWriter, to click **Import 'PrintWriter' (java.io)**:

```
PrintWriter out = response.getWriter();
  PrintWriter cannot be resolved to a type
  10 quick fixes available:
    Import 'PrintWriter' (java.io)
```

30. At the top of the file, click the plus icon to the left of import java.io.IOException; to see that there is now a statement to import the PrintWriter class:

```
import java.io.PrintWriter;
```

31. Select **File – Save**, to save the AlarmSystemServlet.java file.

32. **Right-click** on the AlarmSystemServlet.java file, to select **Run As – Run on Server**.

33. Leave Tomcat v7.0 Server at localhost selected, and click **Finish**.

34. If the Server dialog box appears, select the **Restart server** radio button and click OK.

35. Notice that the application page displays in a browser, with the URL of
http://localhost:8080/alarm-system/status:

Make the DataStax Java driver files available to the project:

36. In Eclipse, **right-click** the alarm-system project, to select **Configure – Convert to Maven Project**.

37. In the Create new POM window, leave the defaults as they are and click **Finish**.

38. Select the Dependencies tab:

39. Click the **Add...** button for the **left** column.

40. For Group Id, enter `com.datastax.cassandra`.

41. For Artifact Id, enter `cassandra-driver-core`.

42. For Version, enter `2.0.2`.

43. Click **OK**.

44. **Save** and close the pom.xml file.

Add code to the servlet that displays a form, queries the home_security.activity table in Cassandra when the form is submitted, and then displays the results on the web page:

45. In the achotl1/class_files/**unit09** folder, open the **laba.txt** file in a text editor:

```
Cluster cluster =
Cluster.builder().addContactPoint("localhost").build();

Session session = cluster.connect();

String homeId = request.getParameter("h_id");
String queryString = "SELECT datetime, event, code_used FROM
home_security.activity WHERE home_id = '" + homeId + "'";

ResultSet result = session.execute(queryString);

PrintWriter out = response.getWriter();

out.println("<!DOCTYPE HTML PUBLIC \"-//W3C//DTD HTML 4.0
Transitional//EN\"><html>");
out.println("<head><title>Alarm System
Status</title></head>");
out.println("<body style=\"font:14px verdana,arial,sans-
serif\">");
out.println("<h1>Alarm System Status</h1>");
out.println("Enter your home id to see the most recent
activity for the system");
out.println("<p> </p>");
out.println("<form id=\"form1\" name=\"form1\" method=\"get\"
action=\"\">");
out.println("Home id: ");
out.println("<input type=\"text\" name=\"h_id\" id=\"h_id\"
/>");
out.println("<input type=\"submit\" name=\"submit\"
id=\"submit\" value=\"Submit\"/>");
out.println("</form>");
out.println("<p> </p>");

if(request.getParameter("h_id") == null)
{
    // blank
}

else if(result.isExhausted())
{
    out.println("<p> </p>");
    out.println("<b>Sorry</b>, no results for home id " +
request.getParameter("h_id"));
}
```

```
else
{
    out.println("<table style=\"font:14px verdana,arial,sans-
serif\" cellpadding=\"4\">");
    for (Row row : result)
    {
        out.println("<tr>");
        out.println("<td>" + row.getString("event") + "</td>");
        out.println("<td>" + row.getDate("datetime") + "</td>");
        out.println("</tr>");
    }
    out.println("</table>");
}

out.println("</body></html>");
```

46. **Notice** the cluster object, for making a connection to the Cassandra cluster.

47. **Notice** the session object, for creating a session, so that CQL queries can be run.

48. **Notice** the CQL query, for retrieving the home alarm activity for the home id entered in the form by the end-user.

49. **Notice** the execute method, for executing the CQL query.

50. **Notice** the result object, for receiving the result of the query.

51. **Notice** the row object in the for loop, for printing a table row for each row of data in the query result.

52. **Copy** all of the code in the laba.txt file.

53. **Replace** the contents of the **doGet** method in the AlarmSystemServlet.java file with the contents of the laba.txt file.

54. **Hover** over the **Cluster** class, to click **Import 'Cluster' (com.datastax.driver.core)**.

55. **Hover** over the **Session** class, to click **Import 'Session' (com.datastax.driver.core)**.

56. **Hover** over the **ResultSet** class, to click **Import 'ResultSet' (com.datastax.driver.core)**.

57. **Hover** over the **Row** class, to click **Import 'Row' (com.datastax.driver.core)**.

58. Save the AlarmSystemServlet.java file and rerun it.

59. See that the form now displays in the browser:

60. Enter H01474777 and press Submit.

61. See the results display:

Add data from the home table to the web page:

62. In the achotl1/class_files/**unit09** folder, open the **labb.txt** file in a text editor:

```
Cluster cluster =
Cluster.builder().addContactPoint("localhost").build();

Session session = cluster.connect();

String homeId = request.getParameter("h_id");
String queryString = "SELECT datetime, event, code_used FROM
home_security.activity WHERE home_id = '" + homeId + "'";
String queryString_hometable = "SELECT contact_name, address,
city, state, zip FROM home_security.home WHERE home_id = '" +
homeId + "'";

ResultSet result = session.execute(queryString);
ResultSet result_hometable =
session.execute(queryString_hometable);

PrintWriter out = response.getWriter();

out.println("<!DOCTYPE HTML PUBLIC \"-//W3C//DTD HTML 4.0
Transitional//EN\"><html>");
out.println("<head><title>Alarm System
Status</title></head>");
out.println("<body style=\"font:14px verdana,arial,sans-
serif\">");
out.println("<h1>Alarm System Status</h1>");
out.println("Enter your home id to see the most recent
activity for the system");
out.println("<p> </p>");
out.println("<form id=\"form1\" name=\"form1\" method=\"get\"
action=\"\">");
out.println("Home id: ");
out.println("<input type=\"text\" name=\"h_id\" id=\"h_id\"
/>");
out.println("<input type=\"submit\" name=\"submit\"
id=\"submit\" value=\"Submit\"/>");
out.println("</form>");
out.println("<p> </p>");

if(request.getParameter("h_id") == null)
    {
       // blank
    }

else if(result.isExhausted())
{
   out.println("<p> </p>");
   out.println("<b>Sorry</b>, no results for home id " +
request.getParameter("h_id"));
}
```

```
else
{
    for (Row row : result_hometable)
    {
        out.println("<p>");
        out.println("<b>" + row.getString("contact_name") +
"</b>, ");
        out.println(row.getString("address") + ", " +
row.getString("city") + ", " + row.getString("state") + ", " +
row.getString("zip"));
        out.println("</p>");
    }

    out.println("<table style=\"font:14px verdana,arial,sans-
serif\" cellpadding=\"4\">");
    for (Row row : result)
    {
        out.println("<tr>");
        out.println("<td>" + row.getString("event") + "</td>");
        out.println("<td>" + row.getDate("datetime") + "</td>");
        out.println("</tr>");
    }
    out.println("</table>");
}

out.println("</body></html>");
```

63. **Notice** the added **queryString_hometable**, **result_hometable**, and **for loop for result_hometable**.

64. **Copy** all of the code in the **labb.txt** file.

65. **Replace** the contents of the **doGet** method in the AlarmSystemServlet.java file with the contents of the labb.txt file.

66. Save the AlarmSystemServlet.java file and rerun it.

67. In the form, enter H01474777 and press Submit.

68. See the results display, including detail from the home table:

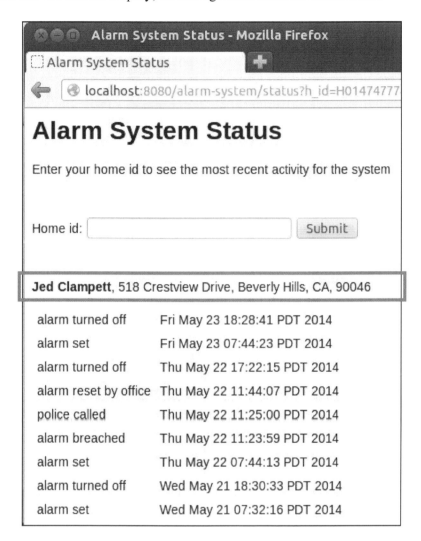

If desired, see the application written in an MVC pattern:

69. In **Eclipse**, close any open files.

70. Select **File – New – Dynamic Web Project**.

71. For Project name, enter `alarm-system-mvc`.

72. For Project location, **deselect** the checkbox for **Use default location**.

73. Click the **Browse...** button.

74. On the left, select **Desktop**.

75. Double-click the **class_files** folder.

76. Double-click the **unit09** folder.

77. Select the **alarm-system-mvc** folder.

78. Click **OK**.

79. Click **Finish**.

80. **See** that the alarm-system-mvc project now exists.

81. Click the triangle to **expand** the project folder:

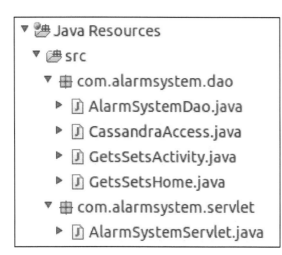

82. Click the triangle to the left of **Java Resources**, to expand it.

83. Click the triangle to the left of **src**, to expand it.

84. Notice the com.alarmsystem.dao and com.alarmsystem.servlet packages.

85. Click the triangles to expand both packages.

86. Notice the files inside:

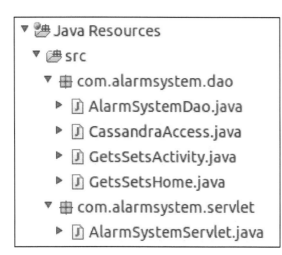

87. Double-click **CassandraAccess.java**, to open the model file.

88. Within the code, **notice** the cluster and session objects, for communicating with the Cassandra cluster:

```
Cluster cluster = Cluster.builder().addContactPoint("localhost").build();
Session session = cluster.connect();
```

89. Double-click **AlarmSystemServlet.java**, to open the view file.

90. **Notice** that there is HTML code, specifying the user interface of the application:

```
out.println("<!DOCTYPE HTML PUBLIC \"-//W3C//DTD HTML 4.0 Transitional//EN\"><html>");
out.println("<head><title>Alarm System Status</title></head>");
out.println("<body style-\"font·14px verdana,arial,sans-serif\">");
out.println("<h1>Alarm System Status</h1>");
out.println("Enter your home id to see the most recent activity for the system");
out.println("<p> </p>");
out.println("<form id=\"form1\" name=\"form1\" method=\"get\" action=\"\">");
out.println("Home id: ");
out.println("<input type=\"text\" name=\"h_id\" id=\"h_id\" />");
out.println("<input type=\"submit\" name=\"submit\" id=\"submit\" value=\"Submit\"/>");
out.println("</form>");
out.println("<p> </p>");

if (request.getParameter("h_id") != null)
{
    AlarmSystemDao asd = new AlarmSystemDao(request.getParameter("h_id"));
    Iterator<GetsSetsActivity> igsa = asd.getResultsIterator();
    Iterator<GetsSetsHome> igsh = asd.getResultsIteratorHome();

    if(igsa.hasNext() == true)
    {
        while (igsh.hasNext())
        {
            GetsSetsHome home = igsh.next();
            out.println("<p>");
            out.println("<b>" + home.getContactName() + "</b>, ");
            out.println(home.getAddress() + ", " + home.getCity() + ", " + home.getStat
            out.println("</p>");
        }

        out.println("<table style=\"font:14px verdana,arial,sans-serif\" cellpadding=\"

        while (igsa.hasNext()) {
            GetsSetsActivity activity = igsa.next();
```

91. Double-click **AlarmSystemDao.java**, to open the controller file.

92. Notice that there are query strings, for retrieving data from Cassandra:

```
protected void getData(String homeId) {
    session = CassandraAccess.getInstance();
    String queryString = "SELECT datetime, event, code_used FROM home_security.
    String queryString_hometable = "SELECT contact_name, address, city, state,
    result = session.execute(queryString);
    result_hometable = session.execute(queryString_hometable);
    resultList = new LinkedList<GetsSetsActivity>();
    resultList_hometable = new LinkedList<GetsSetsHome>();

    for (Row row : result) {
        GetsSetsActivity activity = new GetsSetsActivity();
        activity.setDatetime(row.getDate("datetime").toString());
        activity.setEvent(row.getString("event"));

        resultList.add(activity);
```

93. Double-click **GetsSetsActivity.java**, to open a file with additional controller code, to provide Java encapsulation for columns in the activity table:

```
package com.alarmsystem.dao;

public class GetsSetsActivity {
    private String datetime;
    private String event;

    public String getDatetime() {
        return datetime;
    }
    public void setDatetime(String datetime) {
        this.datetime = datetime;
    }
    public String getEvent() {
        return event;
    }
    public void setEvent(String event) {
        this.event = event;
    }
}
```

94. Double-click **GetsSetsHome.java**, to open a file with additional controller code, to provide Java encapsulation for columns in the home table.

95. Right-click the **AlarmSystemServlet.java** file to select **Run As – Run on Server**.

96. See that the application page displays in a browser, with the URL of **http://localhost:8080/alarm-system-mvc/status-mvc**.

97. Enter H01474777 and press Submit, to see that the MVC application works:

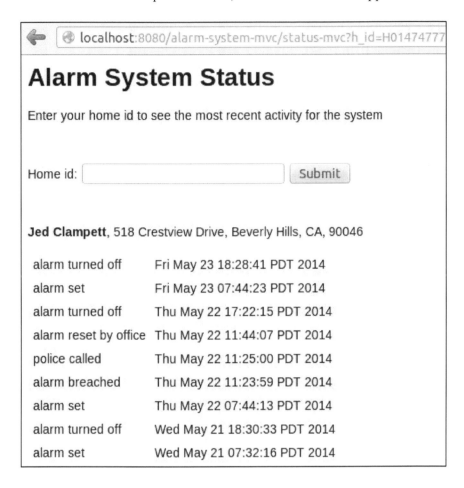

Alternate Lab Steps: Create a Second Application

In this lab exercise, you create an application for a person to be able to remotely check on the status of their home alarm system.

1. Create a new project in Eclipse named `alarm-system`.

2. Use **Apache Tomcat v7.0** as the runtime.

3. In the project, create a servlet named `AlarmSystemServlet` in a package named `com.alarmsystem.servlet`.

4. Write code to have **Vehicle Tracker** display on the web page.

5. Save the servlet and test that it runs in a browser:

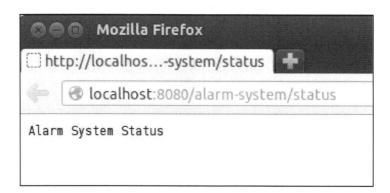

6. Include the DataStax Java driver files in the project, either via Maven or manually.

7. On your desktop, in the achotl1/class_files/**unit09** folder, open the **laba.txt** file.

8. **Review** the code, especially noting the cluster, session, result, and row objects.

9. Copy the code and paste it into the doGet method of the AlarmSystemServlet file, **replacing** what you previously had in the method.

10. Rollover the red underlined classes, importing the needed classes.

11. Save the AlarmSystemServlet file and rerun it.

12. See that the form now displays in the browser:

13. Enter H01474777 and press Submit.

14. See the results display:

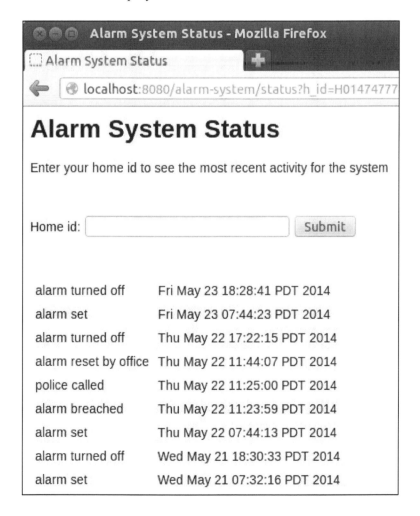

Add data from the home table on the web page:

15. In the achotl1/class_files/**unit09** folder, open the **labb.txt** file in a text editor.

16. **Notice** the added **queryString_hometable**, **result_hometable**, and **for loop for result_hometable**.

17. **Copy** all of the code in the **labb.txt** file.

18. **Replace** the contents of the **doGet** method in the AlarmSystemServlet.java file with the contents of the labb.txt file.

19. **Save** the AlarmSystemServlet.java file and **rerun** it.

20. In the form, enter H01474777 and press Submit.

21. See the results display, including detail from the home table:

If desired, see the application written in an MVC pattern:

22. In **Eclipse**, create a new **Dynamic Web Project**.

23. For Project name, enter `alarm-system-mvc`.

24. For Project location, **deselect** the checkbox for **Use default location**.

25. Use the **Browse...** button to navigate to the alarm-system-mvc folder in the unit 09 folder of the class_files folder.

26. **See** that the alarm-system-mvc project now exists.

27. Click the triangle to **expand** the project folder:

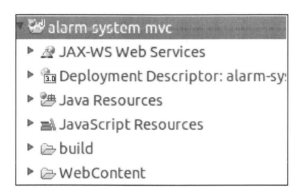

28. Under Java Resources – src, notice the com.alarmsystem.dao and com.alarmsystem.servlet packages.

29. Click the triangles to expand both packages.

30. Notice the files inside:

▼ Java Resources
  ▼ src
    ▼ com.alarmsystem.dao
      ▶ AlarmSystemDao.java
      ▶ CassandraAccess.java
      ▶ GetsSetsActivity.java
      ▶ GetsSetsHome.java
    ▼ com.alarmsystem.servlet
      ▶ AlarmSystemServlet.java

31. Double-click **CassandraAccess.java**, to open the model file.

32. **Notice** the cluster and session objects, for communicating with the Cassandra cluster.

33. Double-click **AlarmSystemServlet.java**, to open the view file.

34. **Notice** that there is HTML code, specifying the user interface of the application.

35. Double-click **AlarmSystemDao.java**, to open the controller file.

36. Notice that there are query strings, for retrieving data from Cassandra.

37. Double-click **GetsSetsActivity.java**, to open a file with additional controller code, to provide Java encapsulation for columns in the activity table.

38. Double-click **GetsSetsHome.java**, to open a file with additional controller code, to provide Java encapsulation for columns in the home table.

39. Right-click the **AlarmSystemServlet.java** file to select **Run As – Run on Server**.

40. See that the application page displays in a browser, with the URL of **http://localhost:8080/alarm-system-mvc/status-mvc**.

41. Enter H01474777 and press Submit, to see that the MVC application works:

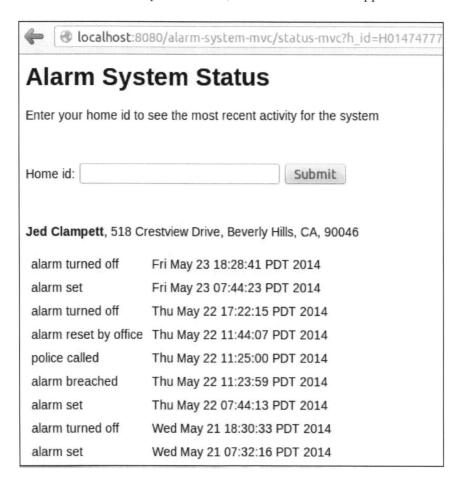

10

· ·

UPDATING AND DELETING DATA

Updating Data

To update row data stored in Cassandra, the UPDATE command can be used to specify the table, the row(s), the column whose value is to be updated, and the value that is to go into the column.

For example, the UPDATE command could be used to update the contact phone number for a home.

```
UPDATE home_security.home SET phone = '310-883-7197' WHERE
home_id = 'H01474777';
```

To update more than one column in the same update, multiple declarations can be specified in the SET clause by separating each with a comma. For example, the following code could be used to update both the phone and the contact_name for a home.

```
UPDATE home_security.home SET phone = '310-883-7197',
contact_name = 'Mr. Drysdale' WHERE home_id = 'H01474777';
```

Exercise 1: Update Data

In this exercise, you use the UPDATE command to update the phone number of a home in the home table.

1. In a terminal window, in **cqlsh**, enter USE home_security; to use the home_security keyspace for subsequent commands.

2. Enter SELECT home_id, address, phone, alt_phone, contact_name FROM home WHERE home_id = 'H01474777'; to view details of a record that you will update:

```
cqlsh:home_security> SELECT home_id, address, phone, alt_phone, contact_name
FROM home WHERE home_id = 'H01474777';

 home_id   | address            | phone        | alt_phone | contact_name
-----------+--------------------+--------------+-----------+--------------
 H01474777 | 518 Crestview Drive | 310-775-4011 |      null | Jed Clampett
```

3. Notice that the phone number is currently 310-775-4011.

4. Enter UPDATE home SET phone = '310-883-7197' WHERE home_id = 'H01474777'; to update the phone number.

5. Rerun SELECT home_id, address, phone, alt_phone, contact_name FROM home WHERE home_id = 'H01474777'; to see that the phone number has been updated to 310-883-7197:

```
 home_id   | address            | phone        | alt_phone | contact_name
-----------+--------------------+--------------+-----------+--------------
 H01474777 | 518 Crestview Drive | 310-883-7197 |      null | Jed Clampett
```

Understanding How Updating Works

When doing an update in Cassandra, unlike relational databases, there is no disk seek to find a record, update its data, and save it. Instead, an update is essentially another write.

For example, the update done in the last exercise (changing the phone number), was simply a write to a memtable, to eventually get flushed to a new SSTable once the memtable is full.

```
vm1@ubuntu:~/cassandra/apache-cassandra-2.0.7$ bin/sstable2json
/var/lib/cassandra/data/home_security/home/home_security-home-jb
-2-Data.db
[
{"key": "483031343734373737","columns": [["phone","310-883-7197"
,1399480188752000]]}
]
```

When a request is made to read the data, Casssandra combines any data from the table's memtable and SSTables that exists for that record. To resolve any conflicts (e.g. a phone number in one write versus a phone number for the same record in another write), Cassandra views the timestamp for each value. Whichever has the latest timestamp is the one that is used to reply to the read request.

Manually Flushing a Memtable

It is possible to manually flush the contents of memtables to disk by using the `nodetool flush` command. In doing so, an SSTable is created for each memtable.

To only flush the memtable for a particular table, a keyspace and table name can be specified with the nodetool flush command. For example, `nodetool flush home_security home` would only flush to disk the contents of the memtable for the home table in the home_security keyspace.

Exercise 2: Get an Inside View into How Updating Works

In this exercise, you get an inside view into how updating works in Cassandra.

1. In a terminal window, at a regular command prompt, enter `cd ~/cassandra/apache-cassandra-2.0.7` to navigate to where Cassandra is installed.

2. Enter `bin/nodetool flush home_security home` to flush the home table's memtable to disk:

```
$ bin/nodetool flush home_security home
```

3. In a separate terminal window, enter `ls /var/lib/cassandra/data/home_security/home` to see the SSTables for the home table:

```
vm1@ubuntu:~$ ls /var/lib/cassandra/data/home_security/home
home_security-home-jb-1-CompressionInfo.db
home_security-home-jb-1-Data.db
home_security-home-jb-1-Filter.db
home_security-home-jb-1-Index.db
home_security-home-jb-1-Statistics.db
home_security-home-jb-1-Summary.db
home_security-home-jb-1-TOC.txt
home_security-home-jb-2-CompressionInfo.db
home_security-home-jb-2-Data.db
home_security-home-jb-2-Filter.db
home_security-home-jb-2-Index.db
home_security-home-jb-2-Statistics.db
home_security-home-jb-2-Summary.db
home_security-home-jb-2-TOC.txt
```

4. In the previous terminal window, in the directory where Cassandra is installed, enter the following to see the contents of the most recent SSTable:

```
bin/sstable2json
/var/lib/cassandra/data/home_security/home/home_security-home-jb-2-Data.db
```

Note: There is a space after sstable2json.

5. See that the SSTable contains the update:

```
vm1@ubuntu:~/cassandra/apache-cassandra-2.0.7$ bin/sstable2json
/var/lib/cassandra/data/home_security/home/home_security-home-jb
-2-Data.db
[
{"key": "4830313437343737","columns": [["phone","310-883-7197"
,1399480188752000]]}
]
```

6. Realize that an update is really a write.

7. Realize that when there is a query, that all of the entries for the requested data are combined (checking timestamps for any conflicting cells) to return the appropriate result.

Deleting Data

There are a number of CQL commands for deleting data in Cassandra, including DELETE, TRUNCATE, and DROP.

Imagine the following table named **messages_by_user** in a keyspace named **playground**:

```
sender | sent                      | body
-------+---------------------------+-----------------------------------
  axel | 2013-07-21 15:34:55-0700  |          for sure! 6:00 at our spot :)
 bobby | 2013-07-21 15:34:01-0700  |                          np, will do
 annie | 2013-07-21 15:31:23-0700  |  will be great to see you guys tonight!
jonesy | 2013-07-21 15:34:03-0700  |                        meet up today?
  juju | 2013-07-21 15:32:58-0700  |                           and mixer!
  juju | 2013-07-21 15:32:16-0700  |               please pick up snacks
```

Deleting a Value

To delete a value, the DELETE command can be used by specifying the name of the column that the unwanted value is in, along with a WHERE clause that specifies which row(s) are to be affected.

```
DELETE body FROM messages_by_user WHERE sender = 'juju' AND sent
= '2013-07-21 15:32:16';
```

Deleting a Row

To delete a row, the DELETE command can be used with a WHERE clause that specifies which row(s) are to be deleted.

```
DELETE FROM messages_by_user WHERE sender = 'juju' AND sent =
'2013-07-21 15:32:16';
```

Deleting All Rows

To delete all of the rows in a table, without deleting the table itself, the TRUNCATE command can be used.

```
TRUNCATE messages_by_user;
```

Deleting a Table

To delete a table, the `DROP` command can be used.

```
DROP TABLE messages_by_user;
```

Deleting a Keyspace

To delete a keyspace, the `DROP` command can be used.

```
DROP KEYSPACE playground;
```

Exercise 3: Delete Data

In this exercise, you create a keyspace and table with data, and then use the DELETE, TRUNCATE, and DROP commands to delete a value, a row, all rows, the table, and the keyspace.

1. In cqlsh, enter the following to create a keyspace name playground:

    ```
    CREATE KEYSPACE playground WITH REPLICATION = {'class' :
    'SimpleStrategy', 'replication_factor' : 1};
    ```

    Note: If the tab key is not providing auto-completion, try exiting cqlsh and then going back in.

2. Enter the following to use the playground keyspace for subsequent commands:

    ```
    USE playground;
    ```

3. Enter the following cqlsh command to run a script that creates a table named messages_by_user, and loads data into the table:

    ```
    SOURCE '/home/vm1/Desktop/class files/unit10/create.cql';
    ```

4. Enter SELECT * FROM messages_by_user; to view the contents of the table:

```
cqlsh:playground> SELECT * FROM messages_by_user;

 sender | sent                       | body
--------+----------------------------+-------------------------------
   axel | 2013-07-21 15:34:55-0700   |          for sure! 6:00 at our spot :)
  bobby | 2013-07-21 15:34:01-0700   |                          np, will do
  annie | 2013-07-21 15:31:23-0700   | will be great to see you guys tonight!
 jonesy | 2013-07-21 15:34:03-0700   |                      meet up today?
   juju | 2013-07-21 15:32:58-0700   |                       and mixer!
   juju | 2013-07-21 15:32:16-0700   |              please pick up snacks
```

5. Enter DELETE body FROM messages_by_user WHERE sender = 'juju' AND sent = '2013-07-21 15:32:16'; to delete the body for the message juju sent at 15:32:16.

6. Rerun `SELECT * FROM messages_by_user;` to see that the value has been deleted:

```
cqlsh:playground> SELECT * FROM messages_by_user;

 sender | sent                       | body
--------+----------------------------+-----------------------------------------
   axel | 2013-07-21 15:34:55-0700 |                 for sure! 6:00 at our spot :)
  bobby | 2013-07-21 15:34:01-0700 |                                     np, will do
  annie | 2013-07-21 15:31:23-0700 | will be great to see you guys tonight!
 jonesy | 2013-07-21 15:34:03-0700 |                               meet up today?
   juju | 2013-07-21 15:32:58-0700 |                                   and mixer!
   juju | 2013-07-21 15:32:16-0700 |                                         null
```

7. Enter `DELETE FROM messages_by_user WHERE sender = 'juju' AND sent = '2013-07-21 15:32:16';` to delete the whole row.

8. Rerun `SELECT * FROM messages_by_user;` to see that the row has been deleted.

```
 sender | sent                       | body
--------+----------------------------+-----------------------------------------
   axel | 2013-07-21 15:34:55-0700 |                 for sure! 6:00 at our spot :)
  bobby | 2013-07-21 15:34:01-0700 |                                     np, will do
  annie | 2013-07-21 15:31:23-0700 | will be great to see you guys tonight!
 jonesy | 2013-07-21 15:34:03-0700 |                               meet up today?
   juju | 2013-07-21 15:32:58-0700 |                                   and mixer!
```

9. Enter `TRUNCATE messages_by_user;` to delete all of the rows in the table.

10. Rerun `SELECT * FROM messages_by_user;` to see that all of the rows have been deleted:

```
cqlsh:playground> TRUNCATE messages_by_user;
cqlsh:playground> SELECT * FROM messages_by_user;

(0 rows)
```

11. Enter `DROP TABLE messages_by_user;` to delete the table.

12. Rerun `SELECT * FROM messages_by_user;` to see that the table has been deleted:

```
cqlsh:home_security> DROP TABLE messages_by_user;
cqlsh:home_security> SELECT * FROM messages_by_user;
Bad Request: unconfigured columnfamily messages_by_user
```

13. Enter `DROP KEYSPACE playground;` to delete the keyspace.

14. Enter `DESCRIBE KEYSPACES;` to see that the playground keyspace is gone:

```
cqlsh:home_security> DROP KEYSPACE playground;
cqlsh:home_security> DESCRIBE KEYSPACES;

system   vehicle_tracker   home_security   system_traces
```

Understanding Tombstones

When a delete is written to Cassandra, what it does is create a tombstone, marking the data for deletion.

A tombstone includes the date for when the data can be deleted.

```
vm1@ubuntu:~/cassandra/apache-cassandra-2.0.7$ bin/sstable2json
/var/lib/cassandra/data/home_security/home/home_security-home-jb
-3-Data.db
        [
{"key": "483032323537323232","metadata": {"deletionInfo": {"mark
edForDeleteAt":1399485775361000,"localDeletionTime":1399485775}}
,"columns": []}
]
```

The reason that data is not immediately deleted is so that there is time for all of the nodes with a replica of the data (like any down nodes) to learn about the mark for deletion. If the deletion were to happen immediately, while a replica node is down, it would be possible for the down node to come back up and replicate the data to the node that had deleted previously deleted it, unaware of the delete.

gc_grace_seconds

The minimum amount of time that must pass before a delete can occur (and its corresponding tombstone) is set in the gc_grace_seconds property for the table. By default, the value of gc_grace_seconds is 864000 (10 days).

Once the gc_grace_seconds amount of time has passed, the data is eligible for deletion.

Compaction

In order for data to actually delete, compaction needs to happen. Compaction is when SSTables are combined, to improve the performance of reads and to reclaim disk space from deleted data.

Compaction is normally done automatically, either via SizeTieredCompactionStrategy or LeveledCompactionStrategy. Detail on both compaction strategies is available in the DataStax Cassandra documentation.

The default compaction strategy is SizeTieredCompactionStrategy, which occurs automatically whenever there are 4 similarly-sized SSTables.

Exercise 4: View a Tombstone

In this exercise, you view a tombstone for a deleted row.

1. At the cqlsh command prompt, enter `USE home_security;` to use the home_security keyspace.

2. Enter `DESCRIBE TABLE home;` to see that gc_grace_seconds is set to 864000 (10 days) and to see that compaction is set to SizeTieredCompactionStrategy:

```
WITH
bloom_filter_fp_chance=0.010000 AND
caching='KEYS_ONLY' AND
comment='' AND
dclocal_read_repair_chance=0.000000 AND
gc_grace_seconds=864000 AND
index_interval=128 AND
read_repair_chance=0.100000 AND
replicate_on_write='true' AND
populate_io_cache_on_flush='false' AND
default_time_to_live=0 AND
speculative_retry='99.0PERCENTILE' AND
memtable_flush_period_in_ms=0 AND
compaction={'class': 'SizeTieredCompactionStrategy'} AND
compression={'sstable_compression': 'LZ4Compressor'};
```

3. Enter `SELECT * FROM home;` to see the rows in the home table:

```
 home_id    | address               | alt_phone    | city
------------+-----------------------+--------------+------------
 H01474777  |     518 Crestview Drive |         null | Beverly Hil
 H01033638  |     129 West 81st Street | 212-483-1072 |     New Yo
 H02257222  | 1164 Morning Glory Circle |       null |     Westpo
 H01545551  |    565 North Clinton Drive |      null |    Milwauk
 H00999943  |     245 East 73rd Street | 212-495-5755 |     New Yo
```

4. Enter `DELETE FROM home WHERE home_id = 'H02257222';` to delete a row in the table.

5. Rerun `SELECT * FROM home;` to see that the row has been deleted:

```
 home_id    | address               | alt_phone    | city
------------+-----------------------+--------------+------------
 H01474777  |     518 Crestview Drive |         null | Beverly Hil
 H01033638  |     129 West 81st Street | 212-483-1072 |     New Yo
 H01545551  |  565 North Clinton Drive |        null |    Milwauk
 H00999943  |     245 East 73rd Street | 212-495-5755 |     New Yo
```

6. In another terminal window, in the directory where Cassandra is installed, enter `bin/nodetool flush home_security home` to flush the home table's memtable to disk:

```
$ bin/nodetool flush home_security home
```

7. Know that an SSTable was created by the flush.

8. Still in the directory where Cassandra is installed, enter the following to see the contents of the new SSTable:

```
bin/sstable2json
/var/lib/cassandra/data/home_security/home/home_security-home-
jb-3-Data.db
```

9. Notice the markedForDeleteAt entry:

```
vm1@ubuntu:~/cassandra/apache-cassandra-2.0.7$ bin/sstable2json
/var/lib/cassandra/data/home_security/home/home_security-home-jb
-3-Data.db
        [
{"key": "4830323233537323232","metadata": {"deletionInfo": {"mark
edForDeleteAt":1399485775361000,"localDeletionTime":1399485775}}
,"columns": []}
]
```

10. Realize this is a tombstone.

Run compaction manually (normally you let compaction happen automatically):

11. In the directory where Cassandra is installed, enter `bin/nodetool compact home_security home` to run compaction manually, to combine the three SSTables into one.

12. Enter the following to view the contents of the combined SSTable:

```
bin/sstable2json
/var/lib/cassandra/data/home_security/home/home_security-home-
jb-4-Data.db
```

13. Notice that the deletion entry still exists, even though compaction has happened:

```
{"key": "30303031303435303632","metadata": {"DeletionInfo":
{"markedForDeleteAt":1397063189388000,"localDeletionTime":13
97063189}},"columns": []},
```

14. Realize that, even though compaction has compacted the three SSTables into one, the tombstone still exists because the gc_grace_seconds period of time has not yet expired.

If desired, see that, because of the compaction, the old SSTables are gone:

15. Enter `ls /var/lib/cassandra/data/home_security/home` to see that there is now just the one SSTable:

```
vm1@ubuntu:~$ ls /var/lib/cassandra/data/home_security/home
home_security-home-jb-4-CompressionInfo.db
home_security-home-jb-4-Data.db
home_security-home-jb-4-Filter.db
home_security-home-jb-4-Index.db
home_security-home-jb-4-Statistics.db
home_security-home-jb-4-Summary.db
home_security-home-jb-4-TOC.txt
```

Using TTLs

TTL stands for Time To Live, and is a way to specify an expiration date for data that is being inserted.

To specify an expiration date, the clause `USING TTL` is included. For example, the following code specifies an expiration of 30 seconds from when the data is inserted.

```
INSERT INTO location (vehicle_id, date, time, latitude,
longitude) VALUES ('AZWT3RSKI', '2014-05-20', '2014-05-20
11:23:55', 34.872689, -111.757373) USING TTL 30;
```

TTL columns are marked with tombstones after they have expired. Once the gc_grace_period of time has passed, the data can then be deleted from disk through compaction.

Updating a TTL

A TTL value can be updated via the `UPDATE` command. For example, to change the expiration date in the code above to 90 days, the following code can be used.

```
UPDATE location USING TTL 7776000 SET latitude = 34.872689,
longitude = -111.757373 WHERE vehicle_id = 'AZWT3RSKI' AND date =
'2014-05-20' AND time='2014-05-20 11:23:55';
```

Exercise 5: Create a TTL

In this exercise, you define a TTL while inserting data in the location table in the vehicle_tracker keyspace.

1. In cqlsh, enter `USE vehicle_tracker;` to change to the vehicle_tracker keyspace.

2. In a terminal window, in the directory where Cassandra is installed, enter `bin/nodetool flush vehicle_tracker location` to flush the location table's memtable to disk (so that we will be able to easily see the TTL markers in Step 8).

3. In cqlsh, enter `INSERT INTO location (vehicle_id, date, time, latitude, longitude) VALUES ('AZWT3RSKI', '2014-05-20', '2014-05-20 11:23:55', 34.872689, -111.757373) USING TTL 30;` to insert a row that will expire in 30 seconds. (Can copy from achot11/class_files/unit10/**ex05a.txt**.)

4. Immediately, enter `SELECT * FROM location;` to see that the row exists:

```
cqlsh:vehicle_tracker> SELECT * FROM location;

 vehicle_id | date       | time                      | latitude
------------+------------+---------------------------+----------
    ME100AAS | 2014-05-19 | 2014-05-19 08:50:00-0700 |   44.749
    ME100AAS | 2014-05-19 | 2014-05-19 08:40:00-0700 |   44.746
    ME100AAS | 2014-05-19 | 2014-05-19 08:30:00-0700 |   44.743
    ME100AAS | 2014-05-19 | 2014-05-19 08:20:00-0700 |   44.728
    ME100AAS | 2014-05-19 | 2014-05-19 08:10:00-0700 |     44.7
    ME100AAS | 2014-05-19 | 2014-05-19 08:00:00-0700 |   44.619
   AZWT3RSKI | 2014-05-20 | 2014-05-20 11:23:55-0700 |   34.873
    FLN78197 | 2014-05-19 | 2014-05-19 08:50:00-0700 |    24.67
    FLN78197 | 2014-05-19 | 2014-05-19 08:40:00-0700 |   24.648
```

5. After 30 seconds, rerun `SELECT * FROM location;` to see that the row no longer displays:

```
cqlsh:vehicle_tracker> SELECT * FROM location;

 vehicle_id | date       | time                      | latitude
------------+------------+---------------------------+----------
    ME100AAS | 2014-05-19 | 2014-05-19 08:50:00-0700 |   44.749
    ME100AAS | 2014-05-19 | 2014-05-19 08:40:00-0700 |   44.746
    ME100AAS | 2014-05-19 | 2014-05-19 08:30:00-0700 |   44.743
    ME100AAS | 2014-05-19 | 2014-05-19 08:20:00-0700 |   44.728
    ME100AAS | 2014-05-19 | 2014-05-19 08:10:00-0700 |     44.7
    ME100AAS | 2014-05-19 | 2014-05-19 08:00:00-0700 |   44.619
    FLN78197 | 2014-05-19 | 2014-05-19 08:50:00-0700 |    24.67
    FLN78197 | 2014-05-19 | 2014-05-19 08:40:00-0700 |   24.648
```

6. In a terminal window, in the directory where Cassandra is installed, enter `bin/nodetool flush vehicle_tracker location` to flush the location table's memtable to disk.

7. In another terminal window, enter `ls /var/lib/cassandra/data/vehicle_tracker/location` to see the SSTable generated:

```
vm1@ubuntu:~$ ls /var/lib/cassandra/data/vehicle_tracker/location
vehicle_tracker-location-jb-1-CompressionInfo.db
vehicle_tracker-location-jb-1-Data.db
vehicle_tracker-location-jb-1-Filter.db
vehicle_tracker-location-jb-1-Index.db
vehicle_tracker-location-jb-1-Statistics.db
vehicle_tracker-location-jb-1-Summary.db
vehicle_tracker-location-jb-1-TOC.txt
vehicle_tracker-location-jb-2-CompressionInfo.db
vehicle_tracker-location-jb-2-Data.db
vehicle_tracker-location-jb-2-Filter.db
vehicle_tracker-location-jb-2-Index.db
vehicle_tracker-location-jb-2-Statistics.db
vehicle_tracker-location-jb-2-Summary.db
vehicle_tracker-location-jb-2-TOC.txt
```

8. Back in the terminal window in the directory where Cassandra is installed, enter `bin/sstable2json /var/lib/cassandra/data/vehicle_tracker/location/vehicle_tracker-location-jb-2-Data.db` to see the contents of the SSTable:

```
vm1@ubuntu:~/cassandra/apache-cassandra-2.0.7$ bin/sstable2json
/var/lib/cassandra/data/vehicle_tracker/location/vehicle_tracker
-location-jb-2-Data.db
[
{"key": "0009415a57543352534b4900000a323031342d30352d323000","co
lumns": [["2014-05-20 11\\:23\\:55-0700:","536b8e33",13995576832
53000,"d"], ["2014-05-20 11\\:23\\:55-0700:latitude","536b8e33",
1399557683253000,"d"], ["2014-05-20 11\\:23\\:55-0700:longitude"
,"536b8e33",1399557683253000,"d"]]}
]
```

9. **Notice** the **d** markers for the columns in the row.

10. Realize that, once their expiration date passed (30 seconds, which it did, as indicated by the d markers, as opposed to e markers), and then the gc_grace_seconds has passed (10 days), the data will be removed when compaction happens.

See e markers:

11. In **cqlsh**, enter `INSERT INTO location (vehicle_id, date, time, latitude, longitude) VALUES ('NERXH276', '2014-05-19', '2014-05-19 13:44:07', 41.129054, -100.921106) USING TTL 180;` to insert a row that will expire in 3 minutes. (Can copy from achot11/class_files/unit10/**ex05b.txt**.)

12. Enter `SELECT * FROM location;` to see that the row exists:

```
 NERXH276 | 2014-05-19 | 2014-05-19 13:44:07-0700 |    41.129 |    -100.92
```

13. In a terminal window, in the directory where Cassandra is installed, enter `bin/nodetool flush vehicle_tracker location` to flush the location table's memtable to disk.

14. Know that an SSTable was generated.

15. Still in the directory where Cassandra is installed, enter `bin/sstable2json /var/lib/cassandra/data/vehicle_tracker/location/vehicle_track er-location-jb-`**3**`-Data.db` to see the contents of the SSTable.

16. **Notice** the **e** markers (for **e**xpiration) for the columns in the row:

```
[
{"key": "00084e4552584832373600000a323031342d30352d313900","colu
mns": [["2014-05-19 13\\:44\\:07-0700:","",1403806341626000,"e",
180,1403806521], ["2014-05-19 13\\:44\\:07-0700:latitude","41.12
9054",1403806341626000,"e",180,1403806521], ["2014-05-19 13\\:44
\\:07-0700:longitude","-100.921106",1403806341626000,"e",180,140
3806521]]}
]
```

17. After 3 minutes have passed from the data insertion, rerun `bin/sstable2json /var/lib/cassandra/data/vehicle_tracker/location/vehicle_track er-location-jb-`**3**`-Data.db` to see that the markers are now d instead of e:

```
[
{"key": "00084e4552584832373600000a323031342d30352d313900","colu
mns": [["2014-05-19 13\\:44\\:07-0700:","53ac6285",1403806341626
000,"d"], ["2014-05-19 13\\:44\\:07-0700:latitude","53ac6285",14
03806341626000,"d"], ["2014-05-19 13\\:44\\:07-0700:longitude","
53ac6285",1403806341626000,"d"]]}
]
```

18. Realize that once the d date (10 days since expiration) has passed, the data can be removed during compaction.

Update the TTL for a column:

19. Calculate the TTL for 90 days (): _____.

    Hint: 60 seconds x 60 minutes x 24 hours x 90 days

20. In cqlsh, enter the following to update the TTL to 90 days for the latitude and longitude values of the row previously inserted:

```
UPDATE location USING TTL 7776000 SET latitude = 41.129054,
longitude = -100.921106 WHERE vehicle_id = 'NERXH276' AND date
= '2014-05-19' AND time='2014-05-19 13:44:07';
```

21. Enter `SELECT * FROM location;` to see that the values are back:

```
NERXH276 | 2014-05-19 | 2014-05-19 13:44:07-0700 |    41.129 |    -100.92
```

If desired, view the e markers in the SSTable:

22. In a terminal window, in the directory where Cassandra is installed, enter `bin/nodetool flush vehicle_tracker location` to flush the location table's memtable to disk.

23. Know that size-tiered compaction happens automatically whenever there are four SSTables of similar size.

24. In another terminal window, enter `ls /var/lib/cassandra/data/vehicle_tracker/location` to see that SSTables 1 to 4 are gone and that there is now just SSTable 5 (i.e. compaction happened automatically, once there were four SSTables of similar size):

```
vm1@ubuntu:~$ ls /var/lib/cassandra/data/vehicle_tracker/location
vehicle_tracker-location-jb-5-CompressionInfo.db
vehicle_tracker-location-jb-5-Data.db
vehicle_tracker-location-jb-5-Filter.db
vehicle_tracker-location-jb-5-Index.db
vehicle_tracker-location-jb-5-Statistics.db
vehicle_tracker-location-jb-5-Summary.db
vehicle_tracker-location-jb-5-TOC.txt
```

25. Back in the previous terminal window, in the directory where Cassandra is installed, enter `bin/sstable2json /var/lib/cassandra/data/vehicle_tracker/location/vehicle_tracker-location-jb-5-Data.db` to see the contents of the SSTable.

26. Scroll up about halfway to see the e markers:

```
ude","41.129054",1402234416207000,"e",7776000,1410010416],
 ["2014-05-19 13\\:44\\:07-0700:longitude","-100.921106",1
402234416207000,"e",7776000,1410010416]]},
```

Summary

The focus of this chapter was on updating and deleting data:

- Updating Data

- Understanding How Updating Works

- Deleting Data

- Understanding Tombstones

- Using TTLs

Unit Review Questions

1) What is the CQL command for updating data?

a. UPDATE

b. UPDATE DATA

c. DATA UPDATE

d. UPDATE NOW

2) What is the CQL command for deleting all of the rows in a table (but leaving the table)?

a. DELETE

b. CLEAR

c. TRUNCATE

d. DROP

3) When does data actually get deleted from disk?

a. As soon as the DELETE command is executed.

b. As soon as the gc_grace_seconds time has elapsed.

c. After the gc_grace_seconds time has elapsed, then during compaction.

d. Data never gets deleted from disk.

4) When does TTL data get deleted from disk?

a. TTL data never gets deleted from disk.

b. As soon as the TTL time has elapsed.

c. As soon as the gc_grace_seconds time has elapsed.

d. After the TTL time has elapsed, then after the gc_grace_seconds time has elapsed, then during compaction.

Lab: Update and Delete Data

In this exercise, you update and delete data.

1. In cqlsh, enter `USE home_security;` to specify the home_security keyspace.

2. Enter `SELECT home_id, address, contact_name FROM home WHERE home_id = 'H01474777';` to view details of a record that you will update:

```
cqlsh:home_security> SELECT home_id, address, contact_name FROM
home WHERE home_id = 'H01474777';

 home_id   | address              | contact_name
-----------+----------------------+--------------
 H01474777 | 518 Crestview Drive  | Jed Clampett
```

3. **Notice** that the contact_name is currently Jed Clampett.

4. At the command prompt, enter `UPDATE home SET contact_name = 'Mr. Drysdale' WHERE home_id = 'H01474777';` to update the contact name.

5. Rerun `SELECT home_id, address, contact_name FROM home WHERE home_id = 'H01474777';` to see that the contact_name has been updated to Mr. Drysdale:

```
cqlsh:home_security> SELECT home_id, address, contact_name FROM
home WHERE home_id = 'H01474777';

 home_id   | address              | contact_name
-----------+----------------------+--------------
 H01474777 | 518 Crestview Drive  | Mr. Drysdale
```

Delete all the activity for home_id H02257222's alarm system:

6. Enter `SELECT home_id, datetime, event, code_used FROM activity;` to see data in the activity table.

7. Notice data for home_id H02257222:

```
 H02257222 | 2014-05-23 18:06:58-0700 | alarm turned off | 1566
 H02257222 | 2014-05-23 07:49:36-0700 |        alarm set | 1566
 H02257222 | 2014-05-22 21:59:44-0700 | alarm turned off | 1566
 H02257222 | 2014-05-21 05:29:47-0700 |        alarm set | 1566
```

8. Enter the following to delete all the activity for the alarm system with the home_id of H02257222:

```
DELETE FROM activity WHERE home_id = 'H02257222';
```

9. Rerun `SELECT home_id, datetime, event, code_used FROM activity;` to see that the activity for home_id H02257222 is gone.

Create and update a TTL:

10. Enter the following to insert an event with an expiration of 20 seconds into the activity table:

```
INSERT INTO activity (home_id, datetime, event) VALUES
('H01033638', '2014-05-22 14:43:07', 'alarm breached') USING
TTL 20;
```

11. Immediately enter `SELECT home_id, datetime, event, code_used FROM activity;` to see the activity in the table.

12. Notice the new row:

```
H01033638 | 2014-05-22 14:43:07-0700 |          alarm breached
```

13. After 20 seconds, rerun `SELECT home_id, datetime, event, code_used FROM activity;` to see that the row is gone.

14. Update the TTL for the inserted data to have an expiration of 6 months:

```
UPDATE activity USING TTL 15552000 SET event = 'alarm
breached' WHERE home_id = 'H01033638' AND datetime = '2014-05-
22 14:43:07';
```

15. Rerun `SELECT home_id, datetime, event, code_used FROM activity;` to see that the row exists:

```
H01033638 | 2014-05-22 14:43:07-0700 |          alarm breached
```

Alternate Lab Steps: Update and Delete Data

In this exercise, you update and delete data.

1. In the **home** table in the **home_security** keyspace, for **home_id** of **H01474777**, update the **contact_name** from Jed Clampett to `Mr. Drysdale`.

2. Check that the update was made:

```
cqlsh:home_security> SELECT home_id, address, contact_name FROM
home WHERE home_id = 'H01474777';

 home_id    | address             | contact_name
------------+---------------------+--------------
 H01474777  | 518 Crestview Drive | Mr. Drysdale
```

3. In the **activity** table in the home_security keyspace, delete all the activity data for **home_id H02257222**.

4. Insert a CQL row of **'H01033638'**, **'2014-05-22 14:43:07'**, and **'alarm breached'** into the **home_id**, **datetime**, and **event** columns of the **activity** table with a TTL of **20 seconds**.

5. Use the SELECT command to check that the row was written:

```
 H01033638 | 2014-05-22 14:43:07-0700 |        alarm breached
```

6. After 20 seconds, check that the row is gone.

7. Update the TTL for the event, to be 6 months.

8. Check that the row is back:

```
 H01033638 | 2014-05-22 14:43:07-0700 |        alarm breached
```

11

SELECTING HARDWARE

Understanding Hardware Choices

Understanding RAM and CPU

Selecting Storage

Deploying in the Cloud

Understanding Hardware Choices

Hardware choices matter for the performance of Cassandra. Although Cassandra does not require special hardware, it is important to ensure that at least the minimum recommendations for RAM, CPU, and storage are met.

Understanding RAM and CPU

The minimum amount of RAM recommended per Cassandra node is 8GB. In production, 32GB of RAM per node is common. The more memory that is available, the better Cassandra's read performance is. This is because, the more data that is already cached, the less chance that time-consuming disk seeks will be needed.

Like RAM, the more CPU power that exists, the better Cassandra's performance will be. Cassandra is highly concurrent and will take advantage of multiple cores. The minimum number of recommended cores is 4. In production, 8 cores is common.

Exercise 1: Check for RAM

In this exercise, you check the amount of RAM that you have on your computer for the upcoming exercises in this course. (At least 8GB of RAM will be needed on your computer for creating our cluster of four nodes. The virtual machines that we will be using each use 1.5GB of RAM.)

If you are using a **Macintosh** computer for this course:

1. Go to the Apple menu (upper-left corner) and select About This Mac.

2. In the window that appears, view the amount of memory that the computer has:

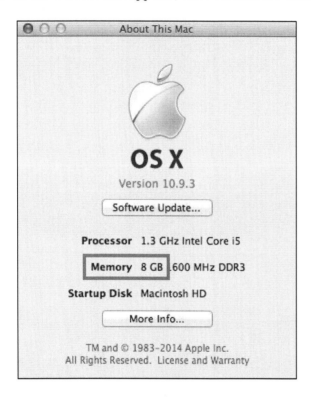

If you are using a **Windows** computer for this course:

Note: the following steps may vary depending on the version of Windows.

1. Right-click on **My Computer** (not C:\), to select **Properties**.

2. In the window that appears, view the amount of memory that the computer has:

Selecting Storage

The type of storage used for Cassandra can greatly affect performance. Storage considerations include whether the storage is shared, type of drive, and capacity.

Shared storage can have a significantly negative effect on the performance of Cassandra. This is because, if the disk head is often being pulled to service others, it will take longer to service the requests to your database. Hence, it is highly recommended to NOT use **shared storage**.

For type of drive, **SSDs** (solid state drives) are preferred. They provide much faster performance than spinning disks. Having said that, either can be used with Cassandra.

With regards to capacity, it is generally better (for performance) to have more nodes in your cluster, with less data on them, rather than just a few nodes in the cluster, with tons of data on them. The recommended amount of data per node varies with the type of disk being used, but is generally from **500GB to 1TB**.

Separate Drive for Commit Log

To provide maximum write performance, it is recommended to have a separate drive for the commit log. By having a separate drive for the commit log, the disk head does not need to move, and so can continuously be used to write commit log entries. It is fine for the commit log disk to be a spinning disk, as the disk head does not need to move.

The location of the commit log is configurable in the cassandra.yaml file on each node.

Exercise 2: View Available Storage on Your Computer

In this exercise, you check the amount of free storage space that you have on your computer for the upcoming exercises in this course. (At least 30GB in total is needed for the four virtual machines we will be using in our cluster.)

If you are using a **Macintosh** computer for this course:

1. Select the **Macintosh HD**.

2. In the **File** menu, select **Get Info**.

3. View the amount of space available:

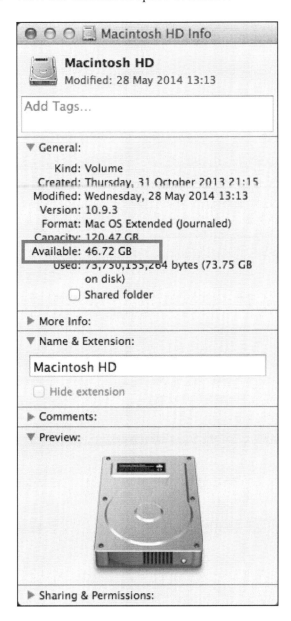

If you are using a **Windows** computer for this course:

1. Right-click **C:**, to select **Properties**.

2. View the amount of free space available:

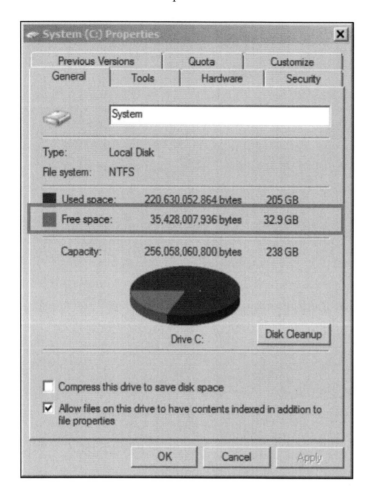

Deploying in the Cloud

Cassandra can be deployed in the cloud. Popular cloud environments for Cassandra include Amazon Web Services and Google Compute Engine, as well as others.

Amazon Web Services

Amazon Web Services offers a wide range of instance types to choose from at various price points.

For up to **1TB** of data per node, **i2.2xlarge** instances with 60GB of RAM and SSDs are recommended.

For up to **100GB** of data per node, **c3.2xlarge** instances with 15GB of RAM and SSDs are recommended.

Amazon's EBS (shared storage) is not recommended, due to the possibility of I/O contention.

Google Compute Engine

Relatively new, Google's cloud offering, Google Compute Engine, is another example of a cloud environment for Cassandra.

For up to **1TB** of data per node, **n1-highmem-16** instances with 104GB of RAM and persistent storage are recommended.

For up to **200GB** of data per node, **n1-standard-8** instances with 30GB of RAM and persistent storage can be used.

Exercise 3: View Cloud Recommendations

In this exercise, you view recommendations for deploying Cassandra in the cloud, as well as on-premise.

1. In a browser, navigate to `http://www.datastax.com/wp-content/uploads/2014/01/WP-DataStax-Enterprise-Reference-Architecture.pdf`.

2. Scan through the table of contents:

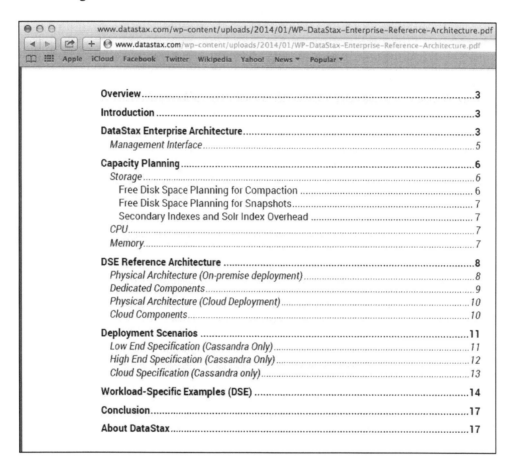

3. To view cloud recommendations, scroll down to page 13.

4. Continue perusing the document, as desired.

Summary

The focus of this chapter was on selecting hardware for Cassandra:

- Understanding Hardware Choices

- Understanding RAM and CPU

- Selecting Storage

- Deploying in the Cloud

Unit Review Questions

1) Cassandra is able to take significant advantage of multiple cores.

a. True

b. False

2) 8GB to 32GB (or more) of RAM per node is recommended for Cassandra.

a. True

b. False

3) Shared storage is recommended for use with Cassandra.

a. True

b. False

4) It is a good idea to have a node's commit log write to a drive that is separate from the drive being used for reads.

a. True

b. False

5) Cassandra can be deployed in the cloud only with Amazon Web Services or Google Compute Engine.

a. True

b. False

12

· ·

ADDING NODES
TO A CLUSTER

Understanding Cassandra Nodes

Each node in a Cassandra cluster has the same functionality as the others. As a result, it is fairly easy to add a node to a Cassandra cluster.

To add a node, it needs to have the same **cluster name** as the other nodes in the Cassandra. Defined in the cassandra.yaml file, the name of a cluster is Test Cluster by default.

```
# The name of the cluster. This is mainly used to prevent
# one logical cluster from joining another.
cluster_name: 'Test Cluster'
```

Along with needing the same cluster name, the nodes need various settings in order to be able to communicate with each other, as described in the next few topics.

Exercise 1: Set up a Second a Node

In this exercise, you set up a second virtual machine, to provide another node for the cluster.

1. In the **achotl1** folder on your desktop, unzip the **achotl1_vmx_64-bit.zip** file.

2. Rename the unzipped file `achotl1_vm2_64-bit`.

   Windows users: rename the achotl1_vmx_64-bit.vmx file in the achotl1_vmx_64-bit.vmwarevm subfolder.

3. **Double-click** the file, to open the virtual machine in VMware.

4. If prompted with a message about other virtual machines running, click **OK**.

5. If prompted, click the **I copied it** button.

6. Enter with the password of `ubuntu`.

In VMware, change the name of the virtual machine to achotl1_vm2_64-bit:

7. Select **Virtual Machine – Settings…**.

   *Windows users: select **Player – Manage – Virtual Machine Settings…**.*

8. Double-click the **General** icon.

   *Windows users: select the **Options** tab.*

9. To the right of Name, **click on** the name (achotl1_vmx_64-bit), to edit it:

10. Change the name to `achotl1_vm2_64-bit`:

11. Close the window.

12. See that the name of the virtual machine has been changed:

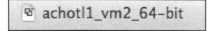

Having a Network Connection

The nodes for a Cassandra cluster need to be in a network that allows them to communicate with each other. In addition, as Cassandra is a distributed database, the faster the network connection between the nodes, the more performant Cassandra can be. Recommended bandwidth is 1000 megabits (or more) per second.

Common ports used in Cassandra:

7000   Cassandra intra-node communication

9042   Cassandra native binary protocol client

9160   Thrift client

7199   JMX monitoring

Working with the Course Virtual Machines

By default, the course virtual machines (created with VMware Fusion 6.0.2) use the network connectivity of the host computer (i.e. your computer) to connect externally (e.g. to www.google.com). On the host computer, each virtual machine is given a dynamic IP address by default. Over time, the dynamic IP address assigned to a virtual machine may change, which stops Cassandra from working. To avoid this problem, static IP addresses can be assigned.

Defining Static IP Addresses

Static IP addresses can be assigned to Ubuntu virtual machines by gathering the network settings for the host computer and then using them in the system settings of the virtual machines.

Exercise 2: Have a Network Connection

In this exercise, you check that your virtual machines can ping each other through their default dynamic IP addresses. Then, you make the hostnames unique and define a static IP address for each virtual machine.

1. In vm**1**, in a terminal window, enter `ifconfig` to see the dynamic IP address currently assigned to vm1:

    ```
    vm1@ubuntu:~$ ifconfig
    eth0      Link encap:Ethernet  HWaddr
              inet addr:192.168.159.215
    ```

2. Write down the IP address of **your vm1**: _____ . _____ . _____ . _____.

3. In vm2, open a terminal window and enter `ifconfig` to see the dynamic IP address currently assigned to this virtual machine:

    ```
    vmx@ubuntu:~$ ifconfig
    eth0      Link encap:Ethernet  HWaddr
              inet addr:192.168.159.207
    ```

4. Write down the IP address of **your vm2**: _____ . _____ . _____ . _____.

5. In vm**2**, enter `ping 192.168.159.215` (substituting in the IP address of your vm1), to ping vm1, to check that your vm2 can communicate with your vm1:

    ```
    vmx@ubuntu:~$ ping 192.168.159.215
    PING 192.168.159.215 (192.168.159.215) 56(84) by
    64 bytes from 192.168.159.215: icmp_req=1 ttl=64
    64 bytes from 192.168.159.215: icmp_req=2 ttl=64
    ```

6. Press **Ctrl-C** to stop pinging.

Gather the network data for defining static IP addresses for your virtual machines:

7. In vm1, in the terminal window where you ran `ifconfig` note the network settings for the virtual machine:

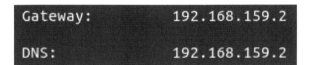

```
vm1@ubuntu:~$ ifconfig
eth0      Link encap:Ethernet  HWaddr 00:0c:29:d7:71:71
          inet addr:192.168.159.215  Bcast:192.168.159.255
 Mask:255.255.255.0
```

8. Write down your **broadcast address**: ____ . ____ . ____ . ____.

9. Write down your **mask**: ____ . ____ . ____ . ____.

10. Enter `nm-tool` to see the gateway IP address and DNS IP address that your virtual machine is using:

```
Gateway:          192.168.159.2

DNS:              192.168.159.2
```

11. Write down your **gateway IP address**: ____ . ____ . ____ . ____.

12. Write down your **DNS IP address**: ____ . ____ . ____ . ____.

13. Using the first three octets from your dynamic IP address, decide that you will create static IP addresses for your four virtual machines with the fourth octet starting at 101:

    *192.168.159.***101**
    *192.168.159.***102**
    *192.168.159.***103**
    *192.168.159.***104**

Change the network settings for the virtual machines to a static IP address:

14. In vm1, close Firefox, close Eclipse, exit cqlsh, flush Cassandra (`bin/nodetool flush`), stop Cassandra (and run `ps aux | grep cass` to check that there are no instances of it running, `kill xxxx` if there are), and close all windows.

15. In the upper-right corner, under the gear icon, select **System Settings**:

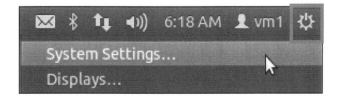

16. Click the **Network** icon.

17. Click the **Options...** button.

18. Select the **IPv4 Settings** tab:

19. For Method, select **Manual**:

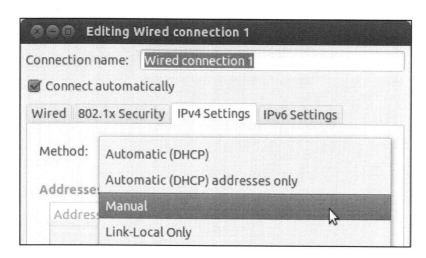

20. In the Addresses, section, click the **Add** button:

21. For **Address**, enter your static IP address for this virtual machine from Step 13 (e.g. *192.168.159.*101).

22. For **Netmask**, enter your mask IP address from Step 9 (e.g. *255.255.255.0*).

23. For **Gateway**, enter your gateway IP address from Step 11 (e.g. *192.168.159.2*).

24. For **DNS servers**, enter your DNS IP address from Step 12 (e.g. *192.168.159.2*).

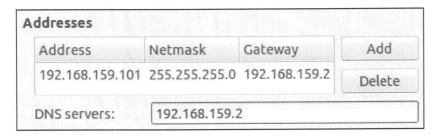

25. Click the **Save** button.

26. If a dialog box with an error message appears, click the **Continue** button.

27. Notice your settings in the Network window:

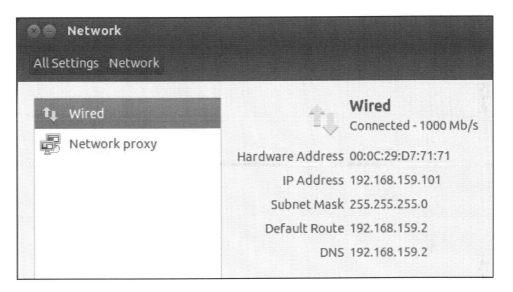

28. **Close** the Network window.

29. **Select Virtual Machine – Restart**, to restart the virtual machine.

*Windows users: select **Player – Power – Restart Guest**.*

30. Once the virtual machine has restarted, open a terminal window and enter `ifconfig` to see the static IP address displayed:

```
⊗⊜◉  vm1@ubuntu: ~
vm1@ubuntu:~$ ifconfig
eth0      Link encap:Ethernet  HWaddr 00:0c:29:d7:71:71
          inet addr 192.168.159.101  Bcast:192.168.159.255  N
          inet6 addr: fe80::20c:29ff:fed7:7171/64 Scope:Link
          UP BROADCAST RUNNING MULTICAST  MTU:1500  Metric:1
          RX packets:0 errors:0 dropped:0 overruns:0 frame:0
          TX packets:64 errors:0 dropped:0 overruns:0 carrier
          collisions:0 txqueuelen:1000
          RX bytes:0 (0.0 B)  TX bytes:10875 (10.8 KB)

lo        Link encap:Local Loopback
          inet addr:127.0.0.1  Mask:255.0.0.0
          inet6 addr: ::1/128 Scope:Host
          UP LOOPBACK RUNNING  MTU:65536  Metric:1
          RX packets:88 errors:0 dropped:0 overruns:0 frame:0
          TX packets:88 errors:0 dropped:0 overruns:0 carrier
          collisions:0 txqueuelen:0
          RX bytes:5500 (5.5 KB)  TX bytes:5500 (5.5 KB)
```

31. Open Firefox to see that you still have Internet access:

```
⊗⊜◉   Ubuntu Start Page - Mozilla Firefox
☐ Ubuntu Start Page                        ✚
← | ◉ Firefox | Search or enter address    ☆ ▾ ℭ  [8]▾ Google   Q

      ubuntu ◉
```

32. **Repeat** steps 15-30 for **vm2**, using your static IP address for vm2 from Step 13.

33. **Ping** from vm1 to vm2:

```
vm1@ubuntu:~$ ping 192.168.159.102
PING 192.168.159.102 (192.168.159.102) 56(
64 bytes from 192.168.159.102: icmp_req=1
64 bytes from 192.168.159.102: icmp_req=2
```

34. Press **Ctrl-C** to stop pinging.

Make the hostnames unique:

35. In **vm1**, enter `sudo vim /etc/hostname`, to edit the hostname for the virtual machine.

36. If prompted for the sudo password, enter `ubuntu`.

37. Press `i` to be able to edit the file.

38. Change the hostname to `vm1`:

39. Press **Esc** and enter `:wq` to save and exit.

40. Enter `sudo vim /etc/hosts` to access the list of hosts.

41. Press `i` to be able to edit the file.

42. **Add** the following entries to the list, **substituting in** your IP addresses for vm1, vm2, vm3, and vm4 (can copy from achotl1/class_files/unit12/**ex02.txt**, substituting in your IP addresses):

43. Press **Esc** and enter `:wq` to save and exit.

44. Close the terminal window and **restart** the virtual machine.

45. **Repeat** steps 35-44 for **vm2**, using the hostname of `vm2`.

46. Ping vm1 from vm2:

```
vmx@vm2:~$ ping vm1
PING vm1 (192.168.159.101) 56(84) bytes of data.
64 bytes from vm1 (192.168.159.101): icmp_req=1
64 bytes from vm1 (192.168.159.101): icmp_req=2
```

47. Ping vm2 from vm1:

```
vm1@vm1:~$ ping vm2
PING vm2 (192.168.159.102) 56(84) bytes of data.
64 bytes from vm2 (192.168.159.102): icmp_req=1
64 bytes from vm2 (192.168.159.102): icmp_req=2
```

Specifying the IP Address of a Node in Cassandra

To specify the IP address of a node in a Cassandra cluster, the listen_address and rpc_address properties in the cassandra.yaml file need to be assigned the IP address of the node.

```
listen_address : 192.168.159.101

rpc_address : 192.168.159.101
```

listen_address

The listen_address is for specifying the IP address of the node so that other nodes in the cluster can communicate with the node.

rpc_address

The rpc_address is for specifying the IP address of the node so that a client application can communicate with the node.

Exercise 3: Specify the IP Address for a Node

In this exercise, you specify an IP address in the cassandra.yaml file of each node.

1. In vm**1**, in a terminal window, enter `ifconfig` to see the IP address for this virtual machine.

2. Enter `vim ~/cassandra/apache-cassandra-2.0.7/conf/cassandra.yaml`, to edit the cassandra.yaml file on vm1:

```
vm1@vm1:~$ vim ~/cassandra/apache-cassandra-2.0.7
/conf/cassandra.yaml
```

3. Scroll down to locate the **listen_address** property (line 297).

4. Read the comments above the listen_address property.

5. Press `i` to be able to edit the property.

6. **Replace** localhost with the IP address of your vm1 virtual machine. (For example, `listen_address:` **192.168.159**.101.)

7. Scroll down to locate the **rpc_address** property (line 335).

8. Read the comments above the rpc_address property.

9. **Replace** localhost with the IP address of your vm1 virtual machine. (For example, `rpc_address:` **192.168.159**.101.)

10. Press **Esc** and enter `:wq` to save and exit.

11. **Repeat** steps 1-10 for vm**2**, entering your vm2 IP address.

Specifying Seed Nodes

Seed nodes are regular nodes that, via their IP address, provide a way for new nodes to join the cluster. The IP address for at least one seed node is needed for a node to be able to join the cluster.

Seed nodes are specified in the cassandra.yaml file of each node in a cluster as a comma-separated list. For example:

```
seeds: "192.168.159.101,192.168.159.102"
```

```
seed_provider:
    # Addresses of hosts that are deemed contact points.
    # Cassandra nodes use this list of hosts to find each other and learn
    # the topology of the ring.  You must change this if you are running
    # multiple nodes!
    - class_name: org.apache.cassandra.locator.SimpleSeedProvider
      parameters:
          # seeds is actually a comma-delimited list of addresses.
          # Ex: "<ip1>,<ip2>,<ip3>"
          - seeds: "192.168.159.101,102.168.159.102"
```

It is common to list the IP address of the first two or three nodes in a cluster, so that if the first node is down, there is an alternative node for any joining nodes to use to get into the cluster.

It is NOT necessary to put the IP address of every node in the cluster in the seed list.

Exercise 4: Specify Seed Nodes

In this exercise, you specify a seed node for the vm1 and vm2 nodes.

1. **Decide** that you will use the first node in the cluster as a seed node.

2. **Gather** the IP address of your vm1 node. (For example, *192.168.159*.101.)

3. In **vm1**, in a terminal window, enter `vim ~/cassandra/apache-cassandra-2.0.7/conf/cassandra.yaml`, to edit the cassandra.yaml file for this node.

4. Scroll down to locate the **seed_provider** property (line 227).

5. Read the comments.

6. Within seed_provider, locate `seeds: "127.0.0.1"`.

7. Press `i` to be able to edit the file.

8. **Change** the value of seeds to the IP address of your vm1. For example:

   `seeds: "192.168.159.101"`

9. Press **Esc** and enter `:wq` to save and exit.

10. **Repeat** steps 3-9 for **vm2**, to also set the value of its seeds property to the IP address of vm1 (so that vm1 can serve as an entry point for vm2 to join the cluster).

Start Cassandra on vm1:

11. In vm**1**, in a terminal window, enter `cd ~/cassandra/apache-cassandra-2.0.7` to navigate to the directory where Cassandra is installed.

12. Enter `bin/cassandra -f` to start Cassandra.

13. Open another terminal window, and navigate to the directory where Cassandra is installed.

14. Enter `watch -n 2 bin/nodetool status` to set up a watch that checks on the status of the cluster every 2 seconds:

```
vm1@vm1:~/cassandra/apache-cassandra-2.0.7$ watch -n 2 bin/nodetool status
```

15. See that the vm1 node is up:

```
vm1@vm1: ~/cassandra/apache-cassandra-2.0.7
Every 2.0s: bin/nodetool status

Note: Ownership information does not include topology; f
Datacenter: datacenter1
========================
Status=Up/Down
|/ State=Normal/Leaving/Joining/Moving
--   Address          Load       Owns    Host ID
UN   192.168.159.101  114.73 KB  100.0%  bcc09b1b-51e1-40
```

Bootstrapping a Node

Adding a node to a cluster is called "bootstrapping". In order to bootstrap a node, it needs to have the same cluster name as the nodes in the cluster it is to join, and it needs to be on a network that allows it to connect to the IP address of at least one of the seed nodes.

Once a node is able to join a cluster, if the auto_bootstrap property is set to true*, the node will start to take on responsibility for the data in its token range(s). (With the default of virtual nodes, defined through the num_tokens property in the cassandra.yaml file, the node will take on responsibility for many small token ranges. If the cluster had instead been configured the old way, with the initial_token property, the node will just take on responsibility for one large token range.)

The node will begin by accepting write requests and then eventually also accept read requests.

If there are multiple nodes to be bootstrapped, give time between each one so that the cluster can smoothly bootstrap each node.

*With Cassandra 1.0 and onwards, `auto_bootstrap : true` is a hidden default. (i.e. It does not show in cassandra.yaml by default, but is in effect.)

Exercise 5: Bootstrap a Node

In this exercise, you add a node to the cluster.

1. In **vm2**, in a terminal window, enter `sudo vim ~/cassandra/apache-cassandra-2.0.7/conf/cassandra.yaml`, to edit the cassandra.yaml file.

1. Scroll down to locate the **cluster_name** property (line 10).

2. **Notice** that the name of the cluster is **Test Cluster**, the same as the cluster name in vm1's cassandra.yaml file.

3. Scroll down to the **num_tokens** property (line 24).

4. Notice that it is set to 256, which means that this node will be responsible for 256 token ranges.

5. Scroll down to line 227, remembering that you provided the IP address of the vm1 node, to serve as a seed node, allowing an entry point for the vm2 node to join the cluster.

6. Press **Esc** and enter `/auto_bootstrap`, to search for the auto_bootstrap property.

7. Notice that the auto_bootstrap property was not found.

8. Realize that the default for auto_bootstrap is true, which means that, once the vm2 node is stable, it will automatically start receiving the data that it is responsible for from other nodes.

9. Press **Esc** and enter `:q` to exit the cassandra.yaml file.

10. In a terminal window, enter `cd ~/cassandra/apache-cassandra-2.0.7` to navigate to the directory where Cassandra is installed.

11. Enter `bin/cassandra -f`, to start Cassandra on vm2.

12. Wait a few seconds and then, in vm1, in the nodetool status watch window, see that the vm2 node is starting to join the cluster:

```
☒ ⊖ ⊡   vm1@vm1: ~/cassandra/apache-cassandra-2.0.7
Every 2.0s: bin/nodetool status

Note: Ownership information does not include topology;
Datacenter: datacenter1
========================
Status=Up/Down
|/ State=Normal/Leaving/Joining/Moving
--   Address          Load        Owns     Host ID
UJ   192.168.159.102  46.71 KB    ?        75151546-2217-49
UN   192.168.159.101  114.73 KB   100.0%   bcc09b1b-51e1-40
```

13. After a few more seconds, see that both nodes are up:

```
Status=Up/Down
|/ State=Normal/Leaving/Joining/Moving
--   Address          Load        Owns    Host ID
UN   192.168.159.102  104.32 KB   50.4%   75151546-2217-49
UN   192.168.159.101  114.73 KB   49.6%   bcc09b1b-51e1-40
```

14. In the **Owns** column, **notice** that they both own approximately 50% of the data.

15. In the **Load** column, realize that, if we were dealing with a larger amount of data (which we will, in the section on cassandra-stress), we would likely see the load for vm2 be approximately half of the load for vm1. This is because the replication factor for the keyspaces in our cluster is currently 1 (hence, vm2 is now responsible for half of the data that had been on vm1), and because Cassandra does not remove data from the old node.

If desired, view the status of the cluster through vm**2**:

16. In vm2, open a new terminal window and navigate to where Cassandra is installed.

17. Enter `bin/nodetool status`.

18. See that the information on the nodes in the cluster is displayed:

```
Status=Up/Down
|/ State=Normal/Leaving/Joining/Moving
--   Address         Load       Owns    Host ID
UN   192.168.159.102 104.32 KB  50.4%   75151546-2217-49
UN   192.168.159.101 114.73 KB  49.6%   bcc09b1b-51e1-40
```

Cleaning Up a Node

When a node auto bootstraps, it does not remove the data from the node that had previously been responsible for the data. This is so that, if the new node were to go down shortly after coming online, the data would still exist.

To tell Cassandra to delete the data that a node is no longer responsible for, the cleanup command can be used. For example, the following command could be run to delete the data that the *192.168.159*.101 node is no longer responsible for.

```
bin/nodetool -h 192.168.159.101 cleanup
```

Exercise 6: Clean Up a Node

In this exercise, you clean up the data that vm1 is no longer responsible for.

1. In a terminal window on vm2, in the directory where Cassandra is installed, run the following command, using your vm1 IP address, to delete any data on vm1 that vm1 is no longer responsible for:

   ```
   bin/nodetool -h 192.168.159.101 cleanup
   ```

2. Watch the nodetool status watch window on vm1 while the cleanup command runs.

3. See if the load size of the vm1 node has reduced:

```
Status=Up/Down
|/ State=Normal/Leaving/Joining/Moving
--  Address          Load       Owns   Host ID
UN  192.168.159.102  104.32 KB  50.4%  75151546-2217-49
UN  192.168.159.101  110.49 KB  49.6%  bcc09b1b-51e1-40
```

Note: If the load for vm1 node did not reduce by much, or not at all, realize that it is likely because of the very small amount of data that we are currently working with. In the next exercise, we load a large amount of data, and then, in the lab exercise, see a visible difference when using the cleanup command.

Using cassandra-stress

The cassandra-stress tool, which comes with Cassandra, is handy for stress-testing a cluster. It can be used to write data, or read data, from a Cassandra cluster.

For example, cassandra-stress could be used to generate and write 100,000 rows of data. Then, when a node is added to a cluster, the effect of the nodetool cleanup command can be clearly seen.

```
tools/bin/cassandra-stress -d 192.168.159.101 -n 100000
```

The cassandra-stress tool has many options, which can be viewed by running cassandra-stress -h.

```
vmx@vm2:~/cassandra/apache-cassandra-2.0.7$ tools/bin/cassandra-stress -h
Usage: ./bin/cassandra-stress [options]

Options:
-D NODESFILE, --nodesfile=NODESFILE
                File containing host nodes (one per line)

-ns, --no-statistics
                Turn off the aggregate statistics that is normally output

-F NUM-DIFFERENT-KEYS, --num-different-keys=NUM-DIFFERENT-KEYS
                Number of different keys (if < NUM-KEYS, the same key will

-ts TRUSTSTORE, --truststore=TRUSTSTORE
                SSL: full path to truststore

-C CARDINALITY, --cardinality=CARDINALITY
                Number of unique values stored in columns, default:50

-L, --enable-cql
```

The executable for cassandra-stress is located in the bin folder of the tools folder, down under where Cassandra is installed.

```
vm1@vm1:~/cassandra/apache-cassandra-2.0.7/tools/bin$ ls
cassandra.in.sh          cassandra-stressd    sstablemetadata.bat
cassandra-stress         sstablelevelreset    token-generator
cassandra-stress.bat  sstablemetadata
```

In using cassandra-stress, a keyspace with a replication factor of 1 named Keyspace1 gets generated. Within Keyspace1, tables named Standard1, Super1, SuperCounter1, Counter1, and Counter3 are generated depending on the cassandra-stress options used.

Exercise 7: Use cassandra-stress

In this exercise, you use cassandra-stress to write 100,000 rows of data to the cluster, so that you will be able to see a more noticeable difference when using the cleanup command during the lab exercise.

1. In vm2 (or vm1), in the directory where Cassandra is installed, run the following, substituting in the IP address of one of your vms, to have cassandra-stress write 100,000 rows of data to the cluster:

```
tools/bin/cassandra-stress -d 192.168.159.101 -n 100000
```

2. In vm1, in the watch nodetool status window, notice the Load column values updating for both nodes, as the data gets written to the cluster:

```
Status=Up/Down
|/ State=Normal/Leaving/Joining/Moving
--  Address          Load      Owns    Host ID
UN  192.168.159.102  11.22 MB  50.4%   75151546-2217-49
UN  192.168.159.101  12.19 MB  49.6%   bcc09b1b-51e1-40
```

Note: It may take a minute or two before you see the numbers updating.

Use cqlsh to view the keyspace generated by cassandra-stress:

3. In vm2, in the directory where Cassandra is installed, enter `bin/cqlsh vm2` to start cqlsh.

4. In cqlsh, enter the following to view the definition of the keyspace generated by cassandra-stress:

```
DESCRIBE KEYSPACE "Keyspace1";
```

5. Notice that the replication factor for the Keyspace1 keyspace is 1:

```
CREATE KEYSPACE "Keyspace1" WITH replication = {
  'class': 'SimpleStrategy',
  'replication_factor': '1'
};
```

6. Scroll down through the keyspace definition to see table definitions for Standard1, Super1, SuperCounter1, Counter1, and Counter3.

7. If desired, enter `SELECT * FROM "Keyspace1"."Standard1" LIMIT 10;` to see data generated by cassandra-stress:

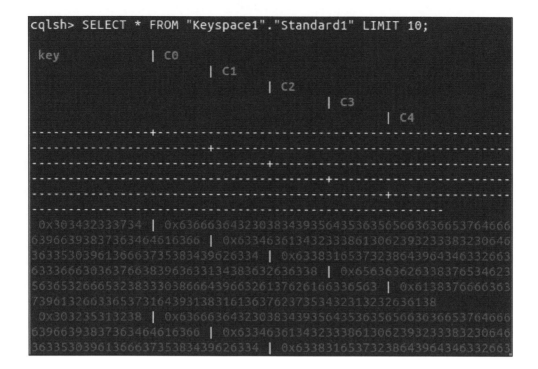

Modify the vehicle-tracker and alarm-system applications to reference the new IP addresses, to be able to connect to the cluster:

1. In vm**1**, open a new terminal window and enter `eclipse/eclipse` to launch Eclipse.

2. If the Workspace Launcher window dialog box displays, click **OK**.

3. On the left, expand the **alarm-system** folder, and then **Java Resources – src – com.alarmsystem.servlet**, to locate the AlarmSystemServlet.java file:

4. Double-click the **AlarmSystemServlet.java** file, to open it.

5. Locate the Cluster cluster line of code.

6. **Replace** the reference to localhost with the IP addresses for your vm1 and vm2 nodes, to provide an initial contact point into the cluster, as well as a backup:

```
Cluster cluster =
Cluster.builder().addContactPoints("192.168.159.101","192.168.
159.102").build();
```

Note the 's' in addContactPoints.

7. **Save** the AlarmSystemServlet.java file.

8. Right-click the file, to select **Run As – Run on Server**.

9. If prompted, click **Finish**.

10. See that the application page displays:

11. Enter `H01545551` and press Submit, to see that the alarm-system application is able to connect to the cluster and retrieve data:

Arthur Fonzarelli, 565 North Clinton Drive, Milwaukee, WI, 53525

alarm turned off	Fri May 23 18:14:53 PDT 2014
alarm set	Fri May 23 08:28:16 PDT 2014
alarm turned off	Thu May 22 18:35:29 PDT 2014
alarm set	Thu May 22 08:32:22 PDT 2014
alarm turned off	Wed May 21 18:41:02 PDT 2014
alarm set	Wed May 21 08:30:14 PDT 2014

12. Repeat step 6 for the **VehicleTrackerServlet.java** file in the **vehicle-tracker** project folder.

13. **Save** and right-click on the VehicleTrackerServlet.java file to select **Run As – Run on Server**.

14. See that the application page displays:

15. Enter `2014-05-19` and `FLN78197` and press Submit, to see that the vehicle-tracker application is able to connect to the cluster and retrieve data:

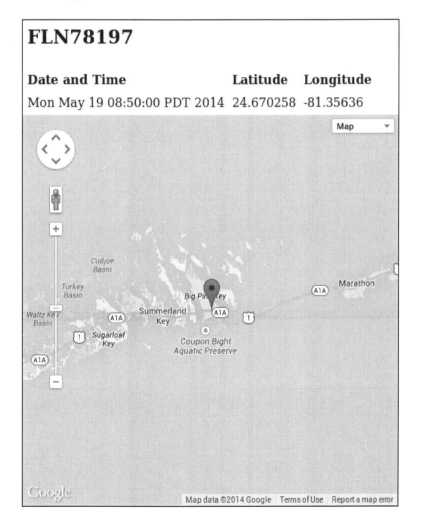

Summary

The focus of this unit was on adding a node to a cluster:

- Understanding Nodes
- Having a Network Connection
- Specifying the IP Address of a Node in Cassandra
- Specifying Seed Nodes
- Bootstrapping a Node
- Cleaning Up a Node
- Using cassandra-stress

Unit Review Questions

1) All of the nodes in a cluster must have the same cluster name.

a. True

b. False

2) In order to add a node to a Cassandra cluster, it is important to register it with the master node.

a. True

b. False

3) As a new node bootstraps, it takes on responsibility for its token range(s) by receiving the data that it is responsible for from other nodes, and then deleting the data off of the other nodes.

a. True

b. False

Lab: Add a Third Node

In this exercise, you add a third node to the cluster.

1. In the **achotl1** folder on your desktop, unzip the **achotl1_vmx_64-bit.zip** file.

2. Rename the unzipped file `achotl1_vm3_64-bit`.

3. **Double-click** achotl1_vm3_64-bit, to open it in VMware.

4. If prompted, click the **I copied it** button.

5. Enter with the password of `ubuntu`.

In VMware, change the name of the virtual machine to achotl1_vm3_64-bit:

6. Select **Virtual Machine – Settings....**

   *Windows users: select **Player – Manage – Virtual Machine Settings....***

7. Click the **General** icon.

   *Windows users: select the **Options** tab.*

8. To the right of Name, click on the name, to edit it.

9. Change the name to `achotl1_vm3_64-bit`:

10. Close the General window.

11. See that the name of the virtual machine has been changed:

Specify a static IP address for the virtual machine:

12. In the upper-right corner, under the gear icon, select **System Settings**:

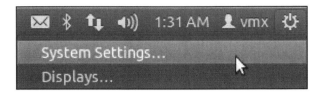

13. Click the **Network** icon:

14. Click the **Options...** button.

15. Select the **IPv4 Settings** tab:

16. For Method, select **Manual**.

17. Click the **Add** button.

18. For **Address**, enter your static IP address from Page 12-6, Step 16 (e.g. *192.168.159*.103).

19. For **Netmask**, enter your mask IP address from Page 12-6, Step 12 (e.g. *255.255.255.0*).

20. For **Gateway**, enter your gateway IP address from Page 12-6, Step 14 (e.g. *192.168.159.2*).

21. For **DNS Servers**, enter your DNS IP address from Page 12-6, Step 15 (e.g. *192.168.159.2*):

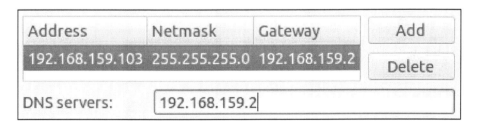

22. Click the **Save** button.

23. If a dialog box with an error message appears, click the **Continue** button.

24. **Notice** your settings in the Network window:

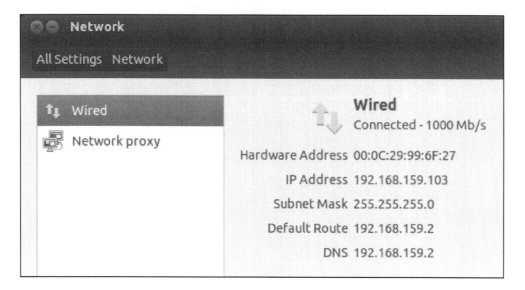

25. **Close** the Network window.

26. Select **Virtual Machine - Restart**, to restart the virtual machine.

27. Once the virtual machine has restarted, enter `ifconfig` in a terminal window to see the static IP address configured:

```
vmx@ubuntu:~$ ifconfig
eth0      Link encap:Ethernet  HWaddr
          inet addr:192.168.159.103  E
```

28. Open Firefox to see that you still have Internet access.

29. **Ping** from vm3 to vm1:

```
vmx@ubuntu:~$ ping 192.168.159.101
PING 192.168.159.101 (192.168.159.101) 56(
64 bytes from 192.168.159.101: icmp_req=1
64 bytes from 192.168.159.101: icmp_req=2
```

30. Press **Ctrl-C** to stop pinging.

31. **Ping** from vm2 to vm3:

```
vmx@vm2:~$ ping 192.168.159.103
PING 192.168.159.103 (192.168.159.103) 56(84) by
64 bytes from 192.168.159.103: icmp_req=1 ttl=64
64 bytes from 192.168.159.103: icmp_req=2 ttl=64
```

32. Press **Ctrl-C** to stop pinging.

Make the hostname unique and known:

33. In vm3, enter `sudo vim /etc/hostname`, to edit the hostname for the virtual machine.

34. Enter the sudo password of `ubuntu` if prompted.

35. Press `i` to be able to edit the file.

36. Change the hostname to `vm3`:

37. Press **Esc** and enter `:wq` to save and exit.

38. Enter `sudo vim /etc/hosts` to add to the list of hosts.

39. Press `i` to be able to edit the file.

40. **Add** the following entries to the list, **substituting in** your IP addresses for vm1, vm2, vm3, and vm4:

41. Press **Esc** and enter `:wq` to save and exit.

42. **Restart** the virtual machine.

43. Once the virtual machine is restarted, enter `ifconfig` in a terminal window to see the hostname displayed:

```
vmx@vm3: ~
vmx(vm3:~$ ifconfig
eth0      Link encap:Ethernet  HWaddr 00:0c:29:
          inet addr:192.168.159.103  Bcast:192.
```

44. In vm2 (or vm1), ping the vm3 host name:

```
vmx@vm2:~$ ping vm3
PING vm3 (192.168.159.103) 56(84) bytes of data.
64 bytes from vm3 (192.168.159.103): icmp_req=1
64 bytes from vm3 (192.168.159.103): icmp_req=2
```

45. Press **Ctrl-C** to stop pinging.

Edit vm3's cassandra.yaml file, to specify the listen_address, rpc_address, and seed nodes:

46. In vm**3**, in a terminal window, enter `vim ~/cassandra/apache-cassandra-2.0.7/conf/cassandra.yaml`, to edit the cassandra.yaml file on vm3.

47. Notice that the **cluster name** is Test Cluster (line 10), the same as the cluster name for vm1 and vm2.

48. Scroll down to locate the **listen_address** property (line 297).

49. Press `i` to be able to edit the property.

50. **Replace** localhost with the IP address of your vm3 virtual machine. (For example, `listen_address: 192.168.159.103.`):

```
listen_address: 192.168.159.103
```

51. Scroll down to locate the **rpc_address** property (line 335).

52. **Replace** localhost with the IP address of your vm3 virtual machine. (For example, `rpc_address: 192.168.159.103`.)

53. Scroll up to locate the **seed_provider** property (line 218).

54. Within seed_provider, locate `seeds: "127.0.0.1"`.

55. Replace the value of seeds with your vm1 and vm2 IP addresses. For example:

    `seeds: "192.168.159.101,192.168.159.102"`

56. Press **Esc** and enter `:wq` to save and exit.

Bootstrap vm3 into the cluster:

57. In vm3, enter `cd ~/cassandra/apache-cassandra-2.0.7` to navigate to the directory where Cassandra is installed.

58. Enter `bin/cassandra -f`, to start Cassandra on vm3.

59. In vm1, in the watch nodetool status window, see the vm3 node joining the cluster:

```
Status=Up/Down
|/ State=Normal/Leaving/Joining/Moving
--   Address          Load       Owns    Host ID
UN   192.168.159.102  11.23 MB   50.4%   75151546-2217-49
UJ   192.168.159.103  14.17 KB   ?       a6a90230-35e1-4c
UN   192.168.159.101  12.22 MB   49.6%   bcc09b1b-51e1-40
```

60. Once the vm3 node is up, look in the **Owns** column, to see that each of the three nodes owns approximately a third of the data:

```
Status=Up/Down
|/ State=Normal/Leaving/Joining/Moving
--   Address          Load       Owns    Host ID
UN   192.168.159.102  14.47 MB   33.9%   75151546-2217-4923-aa
UN   192.168.159.103  9.13 MB    31.6%   a6a90230-35e1-4cf4-a8
UN   192.168.159.101  14.32 MB   34.5%   bcc09b1b-51e1-4034-9b
```

61. In the **Load** column, notice that vm1 and vm2 have a **larger** load size than vm3.

Clean up vm1 and vm2:

62. Still in vm1, in a terminal window, in the directory where Cassandra is installed, enter the following to clean up vm2, **substituting in** your vm2 IP address:

```
bin/nodetool -h 192.168.159.102 cleanup
```

63. In the watch nodetool status window, in the Load column, see that vm2 has been cleaned up (this may take a couple minutes):

```
Status=Up/Down
|/ State=Normal/Leaving/Joining/Moving
--  Address          Load        Owns    Host ID
UN  192.168.159.102  9.77 MB     33.9%   75151546-2217-49
UN  192.168.159.103  9.13 MB     31.6%   a6a90230-35e1-4c
UN  192.168.159.101  14.32 MB    34.5%   bcc09b1b-51e1-40
```

64. Enter the following to clean up vm1, **substituting in** your vm1 IP address:

```
bin/nodetool -h 192.168.159.101 cleanup
```

65. See that vm1 has been cleaned up:

```
Status=Up/Down
|/ State=Normal/Leaving/Joining/Moving
--  Address          Load        Owns    Host ID
UN  192.168.159.102  9.8 MB      33.9%   75151546-2217-49
UN  192.168.159.103  9.13 MB     31.6%   a6a90230-35e1-4c
UN  192.168.159.101  10.05 MB    34.5%   bcc09b1b-51e1-40
```

Alternate Lab Steps: Add a Third Node

In this exercise, you add a third node to the cluster.

1. In the **achotl1** folder on your desktop, unzip the **achotl1_vmx_64-bit.zip** file and rename the unzipped file `achotl1_vm3_64-bit`.

2. **Open** achotl1_vm3_64-bit in VMware.

3. Within VMware, change the name of the virtual machine to achotl1_vm3_64-bit.

4. Using the System Settings in the virtual machine, specify a static IP address for the virtual machine, using the network settings gathered on Page 12-7.

5. Restart the virtual machine and use `ifconfig` to check that vm3 has a static IP address like *192.168.159*.103.

6. Ping vm3 from vm1 and vm2, to make sure they can communicate with it.

7. Use `sudo vim /etc/hostname` to change the hostname of vm3 to `vm3`.

8. Use `sudo vim /etc/hosts` to add to the list of hosts, with entries for vm1, vm2, vm3, and vm4.

9. Edit vm3's cassandra.yaml file, to specify the listen_address, rpc_address, and seed nodes. (Use the IP addresses of vm1 and vm2 as the seed nodes.)

10. Start Cassandra on vm3.

11. In vm1, in the watch nodetool status window, watch vm3 join the cluster:

```
Status=Up/Down
|/ State=Normal/Leaving/Joining/Moving
--   Address          Load       Owns     Host ID
UN   192.168.159.102  11.23 MB   50.4%    75151546-2217-49
UJ   192.168.159.103  14.17 KB   ?        a6a90230-35e1-4c
UN   192.168.159.101  12.22 MB   49.6%    bcc09b1b-51e1-40
```

12. Once the vm3 node is up, look in the **Owns** column, to see that each of the three nodes owns approximately a third of the data:

```
Status=Up/Down
|/ State=Normal/Leaving/Joining/Moving
--  Address          Load        Owns   Host ID
UN  192.168.159.102  14.47 MB    33.9%  75151546-2217-4923-aa
UN  192.168.159.103  9.13 MB     31.6%  a6a90230-35e1-4cf4-a8
UN  192.168.159.101  14.32 MB    34.5%  bcc09b1b-51e1-4034-9b
```

13. Use nodetool cleanup to clean up the vm1 and vm2 nodes.

14. See that the vm1 and vm2 nodes have been cleaned up:

```
Status=Up/Down
|/ State=Normal/Leaving/Joining/Moving
--  Address          Load       Owns   Host ID
UN  192.168.159.102  9.8 MB     33.9%  75151546-2217-49
UN  192.168.159.103  9.13 MB    31.6%  a6a90230-35e1-4c
UN  192.168.159.101  10.05 MB   34.5%  bcc09b1b-51e1-40
```

13

....

MONITORING
A CLUSTER

Understanding Cassandra Monitoring Tools

Using nodetool

Using JConsole

Learning About OpsCenter

Understanding Cassandra Monitoring Tools

Tools for monitoring Cassandra include nodetool, JConsole, and OpsCenter.

Nodetool is a command line tool that comes with Cassandra, JConsole is a tool that comes with JDK (Java Development Kit), and OpsCenter is a GUI application that comes from DataStax.

All of these tools work by communicating with Cassandra through JMX (Java Management Extensions). Through JMX, Cassandra exposes many metrics and commands, which any of these tools can use to monitor and manage a Cassandra cluster.

Using nodetool

Provided with Cassandra, nodetool is available on the command line via its executable, located in the bin subdirectory where Cassandra is installed.

```
vm1@vm1:~/cassandra/apache-cassandra-2.0.7/bin$ ls
cassandra              debug-cql.bat          sstableloader.bat
cassandra.bat          json2sstable           sstablemetadata.bat
cassandra-cli          json2sstable.bat       sstablescrub
cassandra-cli.bat      nodetool               sstablescrub.bat
cassandra.in.sh        nodetool.bat           sstablesplit
cassandra-shuffle      sstable2json           sstablesplit.bat
cassandra-shuffle.bat  sstable2json.bat       sstableupgrade
cqlsh                  sstablekeys            sstableupgrade.bat
cqlsh.bat              sstablekeys.bat        stop-server
debug-cql              sstableloader
```

For example, if Cassandra is installed at ~/cassandra/apache-cassandra-2.0.7, nodetool can be referenced by entering `~/cassandra/apache-cassandra-2.0.7/bin/nodetool`.

nodetool Commands

Many options for monitoring a cluster are available with nodetool. The most common command is `nodetool status`, for monitoring the status of a cluster. Another command is `nodetool info`, for information on a particular node. Others include `nodetool ring`, for seeing which node each token range is assigned to, `nodetool cfstats`, to see statistics for all of the keyspaces and tables, `nodetool cfhistograms` to see the read and write latency for a given table, and `nodetool compactionstats`, to see compaction information.

To see all of the commands for nodetool, nodetool can be run without a command. Alternatively, the commands can be viewed in the DataStax Cassandra documentation.

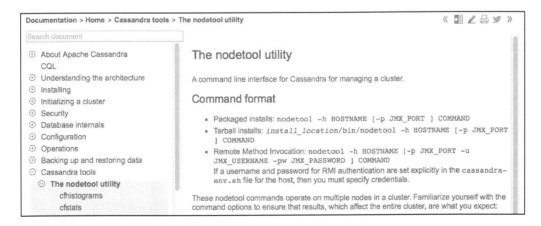

Exercise 1: Use nodetool

In this exercise, you use nodetool with your cluster.

1. In vm**1**, in a terminal window, enter `~/cassandra/apache-cassandra-2.0.7/bin/nodetool` to execute nodetool without an accompanying command.

2. Notice the list of available arguments that displays:

```
vm1@vm1:~$ ~/cassandra/apache-cassandra-2.0.7/bin/nodetool
Command was not specified.
usage: java org.apache.cassandra.tools.NodeCmd --host <arg> <command>

 -a,--include-all-sstables     includes sstables that are already on the
                               most recent version during upgradesstable
 -c,--compact                  print histograms in a more compact format
 -cf,--column-family <arg>     only take a snapshot of the specified tab
                               (column family)
 -dc,--in-dc <arg>             only repair against nodes in the specifie
                               datacenters (comma separated)
 -et,--end-token <arg>         token at which repair range ends
 -h,--host <arg>               node hostname or ip address
```

3. Scroll down to see the list of available commands:

```
Available commands
  cfhistograms <keyspace> <cfname> - Print statistic histograms for
  cfstats [keyspace].[cfname] ... - Print statistics on column famil
  cleanup [keyspace] [cfnames] - Run cleanup on one or more column f
  clearsnapshot [keyspaces...] -t [snapshotName] - Remove snapshots
  compact [keyspace] [cfnames] - Force a (major) compaction on one o
  compactionhistory        - Print history of compaction
  compactionstats          - Print statistics on compactions
  decommission             - Decommission the *node I am connecting to
  describecluster          - Print the name, snitch, partitioner and s
  describering [keyspace] - Shows the token ranges info of a given k
```

4. At the command prompt, enter `~/cassandra/apache-cassandra-2.0.7/bin/nodetool status` to see the status of the ring.

5. See that all three nodes are up, with the data load divided roughly into thirds:

```
Datacenter: datacenter1
========================
Status=Up/Down
|/ State=Normal/Leaving/Joining/Moving
--   Address          Load        Owns    Host ID
UN   192.168.159.102  9.8 MB      33.9%   75151546-2217-49
UN   192.168.159.103  9.18 MB     31.6%   a6a90230-35e1-4c
UN   192.168.159.101  10.05 MB    34.5%   bcc09b1b-51e1-40
```

6. At the command prompt, enter `~/cassandra/apache-cassandra-2.0.7/bin/nodetool ring` to see which nodes the token ranges are assigned to.

7. Notice the long list of token ranges for the 3 nodes, with each having 256 token ranges:

```
192.168.159.103  rack1  Up  Normal  10.42 MB  36.19%  8995959370875111619
192.168.159.101  rack1  Up  Normal  8.8 MB    30.19%  9067420701225382311
192.168.159.101  rack1  Up  Normal  8.8 MB    30.19%  9087437214801154442
192.168.159.102  rack1  Up  Normal  9.74 MB   33.63%  9114799584639192092
192.168.159.101  rack1  Up  Normal  8.8 MB    30.19%  9124927950302931315
192.168.159.102  rack1  Up  Normal  9.74 MB   33.63%  9128195428643885841
192.168.159.102  rack1  Up  Normal  9.74 MB   33.63%  9131758010915769002
192.168.159.103  rack1  Up  Normal  10.42 MB  36.19%  9190440719116978288
192.168.159.102  rack1  Up  Normal  9.74 MB   33.63%  9211350131645519695
```

8. At the command prompt, enter `~/cassandra/apache-cassandra-2.0.7/bin/nodetool info` to see detail about the Cassandra node that you are running nodetool on:

```
vm1@vm1:~$ ~/cassandra/apache-cassandra-2.0.7/bin/nodetool info
Token               : (invoke with -T/--tokens to see all 256 token
ID                  : bcc09b1b-51e1-4034-9b60-e2ef59e276c1
Gossip active       : true
Thrift active       : true
Native Transport active: true
Load                : 10.05 MB
Generation No       : 1403885845
Uptime (seconds)    : 12796
Heap Memory (MB)    : 149.83 / 736.00
Data Center         : datacenter1
Rack                : rack1
```

9. Enter `~/cassandra/apache-cassandra-2.0.7/bin/nodetool -h 192.168.159.102 info`, substituting in your vm2 IP address, to see detail about your vm2 Cassandra node:

```
vm1@vm1:~$ ~/cassandra/apache-cassandra-2.0.7/bin/nodetool -h 192
Token               : (invoke with -T/--tokens to see all 256 tokens
ID                  : 75151546-2217-4923-aac2-f14bc8a631a6
Gossip active       : true
Thrift active       : true
Native Transport active: true
Load                : 9.8 MB
Generation No       : 1403887109
Uptime (seconds)    : 11777
Heap Memory (MB)    : 180.42 / 736.00
Data Center         : datacenter1
Rack                : rack1
```

10. Repeat step 9, substituting in your vm3 IP address, to see detail about your vm3 Cassandra node:

```
vm1@vm1:~$ ~/cassandra/apache-cassandra-2.0.7/bin/nodetool -h 19
Token            : (invoke with -T/--tokens to see all 256 tokens
ID               : a6a90230-35e1-4cf4-a8e8-4d38dd758377
Gossip active    : true
Thrift active    : true
Native Transport active: true
Load             : 9.18 MB
Generation No    : 1403894232
Uptime (seconds) : 4703
Heap Memory (MB) : 25.01 / 736.00
Data Center      : datacenter1
Rack             : rack1
```

Using JConsole

JConsole, which comes with JDK, is a tool for looking inside a Java process.

JConsole can be launched from the command line by entering `jconsole &` from the bin subdirectory where the JDK is installed.

Once open and connected, JConsole provides an interface for exploring exposed metrics.

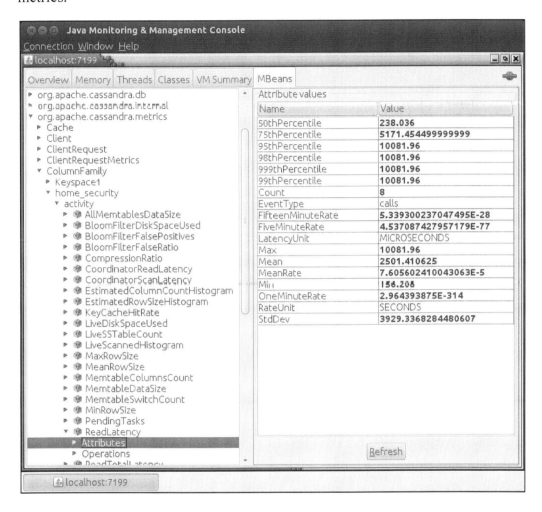

Exercise 2: Use JConsole

In this exercise, you use JConsole to explore metrics for your cluster.

1. In vm**1**, in a terminal window, enter `cd /usr/local/java/jdk1.7.0_55` to navigate to the directory where JDK is installed on vm1.

2. Enter `ls bin` to see the contents of the bin directory.

3. Notice jconsole listed:

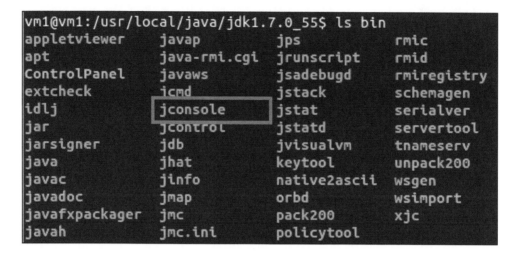

4. At the command prompt, enter `bin/jconsole &` to launch jconsole.

5. See JConsole launch:

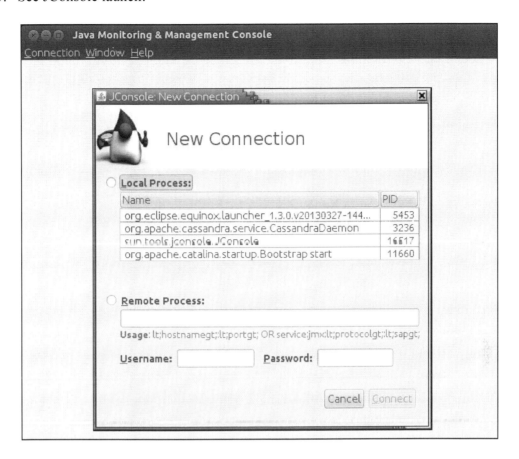

6. Select the **Remote Process** radio button.

7. Enter `localhost:7199`.

8. Click the **Connect** button.

9. Click the Insecure button:

10. See that you have connected and are on the Overview tab:

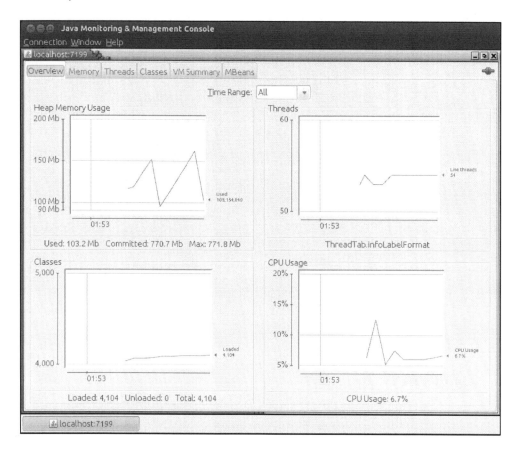

11. Select the **MBeans** tab:

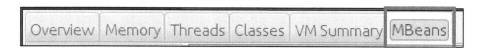

12. Click the triangle to the left of **org.apache.cassandra.metrics**, to expand it:

> ▶ org.apache.cassandra.db
> ▶ org.apache.cassandra.internal
> ▶ org.apache.cassandra.metrics
> ▶ org.apache.cassandra.net
> ▶ org.apache.cassandra.request

13. Click the triangle to the left of **ColumnFamily**, to expand it.

14. Notice the keyspaces in your cluster:

```
▼ org.apache.cassandra.metrics
   ▶ Cache
   ▶ Client
   ▶ ClientRequest
   ▶ ClientRequestMetrics
   ▼ ColumnFamily
      ▶ Keyspace1
      ▶ home_security
      ▶ system
      ▶ system_traces
      ▶ vehicle_tracker
```

15. Click the triangle to the left of **home_security**, to expand it.

16. Notice your tables listed:

```
▼ home_security
   ▶ activity
   ▶ home
```

17. Expand the **activity** table, to see metrics available:

```
▼ activity
   ▶ ⬡ AllMemtablesDataSize
   ▶ ⬡ BloomFilterDiskSpaceUsed
   ▶ ⬡ BloomFilterFalsePositives
   ▶ ⬡ BloomFilterFalseRatio
   ▶ ⬡ CompressionRatio
   ▶ ⬡ CoordinatorReadLatency
   ▶ ⬡ CoordinatorScanLatency
   ▶ ⬡ EstimatedColumnCountHistogram
   ▶ ⬡ EstimatedRowSizeHistogram
   ▶ ⬡ KeyCacheHitRate
   ▶ ⬡ LiveDiskSpaceUsed
   ▶ ⬡ LiveSSTableCount
```

18. Click the triangle to the left of **ReadLatency**, to expand it.

19. Click on **Attributes**, to see the values:

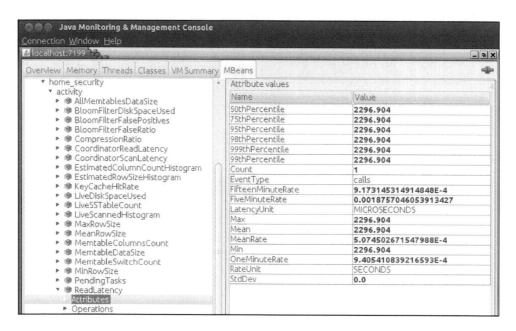

Note: If the values are 0, go to Eclipse, run the AlarmSystemServlet, and enter H01474777 *to generate read metrics. Then click the Refresh button in the Java Monitoring & Management Console window to see the metrics displayed.*

20. Click the triangle to the left of **WriteLatency**, to expand it.

21. Continue perusing JConsole as desired.

22. Close JConsole.

Learning About OpsCenter

DataStax OpsCenter is a GUI web application for monitoring and managing a Cassandra cluster.

Two versions of OpsCenter exist: Community (free) and Enterprise. When using the Enterprise version, the options that were dimmed out in the Community version become available.

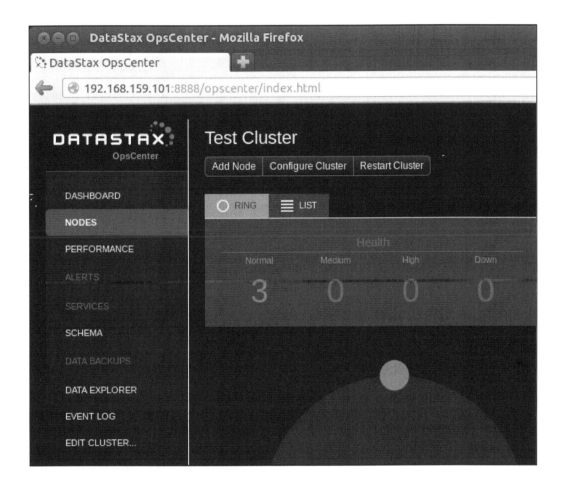

To be able to use OpsCenter, OpsCenter needs to installed on a server (it can be installed on one of the existing nodes in a cluster or on a separate server), and then OpsCenter Agent needs to be installed of each of the nodes in the cluster, so that OpsCenter can communicate with each of the nodes.

Once OpsCenter is installed, it can be accessed by opening a browser window and specifying the IP address of the server that it is installed on, with 8888 as the port number. For example, http://192.168.159.101:8888.

Exercise 3: Learn About OpsCenter

In this exercise, you learn about OpsCenter.

1. In a browser, enter
    `http://www.datastax.com/documentation/opscenter/4.1/opsc/about`
    `_c.html` to access the OpsCenter documentation.

2. Scan the landing page:

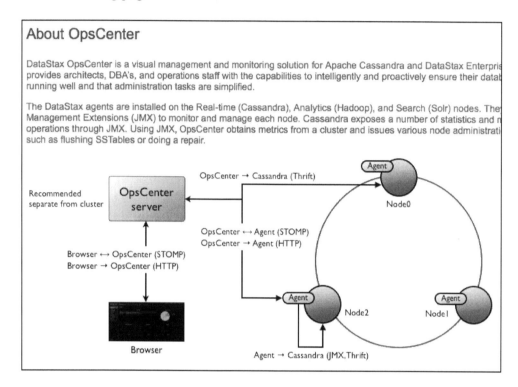

3. Notice that OpsCenter Agent is installed on each node.

4. Realize that OpsCenter can be installed on a separate server, or on one of the
    existing nodes in a cluster.

5. In the left navigation, click through the **Installation** topics as desired:

⊖ **Installation**
    ⊕ Installing OpsCenter
    ⊕ Installing DataStax agents
       OpsCenter and DataStax agent ports
    ⊕ Installation and configuration
       locations
       Starting, restarting, and stopping
       OpsCenter
       Starting and restarting DataStax
       agents

6. In the left navigation, select **Key features**:

⊖ About OpsCenter
    Key features

7. Skim through the key features:

Dashboard

- A Dashboard that displays an overview of commonly watched performance metrics
- Adding your favorite graphs to the dashboard
- An Overview that condenses the dashboards of multiple clusters (not visible when mo

Configuration and administration

- Basic cluster configuration
- Administration tasks, such as adding a cluster, using simple point-and-click actions
- Visual creation of clusters
- Multiple cluster management from a single OpsCenter instance using agents
- Rebalancing data across a cluster when new nodes are added
- Downloadable PDF cluster report

Alerts and performance metrics

- Built-in external notification capabilities
- Alert warnings of impending issues
- Metrics are collected every minute from Cassandra, Analytics, and Search nodes and

Backup operations and restoring from backups

- Automatic backup operations, including scheduling and removing of old backups
- Restoring from backups

Enterprise-only functionality

Enterprise functionality in OpsCenter is only enabled on DataStax Enterprise clusters. The fo
docs page)

- DataStax Enterprise Management Services
- Alerts
- Data Backup and Restore
- Management *en Masse*
- Viewing historical metrics more than one week in the past
- Rebalance
- Diagnostics tarball
- Hadoop jobtracker integration

---

8. Navigate to `http://www.datastax.com/what-we-offer/products-services/datastax-opscenter`.

9. Skim through the page.

10. At the bottom of the page, locate the video:

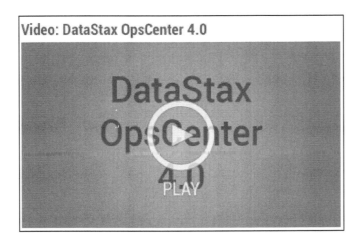

11. Click the **PLAY** button to watch the video, if desired.

Summary

The focus of this chapter was on monitoring a cluster:

- Understanding Cassandra Monitoring Tools

- Using nodetool

- Using JConsole

- Learning About OpsCenter

Unit Review Questions

1) How do the monitoring tools communicate with a Cassandra cluster?

a. BMX

b. JMX

c. KMX

d. XML

2) After installing Cassandra, the installation of nodetool requires additional steps.

a. True

b. False

3) JConsole is provided by:

a. DataStax

b. JRE

c. JDK

d. Apache

4) In order for OpsCenter to communicate with a node, what needs to be installed on the node?

a. OpsCenter Agent

b. Acrobat Reader

c. Hadoop

d. Solr

14

. . . .

REPAIRING NODES

Understanding Repair

Repair is for updating a node's data to be current.

Example of reasons for why data can get outdated on a node include that the node has been down, that the replication factor for a keyspace has been increased (in decreasing the replication factor, you would just do a cleanup), or that the token range(s) for a node have changed.

Repair should be run on each node at least once within the gc_grace_seconds period of time, so that data marked as deleted on one node does not come back to life through another node, because the other node was unaware of the delete (e.g. from being down). Given that the default gc_grace_seconds value is 10 days, running repair at least **once a week** is recommended.

Changing the Replication Factor of a Keyspace

Although it is not common to change the replication factor of a keyspace, it is possible with the ALTER KEYSPACE command.

```
ALTER KEYSPACE "home_security" WITH REPLICATION = {'class':
'SimpleStrategy', 'replication_factor':2};
```

Exercise 1: Modify the Replication Factor of a Keyspace

In this exercise, you increase the replication factor of the home_security keyspace to 2.

1. In vm1 (or any vm in the cluster), in **cqlsh**, enter the following to see the current replication factor for the home_security keyspace:

   ```
   DESCRIBE KEYSPACE home_security;
   ```

2. Scroll up to see that the replication factor is currently set to 1:

   ```
   CREATE KEYSPACE home_security WITH replication = {
     'class': 'SimpleStrategy',
     'replication_factor': '1'
   };
   ```

3. At the cqlsh prompt, enter the following to change the replication factor to 2, so that if one of the nodes in the cluster goes down, all of the data in the keyspace will still be available:

   ```
   ALTER KEYSPACE home_security WITH REPLICATION = {'class':
   'SimpleStrategy', 'replication_factor':2};
   ```

4. Rerun DESCRIBE KEYSPACE home_security; to see that the replication factor is now defined to be 2:

   ```
   CREATE KEYSPACE home_security WITH replication = {
     'class': 'SimpleStrategy',
     'replication_factor': '2'
   };
   ```

5. **Realize** that two replicas will not actually exist until repair is run.

Repairing Nodes

To repair nodes, the nodetool repair command can be used.

```
bin/nodetool -h 192.168.159.101 repair
```

Since repair can put a heavy load on the cluster, it is best to run repair during low-usage hours and to stagger the repairing of nodes so that the system is not overwhelmed with comparing and reconciling all of the data on all of the nodes at the same time.

If using OpsCenter Enterprise, there is an option to have OpsCenter automatically run a continuous repair service in the background, with minimal impact on the performance of the cluster.

Specifying a Keyspace

To specify the repairing of just one keyspace (e.g. after increasing the replication factor of a specific keyspace), the keyspace name can be included in the nodetool repair command.

```
bin/nodetool -h 192.168.159.101 repair home_security
```

Exercise 2: Repair Nodes

In this exercise, you run repair so that the second replicas of data in the home_security keyspace get generated.

1. In vm1 (or any vm in your cluster), in the directory where Cassandra is installed, enter `bin/nodetool -h` *192.168.159*`.101 repair home_security`, substituting in the IP address for your vm1, to repair the vm1 Cassandra node.

2. While repair is running (this will likely take a few minutes), notice the activity in the terminal windows in vm1, vm2, and vm3 where Cassandra is running, as the nodes compare merkle trees and data is streamed to, and received from, vm1.

```
 INFO 02:52:12,359 [repair #354e9e20-003c-11e4-adb1-0d6b4e37025b]
Endpoints /192.168.159.102 and /192.168.159.101 are consistent for
 home
 INFO 02:52:12,361 [repair #354e9e20-003c-11e4-adb1-0d6b4e37025b]
home is fully synced
 INFO 02:52:12,363 [repair #354e9e20-003c-11e4-adb1-0d6b4e37025b]
session completed successfully
 INFO 02:52:12,365 [repair #357eaed0-003c-11e4-adb1-0d6b4e37025b]
requesting merkle trees for activity (to [/192.168.159.102, /192.1
68.159.101])
 INFO 02:52:12,438 [repair #357eaed0-003c-11e4-adb1-0d6b4e37025b]
Received merkle tree for activity from /192.168.159.102
```

Understanding Consistency

Consistency has to do with the accuracy of data when there is more than one instance (a.k.a. replica) of the data.

Consistency is not an overall setting for a cluster or keyspace. A consistency level is specified per read or write request, with a default consistency level set by the client driver. The default consistency level in the client drivers is generally ONE, unless changed.

Along with ONE, examples of consistency levels include TWO, THREE, QUORUM, LOCAL_QUORUM, and ALL. Detail for all of the consistency levels is available in the DataStax Cassandra documentation.

Read Consistency Levels	
Level	**Description**
ALL	Returns the record with the most recent timestamp after all replicas have responded. The read operation will fail if a replica does not respond.
EACH_QUORUM	Returns the record with the most recent timestamp once a quorum of replicas in each data center of the cluster has responded.
LOCAL_SERIAL	Same as SERIAL, but confined to the data center.
LOCAL_QUORUM	Returns the record with the most recent timestamp once a quorum of replicas in the current data center as the coordinator node has reported. Avoids latency of inter-data center communication.
LOCAL_ONE	Available in Cassandra 1.2.11 and 2.0.2 and later. Returns a response from the closest replica, as determined by the snitch, but only if the replica is in the local data center.
ONE	Returns a response from the closest replica, as determined by the snitch. By default, a read repair runs in the background to make the other replicas consistent.
QUORUM	Returns the record with the most recent timestamp after a quorum of replicas has responded regardless of data center.
SERIAL	Allows reading the current (and possibly uncommitted) state of data without proposing a new addition or update. If a SERIAL read finds an uncommitted transaction in progress, it will commit the transaction as part of the read.
TWO	Returns the most recent data from two of the closest replicas.
THREE	Returns the most recent data from three of the closest replicas.

Your needs will determine what the appropriate consistency level is for your write and read requests. For many applications, ONE is adequate. In general, ALL is discouraged, as it would fail if any of the nodes are down that are needed for a read request, and would require that all of the required nodes for storing the replicas must be up in order for a write request to succeed. Instead of ALL, QUORUM is normally used when a strong consistency is required.

CONSISTENCY Command

The cqlsh CONSISTENCY command can be used to view, as well as set, the default consistency level for queries executed through cqlsh.

```
cqlsh> CONSISTENCY;
Current consistency level is ONE.
cqlsh> CONSISTENCY TWO;
Consistency level set to TWO.
```

Exercise 3: Specify Consistency

In this exercise, you set and use consistency levels in cqlsh.

1. In **vm1** (or any vm in your cluster), in **cqlsh**, enter `CONSISTENCY;`, to see the default consistency level for commands executed through cqlsh:

```
cqlsh> CONSISTENCY;
Current consistency level is ONE.
```

2. Enter `CONSISTENCY TWO;` to change the default consistency level for commands executed through cqlsh to two:

```
cqlsh> CONSISTENCY TWO;
Consistency level set to TWO.
```

3. Enter the following to retrieve the activity for the home with id H00999943:

```
SELECT home_id, datetime, event FROM home_security.activity
WHERE home_id = 'H00999943';
```

4. See that the request succeeded:

```
cqlsh> SELECT home_id, datetime, event FROM home_security.
activity WHERE home_id = 'H00999943';

 home_id   | datetime                  | event
-----------+---------------------------+------------------
 H00999943 | 2014-05-23 18:56:23-0700  | alarm turned off
 H00999943 | 2014-05-23 08:52:19-0700  |        alarm set
 H00999943 | 2014-05-22 19:10:56-0700  | alarm turned off
 H00999943 | 2014-05-22 08:55:10-0700  |        alarm set
 H00999943 | 2014-05-21 19:03:33-0700  | alarm turned off
 H00999943 | 2014-05-21 09:05:54-0700  |        alarm set
```

5. Realize that, because the replication factor for the home_security keyspace is 2, specifying a consistency factor of TWO is equivalent to a consistency factor of ALL in this case.

6. Enter CONSISTENCY THREE; to change the consistency level for cqlsh to three.

7. Rerun the previous command:

```
SELECT home_id, datetime, event FROM home_security.activity
WHERE home_id = 'H00999943';
```

8. See that the request failed, because there are only 2 replicas of the data in the home_security keyspace:

```
cqlsh> CONSISTENCY THREE;
Consistency level set to THREE.
cqlsh> SELECT home_id, datetime, event FROM home_security.
activity WHERE home_id = 'H00999943';
Unable to complete request: one or more nodes were unavail
able.
```

9. Enter CONSISTENCY QUORUM; to specify a consistency factor of QUORUM.

10. Rerun the previous command:

```
SELECT home_id, datetime, event FROM home_security.activity
WHERE home_id = 'H00999943';
```

11. See that the request succeeded.

12. Realize that, because the replication factor for the home_security keyspace is 2, and QUORUM requires more than half, this is equivalent to specifying TWO or ALL in this case.

13. Enter CONSISTENCY ONE; to change the consistency level for commands executed through cqlsh back to one.

Try out consistency levels with writing data through cqlsh:

14. Enter CONSISTENCY; to see that the current consistency level is one.

15. Enter the following to write data with cqlsh's consistency of one, which means that only one node needs to acknowledge that it has received the write in order for the write to be considered successfully written to the cluster:

```
INSERT INTO home_security.activity (home_id, datetime, event,
code_used) VALUES ('H00999943', '2014-05-24 08:55:40', 'alarm
set', '1245');
```

16. Notice that the write executed without error:

```
cqlsh> INSERT INTO home_security.activity (home_id, dat
etime, event, code_used) VALUES ('H00999943', '2014-05-
24 08:55:40', 'alarm set', '1245');
cqlsh>
```

17. Enter CONSISTENCY TWO; to change the consistency level for commands executed through cqlsh to two.

18. Enter the following to write data with the consistency level of two, which means that both replica nodes need to acknowledge the write in order for the write to be considered successfully written to the cluster:

```
INSERT INTO home_security.activity (home_id, datetime, event,
code_used) VALUES ('H00999943', '2014-05-24 11:03:17', 'alarm
turned off', '1245');
```

19. Notice that the write executed without error.

20. Enter CONSISTENCY THREE; to change the consistency level for commands executed through cqlsh to three.

21. Enter the following to write data with the consistency level of three, which will fail:

```
INSERT INTO home_security.activity (home_id, datetime, event,
code_used) VALUES ('H00999943', '2014-05-24 12:45:59', 'alarm
set', '1245');
```

22. See that the write failed, because the replication factor for the home_security keyspace is two, which means that there are only two nodes in the cluster responsible for any given row of data in the home_security keyspace:

```
cqlsh> CONSISTENCY THREE;
Consistency level set to THREE.
cqlsh> INSERT INTO home_security.activity (home_id, dat
etime, event, code_used) VALUES ('H00999943', '2014-05-
24 12:45:59', 'alarm set', '1245');
Unable to complete request: one or more nodes were unav
ailable.
```

23. Enter CONSISTENCY ONE; to change the consistency level for commands executed through cqlsh back to one.

View documentation for all of the consistency levels available for reads and writes in Cassandra:

24. In a browser, search on `cassandra 2.0 consistency`:

25. Click the **Configuring data consistency** link, to go to the documentation.

26. **Scroll down** to see the list of **read** consistency levels:

Read Consistency Levels	
Level	Description
ALL	Returns the record with the most recent timestamp after all replicas have responded. The read operation will fail if a replica does not respond.
EACH_QUORUM	Returns the record with the most recent timestamp once a quorum of replicas in each data center of the cluster has responded.
LOCAL_SERIAL	Same as SERIAL, but confined to the data center.
LOCAL_QUORUM	Returns the record with the most recent timestamp once a quorum of replicas in the current data center as the coordinator node has reported. Avoids latency of inter-data center communication.
LOCAL_ONE	Available in Cassandra 1.2.11 and 2.0.2 and later. Returns a response from the closest replica, as determined by the snitch, but only if the replica is in the local data center.
ONE	Returns a response from the closest replica, as determined by the snitch. By default, a read repair runs in the background to make the other replicas consistent.
QUORUM	Returns the record with the most recent timestamp after a quorum of replicas has responded regardless of data center.
SERIAL	Allows reading the current (and possibly uncommitted) state of data without proposing a new addition or update. If a SERIAL read finds an uncommitted transaction in progress, it will commit the transaction as part of the read.
TWO	Returns the most recent data from two of the closest replicas.
THREE	Returns the most recent data from three of the closest replicas.

27. **Scroll back up** to see the list of **write** consistency levels:

Write Consistency Levels	
Level	**Description**
ANY	A write must be written to at least one node. If all replica nodes for the given row key are down, the write can still succeed after a hinted handoff has been written. If all replica nodes are down at write time, an ANY write is not readable until the replica nodes for that row have recovered.
ALL	A write must be written to the commit log and memory table on all replica nodes in the cluster for that row.
EACH_QUORUM	A write must be written to the commit log and memory table on a quorum of replica nodes in *all* data centers.
LOCAL_ONE	Available in Cassandra 1.2.11 and 2.0.2 and later. A write must be sent to, and successfully acknowledged by, at least one replica node in the local datacenter.
LOCAL_QUORUM	A write must be written to the commit log and memory table on a quorum of replica nodes in the same data center as the coordinator node. Avoids latency of inter-data center communication.
LOCAL_SERIAL	A write must be written conditionally to the commit log and memory table on a quorum of replica nodes in the same data center.
ONE	A write must be written to the commit log and memory table of at least one replica node.
QUORUM	A write must be written to the commit log and memory table on a quorum of replica nodes.
SERIAL	A write must be written conditionally to the commit log and memory table on a quorum of replica nodes.
THREE	A write must be written to the commit log and memory table of at least three replica nodes.
TWO	A write must be written to the commit log and memory table of at least two replica nodes.

28. Notice the write consistency level of **ANY**.

Understanding Hinted Handoff

Hinted handoff, which is enabled by default, can provide a way for writes to happen even if one of the nodes that the data is to be written to is down.

This is made possible by having the coordinator node (the node that received the write request) temporarily store the write (for three hours by default) on behalf of the node that is down. Once the down node comes back up, the coordinator node holding the write forwards the write.

A hinted handoff write does **not** count toward the ONE, QUORUM, or ALL consistency levels.

If the consistency level of ANY is specified with a write, the hinted handoff write satisfies the consistency level for the write, even if the write never eventually makes it to the node that owns it (e.g. if the down node is down for more than three hours). Hence, a consistency level of ANY should only be used if it is not critical for the write to be written.

Hinted Handoff Settings

Settings for hinted handoff are located in the cassandra.yaml file. Two key settings are **hinted_handoff_enabled** (default is true) and **max_hint_window_in_ms** (default is 10800000 milliseconds – 3 hours).

Understanding Read Repair

Read repair is an option to have a repair happen as part of a read request. Read repair compares the replicas for the requested data, and then updates any of the replicas that are outdated.

Configured at the table level, read repair is turned on by default, with a value of 10%. With the default setting of 10%, one out of every ten read requests triggers a read repair.

```
cqlsh> DESCRIBE TABLE vehicle_tracker.location;

CREATE TABLE location (
  vehicle_id text,
  date text,
  time timestamp,
  latitude double,
  longitude double,
  PRIMARY KEY ((vehicle_id, date), time)
) WITH CLUSTERING ORDER BY (time DESC) AND
  bloom_filter_fp_chance=0.010000 AND
  caching='KEYS_ONLY' AND
  comment='' AND
  dclocal_read_repair_chance=0.000000 AND
  gc_grace_seconds=864000 AND
  index_interval=128 AND
  read_repair_chance=0.100000 AND
```

The read repair generally happens in the background (unless a consistency of ALL is used, in which case the replicas are repaired before the response to the client is sent), which means that the data from the closest replica is sent, and then the read repair happens.

Exercise 4: View Hinted Handoff and Read Repair Settings

In this exercise, you view the settings for hinted handoff and read repair.

1. In vm1 (or any vm in your cluster), in a terminal window, at a regular command prompt, enter `vim ~/cassandra/apache-cassandra-2.0.7/conf/cassandra.yaml` to view the contents of the cassandra.yaml file for this node.

2. Scroll down to locate the **hinted_handoff_enabled** property (line 36).

3. See that the value is true:

```
hinted_handoff_enabled: true
```

4. Scroll down to locate the **max_hint_window_in_ms** property (line 40).

5. See that the value is 3 hours (10800000 milliseconds):

```
max_hint_window_in_ms: 10800000 # 3 hours
```

6. If desired, in a browser window, navigate to `http://www.datastax.com/documentation/cassandra/2.0/cassandra/dml/dml_about_hh_c.html` to see more detail on hinted handoff.

View the settings for read repair:

7. In **cqlsh**, enter `DESCRIBE TABLE home_security.activity;` to see the read_repair_chance setting.

8. See that read_repair_chance is set to 10%:

```
read_repair_chance=0.100000
```

9. Realize this means that, for one out of every ten read requests, Cassandra will do a background repair of the replicas for the data requested in the read request.

Summary

The focus of this chapter was on repairing nodes:

- Understanding Repair
- Repairing Nodes
- Understanding Consistency
- Understanding Hinted Handoff
- Understanding Read Repair

Unit Review Questions

1) How is it possible for a replica of data to become outdated, compared to other replicas of the data?

a. A node goes down for a day

b. A node storing hinted handoffs goes down permanently

c. A node goes down for any amount of time

d. Any of the above

2) Which consistency level is the default?

a. ANY

b. ONE

c. QUORUM

d. ALL

3) Which consistency level is recommended as a strong, but also fault-tolerant, consistency level?

a. ANY

b. ONE

c. QUORUM

d. ALL

4) Which consistency level could result in a write being acknowledged to the client but not actually being written to a replica node?

a. ANY

b. ONE

c. QUORUM

d. ALL

Lab: Repair Nodes for a Keyspace

In this exercise, you increase the replication factor for the vehicle_tracker keyspace to 2, and then run repair so that the second replicas get created.

1. In vm1 (or any vm in your cluster), in **cqlsh**, enter the following to see the current replication factor for the vehicle_tracker keyspace:

   ```
   DESCRIBE KEYSPACE vehicle_tracker;
   ```

2. Scroll up to see that the replication factor for the vehicle_tracker keyspace is currently set to 1:

   ```
   cqlsh> DESCRIBE KEYSPACE vehicle_tracker;

   CREATE KEYSPACE vehicle_tracker WITH replication = {
      'class': 'SimpleStrategy',
      'replication_factor': '1'
   };
   ```

3. At the cqlsh prompt, enter the following to change the replication factor to 2, so that if one of the nodes in the cluster goes down, all of the data in the keyspace will still be available:

   ```
   ALTER KEYSPACE vehicle_tracker WITH REPLICATION = {'class':
   'SimpleStrategy', 'replication_factor':2};
   ```

4. Rerun `DESCRIBE KEYSPACE vehicle_tracker;` to see that the replication factor is now defined to be 2:

   ```
   CREATE KEYSPACE vehicle_tracker WITH replication = {
      'class': 'SimpleStrategy',
      'replication_factor': '2'
   };
   ```

5. **Realize** that a second replica for the data in the vehicle_tracker keyspace will not actually exist until repair is run.

6. In a terminal window, in the directory where Cassandra is installed, enter
`bin/nodetool -h` *`192.168.159.102`* `repair vehicle_tracker`,
substituting in the IP address for your vm2, to repair the vehicle_tracker keyspace
on the vm2 Cassandra node.

7. While repair is running, notice the activity in the terminal windows in vm1, vm2,
and vm3 where Cassandra is running, as the nodes compare merkle trees and data
is streamed to, and received from, vm2.

Alternate Lab Steps: Repair Nodes for a Keyspace

In this exercise, you increase the replication factor of the vehicle_tracker keyspace to 2, and then run repair so that the second replicas get created.

1. In cqlsh, **see** what the current replication factor is for the vehicle_tracker keyspace.

2. Update the definition of the vehicle_tracker keyspace to change the replication factor of the vehicle_tracker keyspace to **2**.

3. Run **repair** on the vm2 Cassandra node, just for the vehicle_tracker keyspace.

4. While repair is running, notice the activity in the terminal windows in vm1, vm2, and vm3 where Cassandra is running, as the nodes compare merkle trees and data is streamed to, and received from, vm2.

15

....

REMOVING A NODE

Understanding Removing a Node

A node may need to be removed from a cluster for a variety of reasons. For example, the capacity might no longer be needed, or a node may need hardware maintenance, such having more memory added, or a node might be down due to hardware failure.

Designed to be fault-tolerant, Cassandra handles node removal gracefully.

Depending on whether a node is planned for removal or has unexpectedly died, the `nodetool decommission` or `nodetool removenode` commands can be used to handle the node removal.

The `nodetool decommission` command is for a planned removal, whereas the `nodetool removenode` command is for a dead node.

Decommissioning a Node

Decommissioning a node is when you choose to take a node out of service.

To decommission a node, the `nodetool decommission` command can be used.

```
nodetool -h 192.168.159.103 -p 7199 decommission
```

The decommission command assigns the token ranges that the node was responsible for to other nodes, and then streams the data from the node being decommissioned to the other nodes.

Decommissioning a node does not remove data from the decommissioned node. It simply copies data to the nodes that are now responsible for it.

Exercise 1: Decommission a Node

In this exercise, you decommission a node.

1. In vm**1**, in the nodetool status window, see that all three nodes are currently up:

```
Datacenter: datacenter1
=======================
Status=Up/Down
|/ State=Normal/Leaving/Joining/Moving
--  Address         Load      Owns    Host ID
UN  192.168.159.102  9.81 MB   33.9%   75151546-2217-49
UN  192.168.159.103  9.2 MB    31.6%   a6a90230-35e1-4c
UN  192.168.159.101  10.03 MB  34.5%   bcc09b1b-51e1-40
```

2. In another terminal window, in the directory where Cassandra is installed, enter the following to decommission the vm3 node, using your vm3 IP address:

```
bin/nodetool -h 192.168.159.103 -p 7199 decommission
```

3. See that the node is leaving, as indicated by **UL** in the nodetool status window:

```
Status=Up/Down
|/ State=Normal/Leavi
--   Address
UN   192.168.159.102
UL   192.168.159.103
UN   192.168.159.101
```

4. After a while, see that the node is gone and that its load has been assigned to the remaining nodes:

```
Status=Up/Down
|/ State=Normal/Leaving/Joining/Moving
--  Address          Load     Owns
UN  192.168.159.102  14.5 MB  50.4%
UN  192.168.159.101  14.3 MB  49.6%
```

Putting a Node Back into Service

Since data is not removed from a node when it is decommissioned (the data is copied to the other nodes, but not removed from the decommissioned node), it is best to clear the data from the decommissioned node, if the node has been down for any length of time, before putting the node back into service.

In general, it is faster to have the node join as a clean one (with no data), rather than have it join with old data that then needs to be repaired.

Once the data has been deleted from the decommissioned node, the node can join as a new node.

Clearing Data From a Node

To completely remove the data on a Cassandra node, the data, commitlog, and saved_caches directories need to be cleared. This can be done on the command line using the `rm` command.

```
vmx@vm3:~$ cd /var/lib/cassandra
vmx@vm3:/var/lib/cassandra$ ls
commitlog   data   saved_caches
vmx@vm3:/var/lib/cassandra$ rm -r commitlog data saved_caches
```

Exercise 2: Put a Node Back into Service

In this exercise, you put a decommissioned node back into service.

1. In vm**3**, in the terminal window where Cassandra is running, press **Ctrl-C** to stop Cassandra.

2. Enter `ps aux | grep cass` to see that Cassandra is no longer running:

```
vmx@vm3:~/cassandra/apache-cassandra-2.0.7$ ps aux | grep cass
vmx        9999  0.0  0.0  13596   940 pts/1    S+   08:38   0:0
0 grep --color=auto cass
vmx@vm3:~/cassandra/apache-cassandra-2.0.7$
```

3. In another terminal window in vm3, enter `cd /var/lib/cassandra` to navigate to the directory where the node's Cassandra data is stored.

4. Enter `ls` to see the contents of the directory.

5. **Notice** the commitlog, data, and saved_caches directories:

```
vmx@vm3:~$ cd /var/lib/cassandra
vmx@vm3:/var/lib/cassandra$ ls
commitlog  data  saved_caches
```

6. Enter `rm -r commitlog data saved_caches` to delete all three directories, to clear all of Cassandra data stored on this node.

7. Enter `ls` to confirm that the directories have been deleted.

8. Back in the previous terminal window, in the directory where Cassandra is installed, enter `bin/cassandra -f` to start Cassandra running on this node.

9. In vm1, in the nodetool status window, see the vm3 node joining the cluster:

```
Status=Up/Down
|/ State=Normal/Leaving/Joining/Moving
--   Address          Load       Owns     Host ID
UN   192.168.159.102  14.51 MB   50.4%    75151546-
UJ   192.168.159.103  14.17 KB   ?        a7feb8c0-
UN   192.168.159.101  14.3 MB    49.6%    bcc09b1b-
```

10. After awhile, see that the vm3 node is now the owner of approximately a third of the data:

```
Status=Up/Down
|/ State=Normal/Leaving/Joining/Moving
--  Address           Load      Owns     Host ID
UN  192.168.159.102   14.52 MB  33.8%    75151546-
UN  192.168.159.103   9.05 MB   31.2%    a7feb8c0-
UN  192.168.159.101   14.3 MB   34.9%    bcc09b1b-
```

11. Notice that the vm1 and vm2 nodes still have approximately the same Load values as they did before. Realize this is because, although data was copied to the vm3 node for the ranges it owns, that no data was deleted from the vm1 or vm2 nodes.

12. In another terminal window in vm3 (or any node in your cluster), in the directory where Cassandra is installed, enter `bin/nodetool -h 192.168.159.101 -p 7199 cleanup` to cleanup the vm1 node.

13. After awhile, in the nodetool status window, notice that the vm1 node has been cleaned up:

```
Status=Up/Down
|/ State=Normal/Leaving/Joining/Moving
--  Address           Load      Owns     Host ID
UN  192.168.159.102   14.52 MB  33.8%    75151546-
UN  192.168.159.103   9.05 MB   31.2%    a7feb8c0-
UN  192.168.159.101   10.15 MB  34.9%    bcc09b1b-
```

14. Enter `bin/nodetool -h 192.168.159.102 -p 7199 cleanup` to cleanup the vm2 node.

15. After awhile, in the nodetool status window, notice that the vm2 node has been cleaned up:

```
Status=Up/Down
|/ State=Normal/Leaving/Joining/Moving
--  Address           Load      Owns     Host ID
UN  192.168.159.102   9.79 MB   33.8%    75151546-
UN  192.168.159.103   9.05 MB   31.2%    a7feb8c0-
UN  192.168.159.101   10.15 MB  34.9%    bcc09b1b-
```

Removing a Dead Node

Removing a dead node from the cluster is done to reassign the token ranges that the dead node was responsible for to other nodes in the cluster and to populate other nodes with the data that the dead node had been responsible for.

To remove a dead node from the cluster, and reassign its token ranges and data, the nodetool removenode command can be used.

```
bin/nodetool removenode 1c978113-0fbd-425c-83df-353389044bba
```

Note: the host id can be copied from a nodetool status window.

With a dead node being dead, the data that it was responsible for needs to come from other nodes in the cluster, which happens when the `nodetool removenode` command is run.

Watching removenode Happen

The `nodetool removenode status` command can be used to watch removenode happen.

```
Every 2.0s: bin/nodetool ...    Tue Jun  3 11:56:34 2014

RemovalStatus: Removing token (-9129580477490204828).
Waiting for replication confirmation from [/192.168.15
9.102,/192.168.159.101].
```

Exercise 3: Remove a Dead Node

In this exercise, you remove a dead node.

1. In vm**1**, in the nodetool status window, see that all three nodes are currently up:

```
Status=Up/Down
|/ State=Normal/Leaving/Joining/Moving
--  Address           Load       Owns    Host ID
UN  192.168.159.102   9.77 MB    33.8%   75151546-2217-49
UN  192.168.159.103   9.08 MB    31.2%   a7feb8c0-ff78-4a
UN  192.168.159.101   10.17 MB   34.9%   bcc09b1b-51e1-40
```

2. In vm**3**, in the terminal window where Cassandra is running, press **Ctrl-C** to stop Cassandra.

3. In vm**1**, in the window with nodetool status, see that vm3 is now down:

```
Status=Up/Down
|/ State=Normal/Leaving/Joining/Moving
--  Address           Load       Owns    Host ID
UN  192.168.159.102   9.77 MB    33.8%   75151546-2217-49
DN  192.168.159.103   9.08 MB    31.2%   a7feb8c0-ff78-4a
UN  192.168.159.101   10.17 MB   34.9%   bcc09b1b-51e1-40
```

4. In another terminal window on vm1, in the directory where Cassandra is installed, set up a watch for removenode status:

```
$ watch -n 2 bin/nodetool removenode status
```

5. See that the watch command is running every 2 seconds:

```
Every 2.0s: bin/nodetool removenode status

RemovalStatus: No token removals in process.
```

6. In the nodetool status window, highlight and copy the host id of the vm3 node (e.g. a7feb8c0-ff78-4ac1-b043-1517e532b6b9).

7. In yet another terminal window on vm1 (or vm2), in the directory where Cassandra is installed, enter the removenode command below, **substituting in** the host id for your vm3, so that Cassandra will remove the vm3 node from the cluster, assign the token ranges to the other nodes, and replicate the data from the other nodes to the other nodes:

```
bin/nodetool removenode a7feb8c0-ff78-4ac1-b043-1517e532b6b9
```

8. In the remove status watch window, watch the tokens previously assigned to vm3 being assigned to other nodes:

```
Every 2.0s: bin/nodetool ...   Tue Jun  3 11:56:34 2014

RemovalStatus: Removing token (-9129580477490204828).
Waiting for replication confirmation from [/192.168.15
9.102,/192.168.159.101].
```

9. After awhile, in the regular nodetool status window, see that the vm3 node has been removed from the cluster:

```
Status=Up/Down
|/ State=Normal/Leaving/Joining/Moving
--  Address          Load      Owns    Host ID
UN  192.168.159.102  9.77 MB   50.4%   75151546-2217-49
UN  192.168.159.101  10.2 MB   49.6%   bcc09b1b-51e1-40
```

10. Notice that the vm1 and vm2 nodes have taken on the ownership of the token ranges that had been owned by the vm3 node.

11. Know that, because the replication factor of the vehicle_tracker and home_security keyspaces is 2, that the data that was on the vm3 node was able to be regenerated from the remaining nodes.

12. Realize that approximately one third of the data in the Keyspace1 keyspace is missing from the cluster, because, with the replication factor for that keyspace only being 1, and the node dying unexpectedly (rather than being decommissioned), there are no replicas of the data that was on the vm3 node to get from the remaining nodes.

Summary

The focus of this chapter was on removing a node:

- Understanding Removing Nodes

- Decommissioning a Dead Node

- Putting a Node Back into Service

- Removing a Dead Node

Unit Review Questions

1) Which command is for when a node has unexpectedly died?

a. nodetool restore

b. nodetool decommission

c. nodetool live

d. nodetool removenode

2) Which command is for removing a node due to a decreased need for capacity?

a. nodetool restore

b. nodetool decommission

c. nodetool live

d. nodetool removenode

3) It is generally best to delete a node's stored data before putting the node back into service.

a. True

b. False

4) What could potentially be done to get back the Keyspace1 data that was lost in the last exercise?

a. Nothing can be done

b. Run removenode again

c. Delete the stored data on the vm3 node, start the node back up, and run removenode again

d. Start the node back up and, to prevent the problem from happening in the future, change the replication factor for Keyspace1 to 2, and run repair for the keyspace, to generate the second replicas

Lab: Put a Node Back into Service

In this exercise, you remove the stored data on vm3 and put the node back into service. (We don't need the data from Keyspace1, generated by the cassandra-stress tool.)

1. In **vm3**, in a terminal window, enter `cd /var/lib/cassandra` to navigate to the directory where the node's Cassandra data is stored.

2. Enter `ls` to see the contents of the directory.

3. **Notice** the commitlog, data, and saved_caches directories.

4. Enter `rm -r commitlog data saved_caches` to delete all three directories, to clear all of Cassandra data stored on this node.

5. Enter `ls` to confirm that the directories have been deleted.

6. In a terminal window, in the directory where Cassandra was installed, enter `bin/cassandra -f` to start Cassandra running on this node.

7. In vm1, in the nodetool status window, see the vm3 node joining the cluster:

```
Datacenter: datacenter1
=======================
Status=Up/Down
|/ State=Normal/Leaving/Joining/Moving
--  Address          Load      Owns   Host ID
UN  192.168.159.102  9.77 MB   50.4%  75151546-2217-49
UJ  192.168.159.103  14.17 KB  ?      a9910b7d-075f-47
UN  192.168.159.101  10.2 MB   49.6%  bcc09b1b-51e1-40
```

8. See that the vm3 node is now responsible for approximately a third of the data:

```
Datacenter: datacenter1
=======================
Status=Up/Down
|/ State=Normal/Leaving/Joining/Moving
--  Address          Load      Owns   Host ID
UN  192.168.159.102  9.77 MB   33.6%  75151546-2217-49
UN  192.168.159.103  4.55 MB   31.3%  a9910b7d-075f-47
UN  192.168.159.101  10.2 MB   35.0%  bcc09b1b-51e1-40
```

9. Notice that the load values for the vm1 and vm2 nodes did not go down.

10. In another terminal window (in any of the vms in your cluster), in the directory where Cassandra is installed, enter `bin/nodetool -h 192.168.159.101 -p 7199 cleanup` to cleanup the vm1 node.

11. Enter `bin/nodetool -h 192.168.159.102 -p 7199 cleanup` to cleanup the vm2 node.

12. After awhile, in the nodetool status window, see that the vm1 and vm2 nodes have been cleaned up:

```
Datacenter: datacenter1
========================
Status=Up/Down
|/ State=Normal/Leaving/Joining/Moving
--   Address          Load        Owns    Host ID
UN   192.168.159.102  7.47 MB     33.6%   75151546-2217-49
UN   192.168.159.103  4.55 MB     31.3%   a9910b7d-075f-47
UN   192.168.159.101  8.08 MB     35.0%   bcc09b1b-51e1-40
```

Alternate Lab Steps: Put a Node Back into Service

In this exercise, you remove the stored data on vm3 and put the node back into service. (We don't need the data from Keyspace1, generated by the cassandra-stress tool.)

1. In vm3, clear the data, commitlog, and saved_caches directories.

2. In vm3, start Cassandra.

3. In vm1, watch the vm3 node join the cluster.

4. Clean up vm1 and vm2.

5. See that vm3 is part of the cluster, with approximately one third of the ring ownership and approximately one third of the data load:

```
Datacenter: datacenter1
========================
Status=Up/Down
|/ State=Normal/Leaving/Joining/Moving
--   Address          Load      Owns    Host ID
UN   192.168.159.102  7.47 MB   33.6%   75151546-2217-49
UN   192.168.159.103  4.55 MB   31.3%   a9910b7d-075f-47
UN   192.168.159.101  8.08 MB   35.0%   bcc09b1b-51e1-40
```

16

●●●●●●●●●●●●●●●●●●●●●●●●●●●●

REDEFINING A CLUSTER
FOR MULTIPLE DATA CENTERS

Redefining for Multiple Data Centers

Changing Snitch Type

Modify cassandra-rackdc.properties

Changing Replication Strategy

Modifying a Cluster to Span Multiple Data Centers

To modify a cluster so that it can span more than one data center, a few things need to be done. One is that the snitch type cannot be SimpleSnitch. SimpleSnitch is the default snitch for a cluster, but can only be used for a single data center cluster.

Additionally, the data center and rack information for each node in the cluster needs to be specified. This is generally done as part of configuring the snitch type.

Finally, the replication strategy for keyspaces needs to be changed to NetworkTopologyStrategy, which allows for specifying the number of replicas in each data center for a keyspace.

Exercise 1: Set Up a Node

In this exercise, you start setting up a node for a second data center.

1. In the **achotl1** folder on your desktop, unzip the **achotl1_vmx_64-bit.zip** file.

2. Rename the unzipped file `achotl1_vm4_64-bit`.

3. **Double-click** the virtual machine, to open it in VMware.

4. If prompted with a message about other virtual machines running, click **OK**.

5. If prompted, click the **I copied it** button.

6. Enter with the password of `ubuntu`.

Change the title bar name of the virtual machine to achotl1_vm**4**_64-bit:

7. To change the name of the vm in the title bar, select **Virtual Machine – Settings…**.

   *Windows users: select **Player – Manage – Virtual Machine Settings…**.*

8. Click the **General** icon.

   *Windows users: select the **Options** tab.*

9. To the right of Name, **click on** the name (achotl1_vmx_64-bit), to edit it.

10. Change the name to `achotl1_vm4_64-bit`.

11. **Close** the window.

12. See that the title bar name has been changed:

> 🗔 achotl1_vm4_64-bit

Specify a static IP address for the virtual machine:

13. In the upper-right corner, under the gear icon, select **System Settings**:

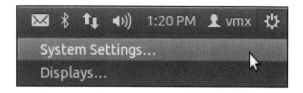

14. Click the **Network** icon.

15. Click the **Options...** button.

16. Select the **IPv4 Settings** tab:

17. For Method, select **Manual**:

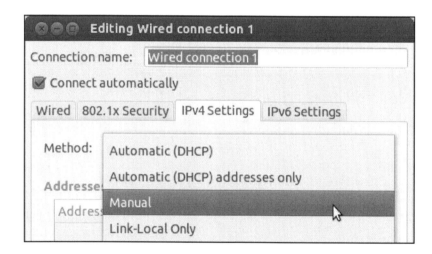

18. In the Addresses, section, click the **Add** button:

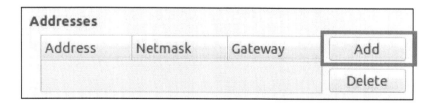

19. For **Address**, enter your static IP address for this virtual machine (e.g. *192.168.159.***104**).

20. For **Netmask**, enter your mask IP address from Page 12-7, Step 9 (e.g. *255.255.255.0*).

21. For **Gateway**, enter your gateway IP address from Page 12-7, Step 11 (e.g. *192.168.159.2*).

22. For **DNS servers**, enter your DNS IP address from Page 12-7, Step 12 (e.g. *192.168.159.2*).

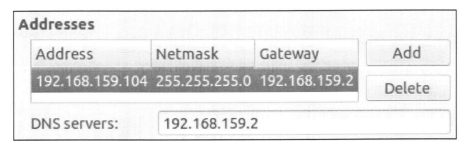

23. Click the **Save...** button.

24. If a dialog box with an error message appears, click the **Continue** button.

25. See the settings in the Network window:

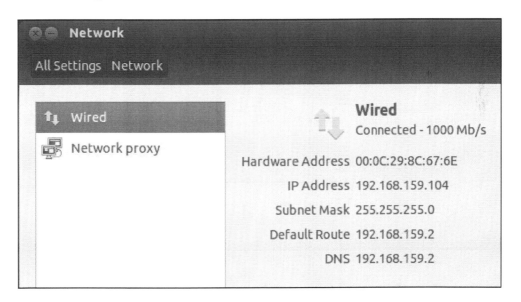

26. **Close** the Network window.

27. **Select Virtual Machine – Restart**, to restart the virtual machine.

*Windows users: select **Player – Power – Restart Guest***.

28. Once the virtual machine has restarted, open a terminal window and enter `ifconfig` to see the static IP address displayed:

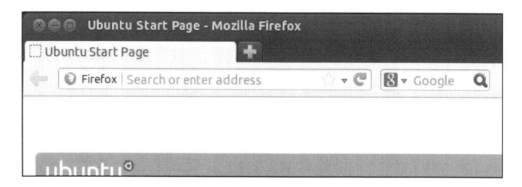

29. Open Firefox to see that you still have Internet access:

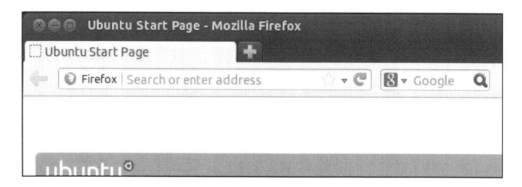

30. Ping from vm4 to vm1:

```
vmx@ubuntu:~$ ping 192.168.159.101
PING 192.168.159.101 (192.168.159.101) 56(84) byt
64 bytes from 192.168.159.101: icmp_req=1 ttl=64
64 bytes from 192.168.159.101: icmp_req=2 ttl=64
```

31. Press **Ctrl-C** to stop pinging.

Make the hostname unique and known:

32. In a terminal window in vm4, enter `sudo vim /etc/hostname`, to edit the hostname for the virtual machine.

33. Enter the sudo password of `ubuntu` if prompted.

34. Press `i` to be able to edit the file.

35. Change the hostname to `vm4`.

36. Press **Esc** and enter `:wq` to save and exit.

37. Enter `sudo vim /etc/hosts` to add to the list of hosts.

38. Press `i` to be able to edit the file.

39. **Add** the following entries to the list, **substituting in** your IP addresses for vm1, vm2, vm3, and vm4:

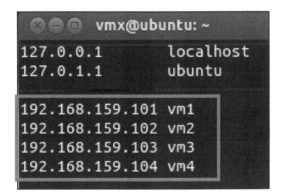

40. Press **Esc** and enter `:wq` to save and exit.

41. **Restart** the virtual machine.

42. Once the virtual machine is restarted, enter `ifconfig` in a terminal window to see the hostname displayed and static IP address still displayed.

Configure the cassandra.yaml file on vm4:

43. Enter `vim ~/cassandra/apache-cassandra-2.0.7/conf/cassandra.yaml`, to edit the cassandra.yaml file on vm4.

44. Notice that the **cluster name** is Test Cluster (line 10), the same as the cluster name for vm1, vm2, and vm3.

45. Scroll down to locate the **listen_address** property (line 297).

46. Press i to be able to edit the property.

47. **Replace** localhost with the IP address of your vm4 virtual machine. (For example, `listen_address: 192.168.159.104`).

48. Scroll down to locate the **rpc_address** property (line 335).

49. **Replace** localhost with the IP address of your vm4 virtual machine. (For example, `rpc_address: 192.168.159.104`.)

50. Scroll up to locate the **seed_provider** property (line 218).

51. Within seed_provider, locate seeds: "127.0.0.1".

52. Replace the value of seeds with your vm1 and vm2 IP addresses. For example:

    `seeds: "192.168.159.101,192.168.159.102"`

53. Press **Esc** and type :wq to save and exit.

Changing Snitch Type

The snitch type is specified in the cassandra.yaml file of each node in the cluster.

Snitch types are:

- Dynamic snitching
- SimpleSnitch
- RackInferringSnitch
- PropertyFileSnitch
- GossipingPropertyFileSnitch
- EC2Snitch
- EC2MultiRegionSnitch

Once the snitch type has been changed in each cassandra.yaml file, any supporting files for the snitch type chosen need to be provided, and then a rolling restart of the nodes can be done. (The cassandra.yaml file is read when a Cassandra node starts up.)

All of the nodes in a cluster must use the same snitch type.

GossipingPropertyFileSnitch

The GossipingPropertyFileSnitch is a popular alternative to the PropertyFileSnitch because, when adding a new node to the cluster, you can simply provide the rack and data center information for the new node in its cassandra-rackdc.properties file, rather than having to update a separate file on every node in the cluster with the information about the new node.

Exercise 2: Changing Snitch Type

In this exercise, you change the snitch type for the cluster to
GossipingPropertyFileSnitch.

1. In vm**1**, in a terminal window, in the directory where Cassandra is installed, enter
    `vim conf/cassandra.yaml` to edit the cassandra.yaml file for this node.

2. Locate the **endpoint_snitch** setting (line 564).

3. Press `i` to be able to edit the text.

4. Change the endpoint_snitch value from SimpleSnitch to
    `GossipingPropertyFileSnitch`:

```
endpoint_snitch: GossipingPropertyFileSnitch
```

5. Press **Esc** and enter `:wq` to save and exit.

6. **Repeat** steps 1-5 for the vm2, vm3, and vm4 nodes.

Modifying cassandra-rackdc.properties

When the endpoint_snitch setting in the cassandra.yaml file is set to
GossipingPropertyFileSnitch, the cassandra-rackdc.properties file is read.

The cassandra-rackdc.properties file, located in the conf directory where
Cassandra is installed, is for specifying the topology of the individual node.

Within the cassandra-rackdc.properties file are two properties: dc, for specifying
the name of the data center that the node is in, and rack, for specifying the name
of the rack that the node is in.

```
dc = DC2
rack   RAC1
```

Exercise 3: Modify cassandra-rackdc.properties

In this exercise, you modify the cassandra-rackdc.properties file in each vm to provide the data center name and rack information for each node in the cluster.

1. In vm1, in a terminal window, in the directory where Cassandra is installed, enter `vim conf/cassandra-rackdc.properties` to edit the cassandra-rackdc.properties file.

2. Notice that that DC1 is set as the data center name and RAC1 is set as the rack name:

```
dc=DC1
rack=RAC1
```

3. Realize that these are the default settings for a node.

4. Press **Esc** and enter `:q` to exit.

5. In vm4, in the directory where Cassandra is installed, enter `vim conf/cassandra-rackdc.properties` to edit the cassandra-rackdc.properties file.

6. Press `i` to be able to edit the text.

7. **Change** the dc value to `DC2`.

8. Press **Esc** and enter `:wq` to save and exit.

Do a rolling restart of the Cassandra nodes:

9. In vm1, in the terminal window where Cassandra is running, enter **Ctrl-C** to stop Cassandra.

10. In the same terminal window, enter `bin/cassandra -f` to start Cassandra.

11. Once the vm1 node is back up, look in the watch nodetool status window to see that it is now in a data center named DC1:

```
Datacenter: DC1
================
Status=Up/Down
|/ State=Normal/Leaving/Joining/Moving
--  Address          Load        Owns     Host ID
UN  192.168.159.101  8.06 MB     35.0%    bcc09b1b-51e1-40
Datacenter: datacenter1
=======================
Status=Up/Down
|/ State=Normal/Leaving/Joining/Moving
--  Address          Load        Owns     Host ID
UN  192.168.159.102  7.46 MB     33.6%    75151546-2217-49
UN  192.168.159.103  4.58 MB     31.3%    a9910b7d-075f-47
```

12. **Repeat** steps 9-11 for vm**2** and vm**3**.

13. In vm**4**, in the terminal window, in the directory where Cassandra is installed, enter `bin/cassandra -f` to start Cassandra.

14. In vm1, in the terminal window with nodetool status, see that the vm4 node is now part of the cluster, in DC2:

```
Datacenter: DC1
================
Status=Up/Down
|/ State=Normal/Leaving/Joining/Moving
--  Address          Load        Owns     Host ID
UN  192.168.159.102  7.49 MB     24.5%    75151546-2217-49
UN  192.168.159.103  4.54 MB     23.7%    a9910b7d-075f-47
UN  192.168.159.101  8.06 MB     27.1%    bcc09b1b-51e1-40
Datacenter: DC2
================
Status=Up/Down
|/ State=Normal/Leaving/Joining/Moving
--  Address          Load        Owns     Host ID
UN  192.168.159.104  14.17 KB    24.8%    e03994dd-7877-40
```

Changing Replication Strategy

In order to specify the number of replicas per data center for a keyspace in a multiple data center cluster, the replication strategy for the keyspace needs to be NetworkTopologyStrategy.

The replication strategy for a keyspace can be updated from SimpleStrategy to NetworkTopologyStrategy by using the `ALTER KEYSPACE` command.

For example, the code below specifies, for the vehicle_tracker keyspace, 2 replicas in DC1 and 1 replica in DC2.

```
ALTER KEYSPACE vehicle_tracker WITH replication = {'class':
'NetworkTopologyStrategy', 'DC1': 2, 'DC2': 1};
```

The number of replicas in each data center does not have to match, and can vary for each keyspace.

Exercise 4: Change Replication Strategy

In this exercise, you change the replication strategy of the keyspaces in the cluster to NetworkTopologyStrategy.

1. In vm1 (or any node in your cluster), in **cqlsh**, enter the following to update the replication factor for the vehicle_tracker keyspace from SimpleStrategy to NetworkTopologyStrategy:

   ```
   ALTER KEYSPACE vehicle_tracker WITH replication = {'class':
   'NetworkTopologyStrategy', 'DC1': 2, 'DC2': 1};
   ```

2. Enter the following to update the replication factor for the home_security keyspace from SimpleStrategy to NetworkTopologyStrategy:

   ```
   ALTER KEYSPACE home_security WITH replication = {'class':
   'NetworkTopologyStrategy', 'DC1': 2, 'DC2': 1};
   ```

3. In a terminal window, in the directory where Cassandra is installed, run repair on the vehicle_tracker keyspace to generate replicas in the second data center for data in the vehicle_tracker keyspace:

   ```
   bin/nodetool -h 192.168.159.104 repair vehicle_tracker
   ```

4. Run repair on the home_security keyspace to generate replicas in the second data center for data in the home_security keyspace:

   ```
   bin/nodetool -h 192.168.159.104 repair home_security
   ```

See that the applications still work:

5. In vm1, in **Eclipse**, right-click on the **AlarmSystemServlet.java** file in the **alarm-system** project and select **Run As – Run on Server**, to run the application.

6. See that the application page displays.

7. Enter H01545551 and press Submit, to see that the application still connects to the cluster and retrieves data.

8. Right-click on **VehicleTrackerServlet.java** file in the **vehicle-tracker** project and select **Run As – Run on Server**, to run the application.

9. See that the application page displays.

10. Enter 2014-05-19 for the date and FLN78197 for the vehicle id, and press Submit, to see that the application still connects to the cluster and retrieves data.

Summary

The focus of this unit was on adding a data center:

- Modifying a Cluster to Span Multiple Data Centers

- Changing Snitch Type

- Modifying cassandra-rackdc.properties

- Changing Replication Strategy

Unit Review Questions

1) The name of the supporting file that is required for the
    GossipingPropertyFileSnitch is:

a. cassandra-env.sh

b. cassandra-topology.properties

c. cassandra-rackdc.properties

d. cassandra-topology.yaml

2) The number of replicas in each data center needs to be the same for all of the
    keyspaces in a cluster.

a. True

b. False

3) The name of the replication strategy that allows a keyspace to be across more than
    one data center is:

a. SimpleStrategy

b. LocalStrategy

c. NetworkTopologyStrategy

d. GNUStrategy

RESOURCES FOR FURTHER LEARNING

Accessing Documentation

Reading Blogs and Books

Watching Video Recordings

Posting Questions

Attending Meetups

Accessing Documentation

The DataStax documentation, available at `http://www.datastax.com/docs`, is a great place to start in gaining more knowledge on Cassandra.

In the 198-page Apache Cassandra 2.0 documentation are details on Cassandra, including the architecture, installation, initializing a cluster, the database internals, configuration, operations, and backing up and restoring data.

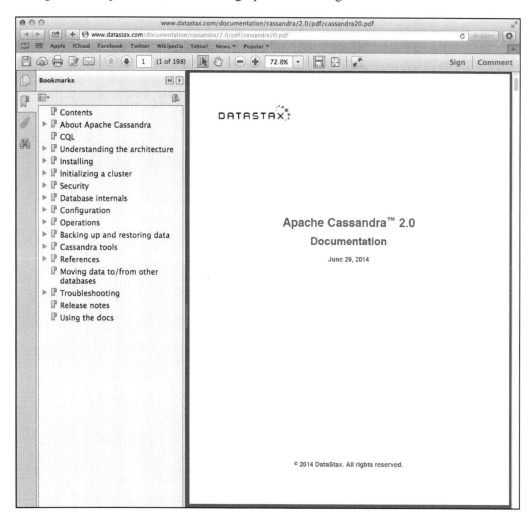

In the 104-page CQL for Cassandra 2.0 documentation are details on using CQL with Cassandra, which also includes a list and description of all the CQL commands that exist.

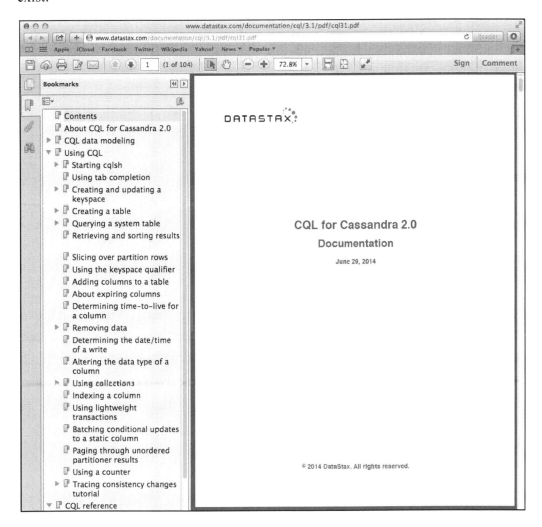

Exercise 1: Access Documentation

In this exercise you access the DataStax documentation for Cassandra.

1. In a browser, navigate to `http://www.datastax.com/docs`:

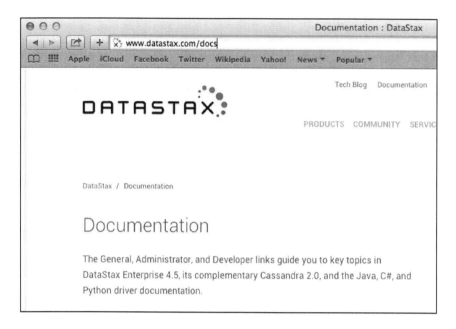

2. Scroll down to the Latest releases section:

Latest releases	
Getting Started with DataStax Enterprise and DataStax Community	PDF
DataStax Enterprise 4.5	PDF
OpsCenter 4.1	PDF
Cassandra 2.0 (used by DataStax Enterprise 4.5)	PDF
Nodetool reference card	PDF
CQL for Cassandra 2.0	PDF
DataStax Java Driver 2.0 for Apache Cassandra (API)	PDF
DataStax C# Driver 2.0 for Apache Cassandra (API)	PDF
DataStax Python Driver 2.0 for Apache Cassandra (API)	PDF

3. Click the **PDF** link for **Cassandra 2.0**.

4. Explore the categories on the left:

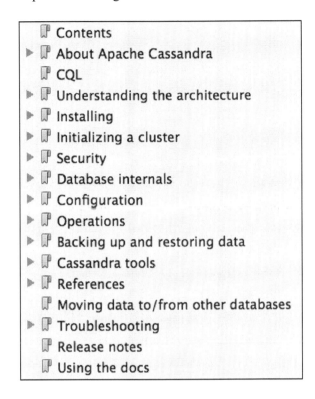

5. Back on the main documentation page at http://www.datastax.com/docs, in the Latest releases section, click the **PDF** link for **CQL for Cassandra 2.0**.

6. Explore the categories on the left:

Reading Blogs and Books

Blogs and books are a great way to supplement your knowledge of Cassandra, often going beyond the documentation in exploring and explaining a topic in depth.

There are a number of Cassandra-focused blogs. A good blog to start with, for gaining more technical knowledge of Casssandra, is the **DataStax Developer Blog** (`http://www.datastax.com/dev/blog`).

The DataStax Developer Blog has entries written by DataStax/Cassandra engineers and technical staff that provide in-depth explanations of Cassandra features.

For example, Aleksey Yeschenko's May 20, 2014 blog post explains the new implementation of counters in Cassandra 2.1, and Ryan McGuire's April 24, 2014 post explains compaction improvements in Cassandra 2.1.

Additional Cassandra blogs include the **Planet Cassandra Blog** (`http://planetcassandra.org/blog/`) with entries on how different companies are using Cassandra, the **DataStax Blog** (`http://www.datastax.com/blog`), and the **Apache Software Foundation Blog** (`https://blogs.apache.org/foundation/tags/cassandra`).

Exercise 2: Read a Blog Post

In this exercise you access the DataStax Developer Blog to read a blog post.

1. In a browser, navigate to `http://www.datastax.com/dev/blog`.

2. **Scroll** down through the list of blog posts, **scanning** the titles.

3. Click on a title that interests you (e.g. the June 5, 2014 blog post titled 4 simple rules when using the DataStax drivers for Cassandra):

---

4 simple rules when using the DataStax drivers for Cassandra

BY ALEX POPESCU · JUNE 5, 2014 | 0 COMMENTS

When using one of the DataStax drivers for Cassandra, either if it's C#, Python, or Java, there are 4 simple rules that should clear up the majority of questions and that will also make your code efficient.

---

4. Skim through the blog post:

---

4 simple rules when using the DataStax drivers for Cassandra

BY ALEX POPESCU · JUNE 5, 2014 | 0 COMMENTS

When using one of the DataStax drivers for Cassandra, either if it's C#, Python, or Java, there are 4 simple rules that should clear up the majority of questions and that will also make your code efficient:

1. Use one `Cluster` instance per (physical) cluster (per application lifetime)
2. Use at most one `Session` per keyspace, or use a single `Session` and explicitly specify the keyspace in your queries
3. If you execute a statement more than once, consider using a `PreparedStatement`
4. You can reduce the number of network roundtrips and also have atomic operations by using `Batches`

In case you are wondering what's behind these rules, keep reading. Otherwise, happy coding!

Cluster

A `Cluster` instance allows to configure different important aspects of the way connections and queries will be handled. At this level you can configure everything from contact points (address of the nodes to be contacted initially before the driver performs node discovery), the request routing policy, retry and reconnection policies, etc. Generally such settings are set once at the application level.

```
cluster = Cluster(['10.1.1.3', '10.1.1.4', '10.1.1.5'],
```

---

5. Peruse additional blog posts, as desired.

Watching Video Recordings

Watching video recordings from Cassandra summits, webinars, and meetups is an easy way to keep learning more about Cassandra.

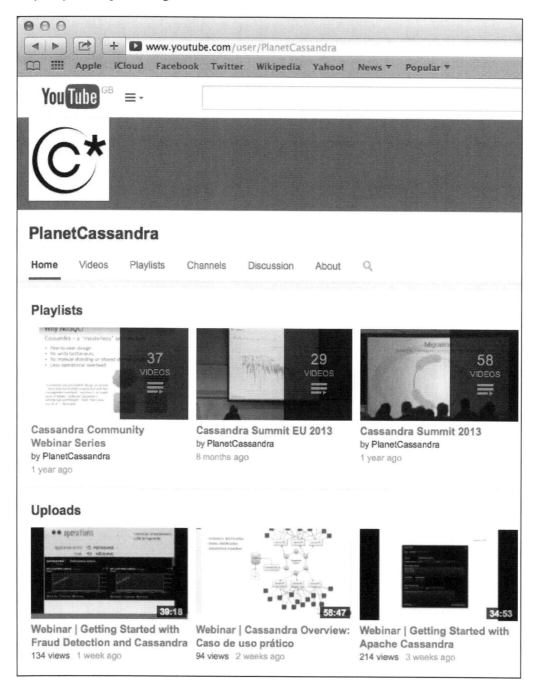

Many Cassandra recordings are available through the YouTube PlanetCassandra channel at `http://www.youtube.com/user/PlanetCassandra.`

Exercise 3: Watch a Video Recording

In this exercise you access the YouTube PlanetCassandra channel to watch a Cassandra Summit video recording.

1. In a browser, navigate to `http://www.youtube.com/user/PlanetCassandra.`

2. Notice the playlists (first row) and uploads (second row).

3. In the playlists row, click the **Cassandra Summit 2013** link.

4. Notice the list of 58 video recordings from the Cassandra summit.

5. Scroll down to locate the recording of Jonathan Ellis's keynote:

6. Click the image, or the title, to start watching the video:

C* Summit 2013: Jonathan Ellis Keynote

7. Continue perusing the PlanetCassandra channel, watching videos as desired.

Posting Questions

For learning more about Cassandra by viewing questions that people are asking, as well as be able to post questions of yours, there are forums as well as a mailing list.

Forums

Stack Overflow is a popular forum for Cassandra, available through `http://stackoverflow.com/questions/tagged/cassandra`.

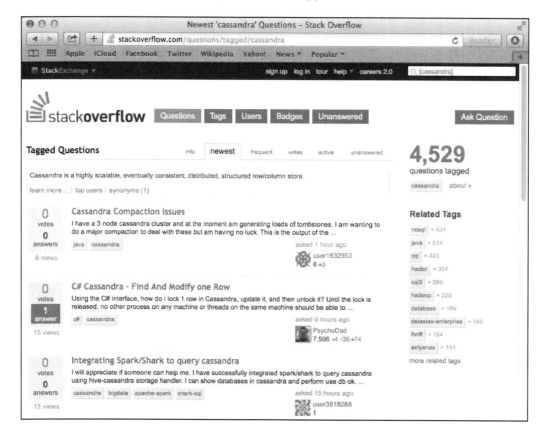

Mailing List

For people who prefer to learn by being part of a mailing list, receiving a few emails each day, the Apache Foundation provides a mailing list that can be subscribed to through `http://cassandra.apache.org`.

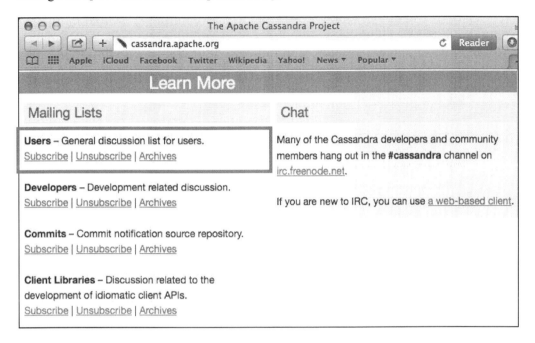

Exercise 4: Post a Question

In this exercise you first go to Stack Overflow to view a forum post. Then you post a question of your own. Then you access the Apache Foundation mailing list for Cassandra users.

1. In a browser, navigate to
   `http://stackoverflow.com/questions/tagged/cassandra.`

2. Notice the Cassandra posts.

3. Click the title of a post that interests you:

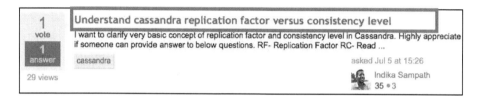

4. Skim through the question and answer(s):

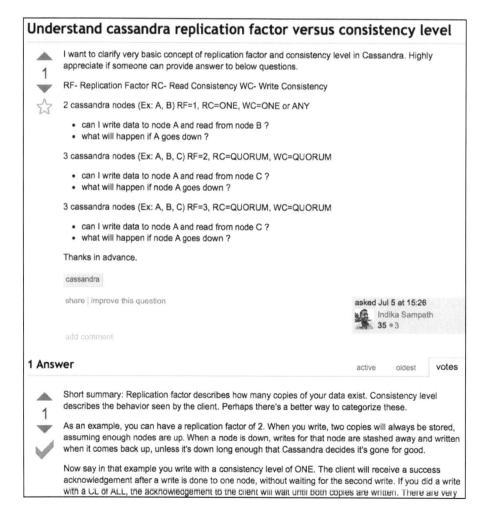

5. View additional posts, as desired.

6. Scroll to the top of the Stack Overflow web page, to see the Ask Question button in the upper-right corner:

7. Click the **Ask Question** button.

8. Click the **Sign up** tab, to create an account:

9. In the Sign up using Stack Exchange section, enter your name, email, and a password.

10. Click the **Sign Up** button.

11. Check your email.

12. In the email message from Stack Overflow, click the link to confirm your email address:

13. Back on the Stack Overflow site, now logged in, click the **Ask Question** button.

14. Read the directions now displayed:

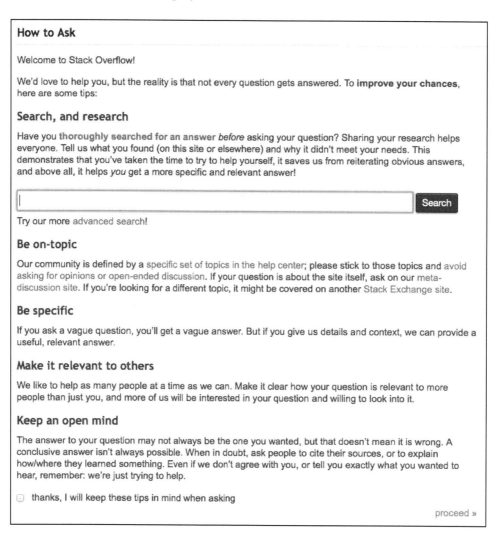

15. Select the checkbox for **thanks, I will keep these tips in mind when asking** and click the **proceed** link in the lower-right corner.

16. See that you can now post a question:

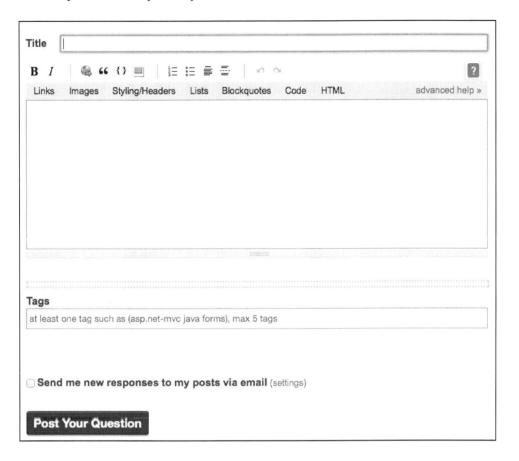

17. If desired, fill out and submit the form to post a question.

Access the Apache Cassandra mailing list:

18. In a browser, navigate to `http://cassandra.apache.org`.

19. Scroll to the bottom of the web page.

20. Under mailing lists, notice the Users section:

Users – General discussion list for users.
Subscribe | Unsubscribe | Archives

21. Click the **Archives** link, to see the archived emails.

22. See the list of emails and responses:

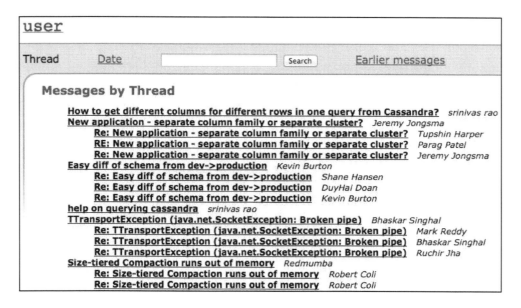

23. Click on one that interests you.

24. Read through the email thread, including the replies.

25. Continue perusing the archived emails, as desired.

26. Back at the bottom of the http://cassandra.apache.org page, in the Users section, see that you can subscribe to the mailing list.

Users – General discussion list for users.
Subscribe | Unsubscribe | Archives

27. If desired, click the **Subscribe** link to subscribe to the mailing list.

Attending Meetups

Cassandra meetups are a great way to continue learning about Cassandra. Along with providing continuing education via knowledgeable speakers, meetups also provide a way for members to ask questions.

To find the closest Cassandra meetup group near you, the map and search form at `http://cassandra.meetup.com` can be used.

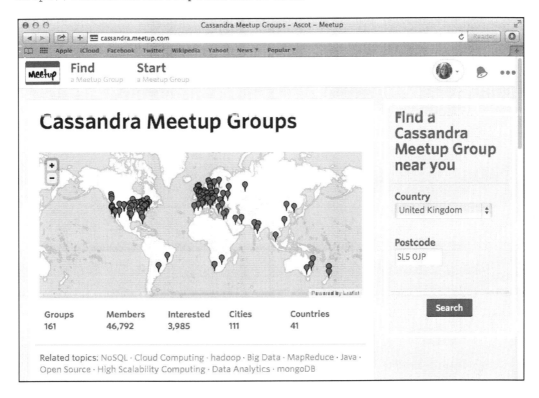

Exercise 5: Join a Meetup

In this exercise, you locate and join the Cassandra meetup group nearest you.

1. In a browser, navigate to http://cassandra.meetup.com.

2. In the search box on the right, enter your country and postcode, and click Search:

3. In the list of results, click a Cassandra meetup group near you:

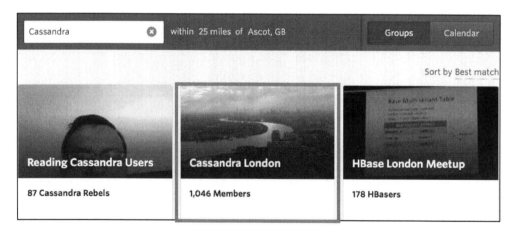

Note: If no Cassandra meetup groups appear in your search results, consider increasing the search radius or creating a Cassandra meetup group in your area.

4. In the upper-right corner of the page for a Cassandra meetup group near you, click the **Join us!** button:

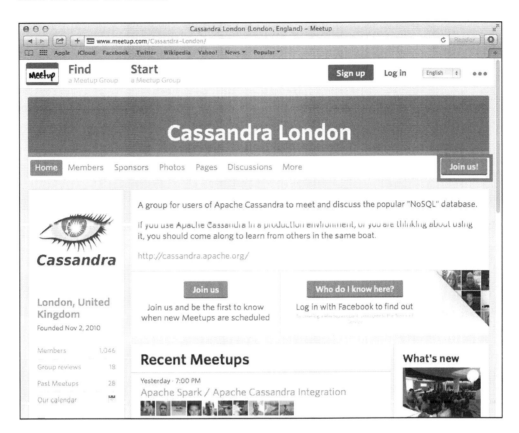

5. In the dialog box that appears, either sign in (if you already have a Meetup account) or fill in your name, email, and a password to create an account.

6. If there is an upcoming meetup listed, sign up for it.

7. If there is not an upcoming meetup listed, know that you will receive an email announcement once the next meetup is scheduled.

8. Attend the meetup, learning from the speaker(s) and talking with fellow members about their experience using Cassandra.

Summary

The focus of this unit was on resources for further learning:

- Accessing Documentation
- Reading Blogs and Books
- Watching Video Recordings
- Posting Questions
- Attending Meetups

ANSWER KEY

Answer Key to Unit Questions

Unit 1: End of Unit

1) c

2) d

Unit 2: Exercise 2

1) d

2) b

3) a

Unit 2: End of Unit

1) c

2) d

3) b

4) b

Unit 3: End of Unit

1) c

2) b

3) d

4) b

Unit 4: End of Unit

1) b

2) c

Unit 5: End of Unit

1) d

2) b

3) b

Unit 6: End of Unit

1) c

2) d

3) a

Unit 7: End of Unit

1) c

2) b

3) a

4) b

Unit 8: End of Unit

1) a

2) b

3) b

4) d

Unit 9: End of Unit

1) b

2) b

3) a

4) a

5) d

Unit 10: End of Unit

1) a

2) c

3) c

4) d

Unit 11: End of Unit

1) a

2) a

3) b

4) a

5) b

Unit 12: End of Unit

1) a

2) b

3) b

Unit 13: End of Unit

1) b

2) b

3) c

4) d

Unit 14: End of Unit

1) d

2) b

3) c

4) a

Unit 15: End of Unit

1) d

2) b

3) a

4) d

Unit 16: End of Unit

1) c

2) b

3) c

SETTING UP THE STUDENT COMPUTERS

Understanding the System Requirements

Getting the Course Virtual Machines

Getting the Course Files

Understanding the System Requirements

In this course, each student will create a Cassandra cluster on their computer, using virtual machines. In order to do this, the student computers need to be fairly high spec.

Hardware

Each computer (one computer per student) needs to be **64-bit**, needs to have **8 GB** or more of **RAM**, needs to have **30 GB** or more of **free hard drive space**, and needs a **USB port** (for the instructor to copy the virtual machines and class files from a USB drive to the student computers before the start of class).

Software

Each computer needs to have a **64-bit operating system**, needs the latest version of **VMware Player** installed and working, needs **Acrobat Reader** (or equivalent, for viewing a .pdf file), and needs a way to **unzip** files.

VMware Player

The latest version of VMware Player is required in order to run the VMware virtual machines used in the course.

Macintosh: VMware does not have a separate VMware Player for the Macintosh. However, VMware Fusion, which is VMware's product for the Macintosh, can be used. VMware Fusion is available online for purchase or as a 30-day trial.

Windows: VMware Player for Windows can be downloaded for free from `http://www.vmware.com/support/download-player.html`.

Once the latest Windows VMware Player has been download and installed, if VMware Player does not allow 64-bit virtual machine images to open, it may be that Virtualization Technology (required by the Windows VMware Player) is not turned on in BIOS. The steps for turning Virtualization Technology on in BIOS vary, depending on the computer manufacturer. (For detail, use Google, or any search engine, to search on "enable virtualization technology".) For example, the sequence might be: restart the computer and hold down the F10 key while it is booting, then press Escape, then choose System Configuration, then Device Configurations, then Virtualization Technology, then change the value to enable, then Save.

Linux: VMware Player for Linux can be downloaded for free from `http://www.vmware.com/support/download-player.html`.

Exercise: Check for the System Requirements

In this exercise you check that the student computers you are thinking to use for class meet the minimum system requirements.

For any **Macintosh** computers:

1. Go to the Apple menu (upper-left corner) and select **About This Mac**.

2. Notice the **Processor** value:

3. Check the Processor value against this list, ensuring that it is **64-bit**:

Processor Name	32- or 64-bit
Intel Core Solo	32 bit
Intel Core Duo	32 bit
Intel Core 2 Duo	64 bit
Intel Quad-Core Xeon	64 bit
Dual-Core Intel Xeon	64 bit
Quad-Core Intel Xeon	64 bit
Core i3	64 bit
Core i5	64 bit
Core i7	64 bit

4. Also in the About This Mac window, check that the **Memory** value is at least **8 GB**:

5. Select the **Macintosh HD**.

6. In the **File** menu, select **Get Info**.

7. Check **Available** value to see that the amount of space available is at least **30 GB**:

8. Proceed to the next topic, to acquire the course virtual machines, check that files can be unzipped, and test that VMware Player is installed and working.

For any **Windows** computers:

Note: the following steps may vary depending on the version of Windows.

1. Right-click on **My Computer** (not C:\), to select **Properties**.

2. In the window that appears, check that the System type is **64-bit**:

3. Check that the Installed memory (RAM) is at least 8 GB:

Installed memory (RAM):	16.0 GB	(15.9 GB usable)

4. Right-click **C:**, to select **Properties**.

5. Check that the amount of free space available is at least 30 GB:

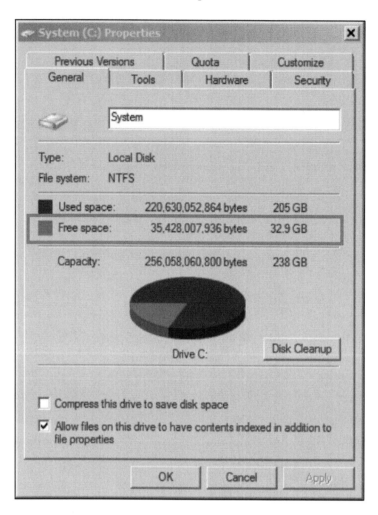

6. Proceed to the next topic, to acquire the course virtual machines, check that files can be unzipped, and test that VMware Player is installed and working.

Getting the Course Virtual Machines

The virtual machine images for the course can be downloaded from
`http://www.ruthstryker.com/books/achotl1`:

Downloads for Course
achotl1_vm1_64-bit.zip **California** (2.4 GB, virtual machine, needed for Units 1-16)
achotl1_vmx_64-bit.zip **California** (1.5 GB, second virtual machine, needed for Units 12-16)
class_files.zip **California** (18 MB, class files, needed for Units 1-16)
achotl1_vm1_64-bit.zip **Ireland** (2.4 GB, virtual machine, needed for Units 1-16)
achotl1_vmx_64-bit.zip **Ireland** (1.5 GB, second virtual machine, needed for Units 12-16)
class_files.zip **Ireland** (18 MB, class files, needed for Units 1-16)
achotl1_vm1_64-bit.zip **Singapore** (2.4 GB, virtual machine, needed for Units 1-16)
achotl1_vmx_64-bit.zip **Singapore** (1.5 GB, second virtual machine, needed for Units 12-16)
class_files.zip **Singapore** (18 MB, class files, needed for Units 1-16)

There are two virtual machine images for the course. One is **achotl1_vm1_64-bit**, which is used for Units 1-16. The second virtual machine, **achotl1_vmx_64-bit**, is used for Units 12-16.

Both virtual machine images are needed for the course.

Multiple copies of the download files are provided so that the closest location can be selected, to provide the fastest download.

Exercise: Get the Course Virtual Machines

In this exercise you set up a class folder on the desktop of a student computer and then download the course virtual machines into the folder.

Instructor note: As the files are very large, you will likely want to do the following steps to download the files onto one student computer and then copy the files to the other student computers via a USB drive. You will want to do this at least one day in advance of the class, as the downloading can take awhile. (Files are 2.4 GB, 1.5 GB, and 18 MB.)

1. On the **desktop** of a student computer, **create a folder** named `achotl1`.

2. In a browser, navigate to `http://www.ruthstryker.com/books/achotl1` (apache cassandra hands-on training level 1).

3. Notice the links for the achotl1_vm1_64-bit.zip and achotl1_vmx_64-bit.zip virtual machines:

Downloads for Course

achotl1_vm1_64-bit.zip **California** (2.4 GB, virtual machine, needed for Units 1-16)

achotl1_vmx_64-bit.zip **California** (1.5 GB, second virtual machine, needed for Units 12-16)

class_files.zip **California** (18 MB, class files, needed for Units 1-16)

4. Right-click the **achotl1_vm1_64-bit.zip** link for the region that is closest to you (e.g. California, Ireland, or Singapore), to select **Download Linked File As...** (or equivalent in your browser, such as **Save Target As...**):

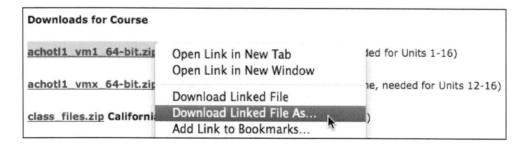

5. In the dialog box that appears, select the desktop **achotl1** folder as the save destination.

6. Click the **Save** button, to start downloading the file to the achotl1 folder.

7. Once the file has finished downloading, see that it is in the achotl1 folder on the desktop:

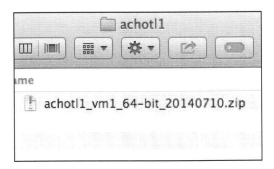

8. **Repeat** steps 4-6 to also download the **achotl1_vmx_64-bit.zip** file to the achotl1 folder.

9. If there is a date in the zip file names, remove the date. (e.g. Change achotl1_vm1_64-bit_20140710.zip to `achotl1_vm1_64-bit.zip`.):

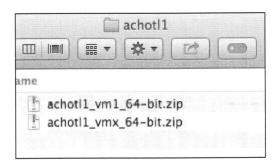

Check that the latest version of VMware player is installed and set up on the student computer:

10. In the achotl1 folder, **unzip** the **achotl1_vm1_64-bit.zip** file. (e.g. If on a Macintosh, double-click the .zip file. Or, if on Windows, right-click the .zip file and select Extract All….)

11. Once the file is unzipped, **double-click** the **achotl1_vm1_64-bit** file, to check that it opens in VMware.

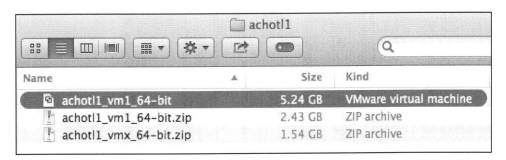

*If on Windows: look in the **achotl1_vm1_64-bit.vmwarevm** subfolder to locate and double-click the **achotl1_vm1_64-bit.vmx** file:*

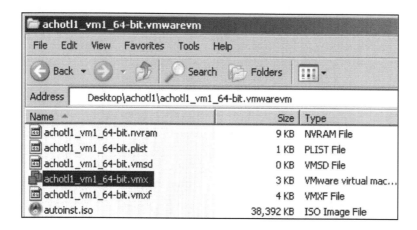

Note: If the achotl1_vm1_64-bit.vmx file does not open in VMware Player, it may be that the latest version of VMware Player is not installed, or that Virtualization Technology is not turned on in BIOS. For details, see page C-2.

12. If prompted, click the **I copied it** button.

13. See that the login screen for the virtual machine displays:

14. Select **Virtual Machine – Shut Down**, to shut down the virtual machine.

    *If on Windows: select **Player – Power – Shut Down Guest**.*

15. Proceed to the next topic to get the course files and check that Acrobat Reader is installed on the student computer.

Getting the Course Files

Throughout the course, along with the virtual machines, various files are needed. These files are provided in a folder named class_files.

The class_files folder is available by downloading the class_files.zip file from `http://www.ruthstryker.com/books/achotl1`.

Downloads for Course

<u>achotl1_vm1_64-bit.zip</u> **California** (2.4 GB, virtual machine, needed for Units 1-16)

<u>achotl1_vmx_64-bit.zip</u> **California** (1.5 GB, second virtual machine, needed for Units 12-16)

<u>class_files.zip</u> **California** (18 MB, class files, needed for Units 1-16)

Within the class_files folder, the files are organized by unit.

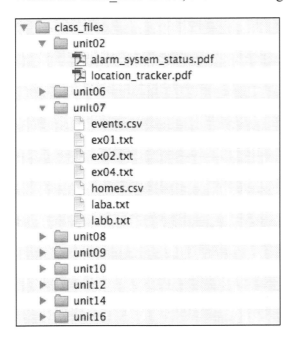

Exercise: Get the Course Files

In this exercise, you download the class_files.zip file to the achotl1 folder on the desktop of the student computer.

1. In the browser window, still on the `http://www.ruthstryker.com/books/achotl1` web page, notice the class_files.zip link:

    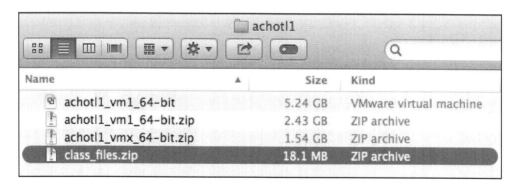

    Downloads for Course

    achotl1_vm1_64-bit.zip California (2.4 GB, virtual machine, needed for Units 1-16)

    achotl1_vmx_64-bit.zip California (1.5 GB, second virtual machine, needed for Units 12-16)

    class_files.zip California (18 MB, class files, needed for Units 1-16)

2. Right-click the **class_files.zip** link for the region that is closest to you (e.g. California, Ireland, or Singapore), to select **Download Linked File As...** (or the equivalent in your browser, such as **Save Target As...**).

3. In the dialog box that appears, select the desktop **achotl1** folder as the save destination.

4. Click the **Save** button, to start downloading the file to the achotl1 folder.

5. Once the file has finished downloading, see that it is in the achotl1 folder:

Name	Size	Kind
achotl1_vm1_64-bit	5.24 GB	VMware virtual machine
achotl1_vm1_64-bit.zip	2.43 GB	ZIP archive
achotl1_vmx_64-bit.zip	1.54 GB	ZIP archive
class_files.zip	18.1 MB	ZIP archive

6. **Unzip** the class_files.zip file. (e.g. If on a Macintosh, double-click the .zip file. Or, if on Windows, right-click the .zip file and select Extract All....)

7. See that the class_files folder now exists:

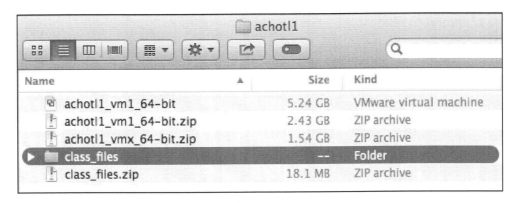

8. Expand the class_files folder to see the unit folders and files:

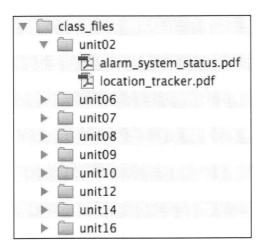

9. In the **unit02** folder, double-click the **alarm_system_status.pdf** file to open it, to check that Acrobat Reader (or equivalent) is installed:

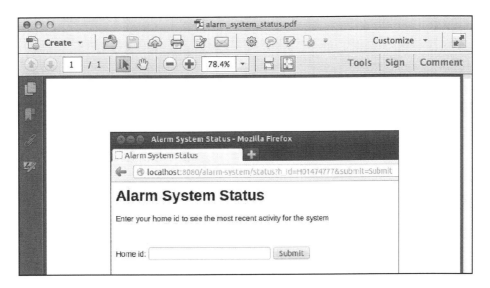

10. **Delete** the class_files.zip file.

11. Check the contents of the achotl1 folder, ready for the start of class:

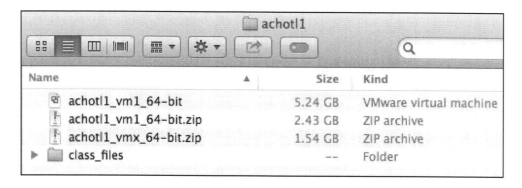

Name	Size	Kind
achotl1_vm1_64-bit	5.24 GB	VMware virtual machine
achotl1_vm1_64-bit.zip	2.43 GB	ZIP archive
achotl1_vmx_64-bit.zip	1.54 GB	ZIP archive
▶ class_files	--	Folder

HOW THE COURSE VIRTUAL MACHINES WERE BUILT

How the Main Virtual Machine was Built

How the Second Virtual Machine was Built

How the Main Virtual Machine was Built

The main course virtual machine (vm1), downloadable through
`http://www.ruthstryker.com/books/achot11` (apache cassandra hands-on
training level 1), was built using VMware to provide a virtual machine that can be
run on Windows, Mac, or Linux.

For people curious to know exactly how the virtual machine was created, the steps
that were done (using VMware Fusion 6 on a Mac in May 2014) are provided in this
appendix. (Realize that, if you go to reproduce these steps at a later date, some of the
open source software versions and URLs may have moved on.)

At a high level, the steps done to create the main virtual machine were:

1. Acquired VMware Fusion (to be able to create a virtual machine).

2. Acquired Ubuntu ISO disk image (to have an operating system as a base for
   creating a virtual machine).

3. Used VMware Fusion to create a virtual machine from the disk image.

4. Installed vim (a text editor) on the virtual machine.

5. Installed curl (for referencing URLs on the command line).

6. Installed Oracle JDK (to be able to create and run Java applications).

7. Installed Apache Maven (for managing dependencies when developing an
   application).

8. Installed Eclipse (to have a development environment for writing a Java
   application).

9. Installed Tomcat (to be able to host and serve a Java application).

10. Downloaded Apache Cassandra to the virtual machine.

*Note: It is not necessary to build the virtual machine yourself. You can download it
through* `http://www.ruthstryker.com/books/achot11`.

Steps Used to Build the Main Virtual Machine

These are the steps that were used to build the vm1 virtual machine.

1. Acquired and installed **VMware Fusion**.

2. Downloaded the **Ubuntu ISO file** (64-bit Ubuntu 12.04 LTS used), from
   `http://www.ubuntu.com/download/desktop`.

Created a **virtual machine** in VMware Fusion using the Ubuntu ISO file:

3. In VMware Fusion, selected **File – New…**.

4. With **Install from disc or image** selected, clicked the **Continue** button.

5. Clicked the **Use another disc or disc image…** button.

6. **Selected** the ISO image downloaded in step 2.

7. Clicked the **Continue** button.

8. For Display Name, entered `vm1`.

9. For Account Name, entered `vm1`.

10. For Password, entered `ubuntu`.

11. For Confirm Password, entered `ubuntu`.

12. Left the checkbox for Make your home folder accessible to the virtual machine **deselected**.

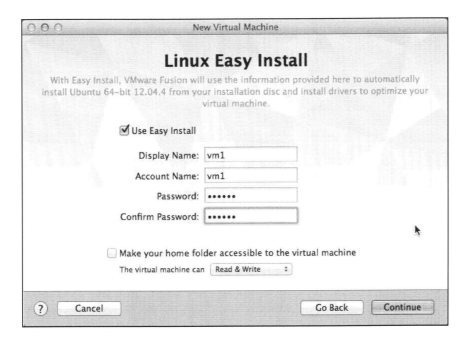

13. Clicked **Continue**.

14. Clicked the **Download Tools** button. (Does not show if they have already been downloaded.)

15. Clicked the **Customize Settings** button.

16. Entered `achotl1_vm1_64-bit` as the file name.

17. Clicked **Save**.

18. Double-clicked the **Processors & Memory** icon.

19. Increased the memory to **1536** MB.

20. Closed the Processors & Memory window.

21. Clicked the **Play** button, to start the virtual machine.

22. Watched the virtual machine install needed files.

23. When prompted, entered `ubuntu` for Password:

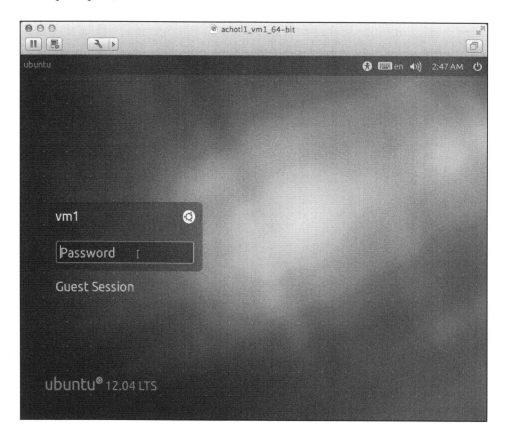

24. In the upper-right corner, under the gear icon, selected **Displays**....

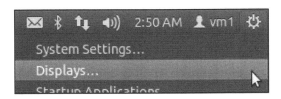

25. For Resolution, selected **1024 x 768**.

26. Clicked **Apply**.

27. Clicked **Keep This Configuration**.

28. **Closed** the Displays window. (Hovered over Displays in the upper-left corner to be able to see the close button.)

Installed text editor **vim**:

29. Opened a terminal window by clicking the Dash Home icon (upper-left), and typing `Ter` to then select the **Terminal** application:

30. At the command prompt, entered `sudo apt-get install vim` to install vim:

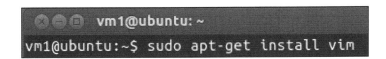

31. Entered the sudo password of `ubuntu` when prompted.

32. Entered `Y` when prompted.

Installed **curl** (for referencing URLs on the command line):

33. At the command prompt, entered `sudo apt-get install curl` to install curl.

Downloaded and installed **Oracle JDK**, for allowing Cassandra to run (Oracle JRE or JDK required), and to be able to create Java applications (Unit 9, JDK required):

34. In the virtual machine, opened a **browser** (Firefox icon, on the left) and navigated to `http://www.oracle.com/technetwork/java/javase/downloads`.

35. Clicked on the **Download** button for **JDK 7**:

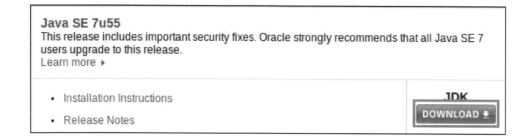

36. Selected the **Accept License Agreement** radio button.

37. For **Linux x64**, clicked the **jdk-7u55-linux-x64.tar.gz** link, to download the tarball file.

38. Selected the **Save File** radio button.

39. Clicked **OK**, to download the tarball to the Downloads directory.

40. In the terminal window, entered `cd Downloads` to navigate to the Downloads directory.

41. Entered `ls`, to see that the JDK tarball is there:

```
vm1@ubuntu:~$ cd Downloads
vm1@ubuntu:~/Downloads$ ls
jdk-7u55-linux-x64.tar.gz
```

42. Entered `sudo mkdir -p /usr/local/java` to create a directory for the JDK.

43. Entered `sudo mv jdk-7u55-linux-x64.tar.gz /usr/local/java` to move the tarball to the java directory.

44. Entered `cd /usr/local/java` to navigate to the java directory.

45. Entered `ls` to see the tarball file.

46. Entered `sudo tar zxvf jdk-7u55-linux-x64.tar.gz` to unpack the tarball.

47. Entered `ls` to see the unpacked directory:

```
vm1@ubuntu:/usr/local/java$ ls
jdk1.7.0_55   jdk-7u55-linux-x64.tar.gz
```

48. Entered `ls jdk1.7.0_55` to see the **jre** subdirectory (to see that the JRE is included with the JDK):

```
vm1@ubuntu:/usr/local/java$ ls jdk1.7.0_55
bin          lib          src.zip
COPYRIGHT    LICENSE      THIRDPARTYLICENSEREADME-JAVAFX.txt
db           man          THIRDPARTYLICENSEREADME.txt
include      README.html
jre          release
```

49. Entered `sudo update-alternatives --install  "/usr/bin/java" "java" "/usr/local/java/jdk1.7.0_55/bin/java" 1` so that Ubuntu knows about the new Java runtime.

50. Entered `java -version` to check that Oracle JRE is being used as the default runtime:

```
vm1@ubuntu:/usr/local/java$ java -version
java version "1.7.0_55"
Java(TM) SE Runtime Environment (build 1.7.0_55-b13)
Java HotSpot(TM) 64-Bit Server VM (build 24.55-b03, mixed mode)
```

51. Entered `sudo update-alternatives --install  "/usr/bin/javac" "javac" "/usr/local/java/jdk1.7.0_55/bin/javac" 1` so that Ubuntu knows about the new Java compiler.

52. Entered `javac -version` to check that Oracle JDK is being used as the default compiler:

```
vm1@ubuntu:/usr/local/java$ javac -version
javac 1.7.0_55
```

Modified **JAVA_HOME** and **JDK_HOME** in the java.sh file so that java -version and javac -version would still reference Oracle JRE and JDK even after a restart:

53. At the command prompt, entered `sudo vim /etc/profile.d/java.sh`.

54. Pressed `i` (insert), to edit the file.

55. Typed `export JDK_HOME=/usr/local/java/jdk1.7.0_55`.

56. Pressed the **Enter** key to create a new line.

57. Typed `export JAVA_HOME=/usr/local/java/jdk1.7.0_55`.

58. Pressed the **Esc** key and then entered `:wq` to save the file and quit.

59. Back at the command prompt, entered `sudo chmod +x /etc/profile.d/java.sh` to change the permissions for the java.sh file, so that it could be executed.

60. Entered `source /etc/profile.d/java.sh` to execute the file.

61. Entered `echo $JAVA_HOME` to see that the JAVA_HOME variable has been set to the location of the Oracle JDK.

62. Closed all windows in the virtual machine and selected **Virtual Machine – Restart**, to restart the virtual machine.

63. Waited for the virtual machine to restart.

64. When prompted to log in, entered `ubuntu` as the password.

65. Opened a terminal window.

66. Entered `java -version` to see that it is still set up.

67. Entered `javac -version` to see that it is still set up.

Installed **Apache Maven**, a software build tool that manages dependencies (optionally used in Unit 9, when creating a Java application that uses the DataStax Java driver to communicate with a Cassandra cluster):

68. At the command prompt, entered `sudo apt-get install maven2`.

69. Entered `ubuntu` when prompted for the sudo password.

70. Entered `Y` when prompted.

71. Waited for Maven to install.

72. Entered `mvn -version` to see that Maven installed:

```
vm1@ubuntu:~$ mvn -version
Apache Maven 2.2.1 (rdeblan-8)
Java version: 1.7.0_55
Java home: /usr/local/java/jdk1.7.0_55/jre
Default locale: en_US, platform encoding: UTF-8
OS name: "linux" version: "3.11.0-15-generic" arch:
```

73. Entered `java -version` to check the default runtime:

```
vm1@ubuntu:~$ java -version
java version "1.6.0_30"
OpenJDK Runtime Environment (IcedTea6 1.13.1) (6b30-1.13.1
OpenJDK 64-Bit Server VM (build 23.25-b01, mixed mode)
```

74. Noticed that the Maven installation changed the default runtime to OpenJDK.

75. Entered `sudo update-alternatives --config java` to change the default Java runtime.

76. Entered `2`, to select the Oracle runtime (installed at /usr/local/java/jdk1.7.0_55/bin/java).

77. Entered `java -version` to see that the default runtime is back to using the Oracle Java runtime.

78. Entered `sudo apt-get remove openjdk*` to remove OpenJDK from the virtual machine.

79. Entered `Y` when prompted.

Installed **Eclipse**, a development environment commonly used for creating Java applications (used in Unit 9):

80. Inside the virtual machine, opened a browser window and navigated to `https://www.eclipse.org/downloads`.

81. To the right of **Eclipse IDE for Java EE Developers**, clicked the **Linux 64 Bit** link.

82. Clicked the green **download arrow**, selected the **Save File** radio button, and clicked the **OK** button, to download the Eclipse tarball file to the Downloads directory.

83. Watched the status icon in the upper-right corner, waiting until the Eclipse tarball finished downloading:

84. In the terminal window, entered `cd ~/Downloads` to navigate to the Downloads directory.

85. Entered `ls` to see that the Eclipse tarball was there.

86. Entered `cd` to navigate to the default home directory (/home/vm1).

87. Entered `sudo mv ~/Downloads/eclipse-jee-kepler-SR2-linux-gtk-x86_64.tar.gz .` to move the Eclipse tarball to the default home directory.

88. Entered `tar xvf eclipse-jee` (and the **Tab** key, to autocomplete) to unpack the tarball.

89. Entered `cd eclipse`, to navigate to the unpacked eclipse directory.

90. Entered `./eclipse`, to start the Eclipse application.

91. In the Workspace Launcher window, clicked **OK** to accept the default workspace directory.

92. Clicked the **X** in the Welcome tab, to close the Welcome window.

Installed **Apache Tomcat** (used in Unit 9), a web server and servlet container, from within Eclipse:

93. Still in Eclipse, selected **File – New – Dynamic Web Project**.

94. For Project name, entered `temporary`.

95. In the Target runtime section, clicked the **New Runtime...** button.

96.   In the list of versions, selected **Apache Tomcat v7.0**.

97. Selected the checkbox for **Create a new local server**.

98. Clicked **Next**.

99. In the Tomcat installation directory section, click the **Download and Install...** button.

100. Selected the radio button for **I accept the terms of the license agreement** and clicked **Finish**.

101. Selected the **vm1** folder (on the left) and clicked **OK**.

102. **Noticed** that the Finish button was dimmed out until Tomcat was done installing.

103. After the **Finish** button became available, selected it.

104. Clicked the **Cancel** button (to get out of the project wizard).

105. In the left panel, **notice** the Servers folder with Tomcat v7.0 Server inside it.

106. **Close** Eclipse.

Downloaded the **Apache Cassandra tarball** to the virtual machine:

107. In the virtual machine, in the browser window, navigated to `http://cassandra.apache.org`.

108. Clicked the **Download options** link, to go to the download page.

109. Clicked the **apache-cassandra-2.0.7-bin.tar.gz** link.

110. Noticed the list of mirror sites.

111. Clicked the first link, to use the suggested download server.

112. Left the **Save File** radio button selected, and clicked **OK**.

113. In a terminal window, entered `ls ~/Downloads` to see that the tarball downloaded.

Copied the **class files** folder to the virtual machine's desktop:

114. Copied the **class_files** folder (after downloading from
`http://www.ruthstryker.com/books/achotl1` and unzipping) to the
desktop of the virtual machine:

Shut down and **zipped** the virtual machine:

115. **Closed all** of the open windows in the virtual machine.

116. Selected **Virtual Machine – Shut Down**.

117. Clicked the **Shut Down** button.

118. **Closed** the window for the virtual machine.

119. Selected **VMware Fusion – Quit VMware Fusion**.

120. **Located** the saved virtual machine file (achotl1_vm1_64-bit).

121. **Zipped** the virtual machine file, to make it smaller for distribution.

How the Second Virtual Machine Was Built

The second virtual machine (vmx), also downloadable through `http://www.ruthstryker.com/books/achotl1`, was created for use in Unit 12 (Adding Nodes to a Cluster) and onwards. It is a slim virtual machine, with Cassandra installed but without Java development tools like Eclipse, Tomcat, Maven, and JDK.

At a high level, the steps done to create the second virtual machine were:

1. Used VMware Fusion to create a virtual machine from the Ubuntu disk image.

2. Installed vim (a text editor) on the virtual machine.

3. Installed Oracle JRE (to be able to run Cassandra).

4. Downloaded and installed Apache Cassandra on the virtual machine.

Note: It is not necessary to build this virtual machine yourself. You can download it through `http://www.ruthstryker.com/books/achotl1`.

Steps Used to Build the Second Virtual Machine

These are the steps that were used to build the second virtual machine (vmx).

Created a **virtual machine** in VMware Fusion using the Ubuntu ISO file:

1. In VMware Fusion, selected **File – New...**.

2. With **Install from disc or image** selected, clicked the **Continue** button.

3. Clicked the **Use another disc or disc image...** button.

4. **Selected** the **Ubuntu ISO file** previously downloaded.

5. Clicked the **Open** button.

6. Clicked the **Continue** button.

7. For Display Name, entered vmx.

8. For Account Name, entered vmx.

9. For Password, entered ubuntu.

10. For Confirm Password, entered ubuntu.

11. Left the checkbox for Make your home folder accessible to the virtual machine **deselected**.

12. Clicked **Continue**.

13. Clicked the **Customize Settings** button.

14. Entered achot11_vmx_64-bit as the file name.

15. Clicked **Save**.

16. Double-clicked the **Processors & Memory** icon.

17. Increased the memory to **1536** MB.

18. Closed the Processors & Memory window.

19. Clicked the **Play** button, to start the virtual machine.

20. Watched the virtual machine install needed files.

21. When prompted to log in, entered ubuntu for the password.

22. In the upper-right corner, under the gear icon, selected **Displays...**.

23. For Resolution, selected **1024 x 768**.

24. Clicked **Apply**.

25. Clicked **Keep This Configuration**.

26. **Closed** the Displays window. (Hovered over the word Displays in the upper-left corner to be able to see the close button.)

Installed text editor **vim**:

27. Opened a terminal window.

28. At the command prompt, entered `sudo apt-get install vim` to install vim, a text editor.

29. Entered the sudo password of `ubuntu` when prompted.

30. Entered `Y` when prompted.

Downloaded and installed **Oracle JRE**, for running Cassandra:

31. In the virtual machine, opened a **browser** (Firefox icon, on the left) and navigated to `http://www.oracle.com/technetwork/java/javase/downloads`.

32. Clicked on the Download button for **JRE 7**:

33. Selected the **Accept License Agreement** radio button.

34. For **Linux x64**, clicked the **jre-7u55-linux-x64.tar.gz** link, to download the tarball file.

35. Selected the **Save File** radio button.

36. Clicked **OK**, to download the tarball to the Downloads directory.

37. In the terminal window, entered `cd Downloads` to navigate to the Downloads directory.

38. Entered `ls`, to see the JRE tarball listed:

```
vmx@ubuntu:~/Downloads$ ls
jre-7u55-linux-x64.tar.gz
```

39. Entered `sudo mkdir -p /usr/local/java` to create a directory for the JRE.

40. Entered `sudo mv jre-7u55-linux-x64.tar.gz /usr/local/java` to move the tarball to the java directory.

41. Entered `cd /usr/local/java` to navigate to the java directory.

42. Entered `ls` to see the tarball file.

43. Entered `sudo tar zxvf jre-7u55-linux-x64.tar.gz` to unpack the tarball.

44. Entered `ls` to see the unpacked directory.

45. Entered `ls jre1.7.0_55` to see the contents of the directory:

```
vmx@ubuntu:/usr/local/java$ ls
jre1.7.0_55  jre-7u55-linux-x64.tar.gz
vmx@ubuntu:/usr/local/java$ ls jre1.7.0_55
bin        man      THIRDPARTYLICENSEREADME-JAVAFX.txt
COPYRIGHT  plugin   THIRDPARTYLICENSEREADME.txt
lib        README   Welcome.html
LICENSE    release
```

46. Entered `sudo update-alternatives --install "/usr/bin/java" "java" "/usr/local/java/jre1.7.0_55/bin/java" 1` so that Ubuntu would know about the new Java runtime.

47. Entered `java -version` to check that Oracle JRE is being used as the default runtime:

```
vmx@ubuntu:/usr/local/java$ java -version
java version "1.7.0_55"
Java(TM) SE Runtime Environment (build 1.7.0_55-b13)
Java HotSpot(TM) 64-Bit Server VM (build 24.55-b03, mixed mode)
```

Modified **JAVA_HOME** in the java.sh file so that java -version would still reference Oracle JRE even after a restart:

48. At the command prompt, entered `sudo vim /etc/profile.d/java.sh`.

49. Pressed `i` (insert), to edit the file.

50. Typed `export JAVA_HOME=/usr/local/java/jre1.7.0_55`.

51. Pressed the **Esc** key and then entered `:wq` to save the file and exit it.

52. Back at the command prompt, entered `sudo chmod +x /etc/profile.d/java.sh` to change the permissions for the java.sh file, so that it could be executed.

53. Entered `source /etc/profile.d/java.sh` to execute the file.

54. Entered `echo $JAVA_HOME` to see that the JAVA_HOME variable has been set to the location of the Oracle JRE.

55. Closed all windows in the virtual machine and selected **Virtual Machine – Restart**, to restart the virtual machine.

56. Clicked the **Restart** button.

57. When prompted to log in, entered `ubuntu` as the password.

58. Opened a terminal window.

59. Entered `java -version` to see that it is still set up:

```
 vmx@ubuntu: ~
vmx@ubuntu:~$ java -version
java version "1.7.0_55"
Java(TM) SE Runtime Environment (build 1.7.0_55-b13)
Java HotSpot(TM) 64-Bit Server VM (build 24.55-b03, mixed mode)
vmx@ubuntu:~$
```

Downloaded the **Apache Cassandra tarball** to the virtual machine:

60. In the virtual machine, in a browser, navigated to
    `http://cassandra.apache.org`.

61. Clicked the **Download options** link, to go to the download page.

62. Clicked the **apache-cassandra-2.0.7-bin.tar.gz** link.

63. Noticed the list of mirror sites.

64. Clicked the first link, to use the suggested download server.

65. Left the **Save File** radio button selected, and clicked **OK**.

66. Watched the download progress in the upper-right corner.

67. In a terminal window, entered `ls ~/Downloads` to see that the tarball
    downloaded.

68. Entered `mkdir cassandra` to create a subdirectory, to install Cassandra into.

69. Entered `cd cassandra` to go into the subdirectory.

70. Entered `mv ~/Downloads/apache-cassandra-2.0.7-bin.tar.gz .` to
    move the tarball file from the Downloads directory to this directory.

71. Entered `ls` to see that the file had moved:

```
vmx@ubuntu:~/cassandra$ ls
apache-cassandra-2.0.7-bin.tar.gz
```

72. Entered `tar -xvzf apache-cassandra-2.0.7-bin.tar.gz` to unpack the
    file.

73. Entered `ls` to see the new directory:

```
vmx@ubuntu:~/cassandra$ ls
apache-cassandra-2.0.7    apache-cassandra-2.0.7-bin.tar.gz
```

74. Entered `cd apache-cassandra-2.0.7` to navigate to the new directory.

75. Entered `ls` to see the contents of the directory:

```
vmx@ubuntu:~/cassandra/apache-cassandra-2.0.7$ ls
bin              interface    LICENSE.txt    pylib
CHANGES.txt      javadoc      NEWS.txt       README.txt
conf             lib          NOTICE.txt     tools
```

Created directories and provided Cassandra with **permission** to write:

76. Entered `sudo mkdir /var/lib/cassandra` to create a cassandra subdirectory under the /var/lib directory.

77. Entered `sudo mkdir /var/log/cassandra` to create a cassandra subdirectory under the /var/log directory.

78. Entered `sudo chown -R $USER:$GROUP /var/lib/cassandra` to allow Cassandra to write to the /var/lib/cassandra directory.

79. Entered `sudo chown -R $USER:$GROUP /var/log/cassandra` to allow Cassandra to write to the /var/log/cassandra directory.

Shut down and **zipped** the virtual machine:

80. **Closed all** of the open windows in the virtual machine.

81. Selected **Virtual Machine – Shut Down**.

82. Clicked the **Shut Down** button.

83. **Closed** the window for the virtual machine.

84. Selected **VMware Fusion – Quit VMware Fusion**.

85. **Located** the saved virtual machine file (achotl1_vmx_64-bit).

86. **Zipped** the virtual machine file, to make it smaller for distribution.

About the Author

Ruth Stryker is a long-time trainer who enjoys teaching in a clear and easy-to-understand manner, providing people who are new to a technology with a solid foundation as they move forward. Her all-time favorite student quote is, "Ruth rocks!" With 20 years of experience delivering technical training throughout the San Francisco Bay Area and the U.S., Ruth now lives in London, providing training on Apache Cassandra worldwide. She can best be contacted via email (ruth@ruthstryker.com), LinkedIn (http://www.linkedin.com/in/ruthstryker), or Twitter (@ruthstryker).

Ruth Stryker
Technical Trainer

7409937R00224

Printed in Great Britain
by Amazon.co.uk, Ltd.,
Marston Gate.